Internal Marketing

The Chartered Institute of Marketing/Butterworth-Heinemann Marketing Series is the most comprehensive, widely used and important collection of books in marketing and sales currently available worldwide.

As the CIM's official publisher, Butterworth-Heinemann develops, produces and publishes the complete series in association with the CIM. We aim to provide definitive marketing books for students and practitioners that promote excellence in marketing education and practice.

The series titles are written by CIM senior examiners and leading marketing educators for professionals, students and those studying the CIM's Certificate, Advanced Certificate and Postgraduate Diploma courses. Now firmly established, these titles provide practical study support to CIM and other marketing students and to practitioners at all levels.

The Chartered
Institute of Marketing

Formed in 1911, the Chartered Institute of Marketing is now the largest professional marketing management body in the world with over 60 000 members located worldwide. Its primary objectives are focused on the development of awareness and understanding of marketing throughout UK industry and commerce, and in the raising of standards of professionalism in the education, training and practice of this key business discipline.

Books in the series

Internal Marketing

Tools and concepts for customer-focused management

Pervaiz K. Ahmed and Mohammed Rafiq

Published in association with The Chartered Institute of Marketing

OXFORD AMSTERDAM BOSTON LONDON NEW YORK PARIS
SAN DIEGO SAN FRANCISCO SINGAPORE SYDNEY TOKYO

Butterworth-Heinemann
An imprint of Elsevier Science
Linacre House, Jordan Hill, Oxford OX2 8DP
225 Wildwood Avenue, Woburn, MA 01801-2041

First published 2002

British Library Cataloguing in Publication Data
A catalogue record for this book is available from the British Library

Library of Congress Cataloguing in Publication Data
A catalogue record for this book is available from the Library of Congress

ISBN 0 7506 4838 4

For information on all Butterworth-Heinemann publications visit our
website at www.bh.com

Printed and bound in Great Britain by Biddles Ltd
www.biddles.co.uk

Contents

Acknowledgements

This book is based on some of our previously published research and research conducted specifically for this book, but the book would not have been possible without the work of the numerous internal marketing scholars whose work we cite, to whom we are grateful. The work of Leonard Berry and colleagues, William George, Christian Grönroos and Nigel Piercy has been particularly influential in the development of internal marketing, and this book is no exception. We would also like to thank Charlie Shepherd, Vice President of Quality, NCR, for allowing us to use some of his material on innovation. We are also grateful to the numerous other individuals for providing their insights, thoughts and sharing their corporate experiences. In particular, we are indebted to staff at Butterworth-Heinemann for encouraging us to undertake this project and supporting us throughout.

Introduction

The internal marketing (IM) concept was first proposed in the mid 1970s as a way of achieving consistent service quality – a major problem in the services area. Its basic premise was '*to have satisfied customers, the firm must also have satisfied employees*' and that this could be best achieved by treating employees as customers, i.e. by applying the principles of marketing to job design and employee motivation. Since then, the concept has seen a number of major developments and its application is no longer confined to the services area. It has been shown that any type of organization can use IM to facilitate the implementation of its external marketing strategy or any other organizational strategies. However, despite nearly 25 years of development, the concept has not achieved the widespread recognition amongst mangers that it deserves. The major reason for this, we believe, is that the concept was well ahead of its time.

Internal marketing requires:

■ the acceptance of marketing techniques and philosophy;
■ customer orientation/market orientation;
■ a participative approach to management;
■ a strategic approach to human resource management (HRM) to ensure the alignment of HRM strategy with organizational strategy;
■ the co-ordination of all management activity to achieve customer or market orientation or customer/market-focused management.

Marketing and the marketing philosophy came into prominence in the 1960s, yet it was not until the 1980s that it became widely accepted, practised and seen by most organizations as indispensable. Similarly, participative management gained wide acceptance in the 1980s, and the 1990s saw the emergence of the strategic approach to HRM. The need to align human resources to the organizational strategy is widely accepted and, more recently, the need to focus organizational resources towards customer/market orientation has gained ground in the emergence of market-focused management. These developments mean that conditions for the adoption of IM are optimal. This can be seen in the growth of interest in IM by managers and the rapid growth in the numbers of organizations adopting IM management practices. This is because IM tackles the issues and problems of implementing organizational strategies head on. This issue is neglected in most discussions of strategic management and marketing strategy. Numerous firms and organizations have discovered to their cost that formulation of brilliant strategies is next to useless without effective implementation.

The purpose of this book is to introduce readers to the concept of IM and help them to implement it within their own organization. The main features of the book are:

- it presents the state-of-the-art thinking and research in the IM area;
- it shows how IM strategy can be used to implement such diverse strategies as implementing marketing strategy, total quality management (TQM), new product development and knowledge management;
- it equips readers with IM techniques to enable them to use IM within their own organization;
- it includes practical case studies showing how IM is already being used within leading companies.

For convenience, the book is divided into three sections. Section I explains what internal marketing is all about, how it works, introduces the main internal marketing techniques, discusses the role of HRM in internal marketing, and discusses a framework for empowerment of employees. Section II provides detailed discussion of the implementation of internal marketing in three areas, namely TQM, new product development and the rapidly developing area of knowledge management. Section III contains a number of case studies showing how internal marketing was used to tackle specific management issues. Whilst we have included illustrations and examples throughout the text, we believe that the variety of approaches illustrated in the case studies is useful for illustrating the variety of approaches to internal marketing.

Section I

Internal Marketing Theory

chapter one

What is internal marketing?

Introduction

More than 25 years ago, internal marketing (IM) was first proposed as a solution to the problem of delivering consistently high service quality by Berry et al.[1]. However, despite the rapidly growing literature on IM, relatively few organizations actually apply the concept in practice. One of the main problems contributing to this is that there does not exist a single unified concept of what is meant by IM. There are a variety of meanings attributed in the literature as to exactly what IM is, what it is supposed to do, how it is supposed to do it, and who is supposed to do it. This variety of interpretations as to what IM constitutes has led to a diverse range of activities being grouped under the umbrella of IM. This diversity of interpretations and definitions in turn has led to difficulties in the implementation and widespread adoption of the concept. Most importantly, these problems create contradictions at the conceptual level with respect to defining the precise domain of IM, and make meaningful investigations of the concept more difficult.

In order for IM to be effectively operationalized as a paradigm of organizational change, management and implementation of strategies, a clarification at the definitional level is necessary. What is required is a precise specification of those activities that can be taken to constitute IM and those that do not, since definition and classification are fundamental prerequisites to marketing analysis. The purpose of this chapter is to critically examine the IM concept and outline its scope by tracing the major developments in the concept to date. It proposes a definition and a set of core criteria that are essential features of an internal marketing programme. Managerial implications arising from the proposed definition of internal marketing are also discussed.

Phases in the development and evolution of the internal marketing concept

Despite the array of interpretations mentioned above, a careful examination of the literature over the last 25 years indicates the existence of three separate yet closely intertwined strands of development of the IM concept, namely an employee satisfaction phase, a customer orientation phase and a strategy implementation/change management phase. We discuss the evolution of these phases below.

Phase 1: employee motivation and satisfaction

In the early developmental phase, the majority of the work on internal marketing focused upon the issue of employee motivation and satisfaction. The major reason behind this was the fact that the roots of the internal marketing concept lie in efforts to improve service quality. Not being machines, individuals exhibit inconsistencies in the performance of service tasks and as a consequence cause variation in the level of delivered service quality. The problem of 'variability' focused organizational efforts on getting employees to deliver consistently high quality service. The overall effect of this was to bring to the fore the issue of employee motivation and satisfaction. From this starting point, the importance of employee satisfaction as an important parameter impacting upon customer satisfaction was hypothesized.

The term internal marketing appears to have been first used by Berry et al. as previously mentioned, and later by George[2], Thompson et al.[3] and Murray[4]. Even though the term internal marketing was not directly used by them, the idea of internal marketing was also present in Sasser and Arbeit's 1976 article[5]. However, it was not until the publication of Leonard Berry's 1981 seminal article in which he defined internal marketing as '*viewing employees as internal customers, viewing jobs as internal products that satisfy the needs and wants of these internal customers while addressing the objectives of the organization*'[6] that the term entered popular management discourse.

A key assumption underlying this view of IM is based upon the notion that '*to have satisfied customers, the firm must also have satisfied employees*'[7]. Sasser and Arbeit took this line of argument a step further by contending that personnel is the most important market of a service company[8]. The deployment of marketing techniques in the personnel area is also indicated by Sasser and Arbeit by their depiction of jobs as products and employees as customers:

> *'Viewing their job offerings as products and their employees as customers forces managers to devote the same care to their jobs as they devote to the purchasers of their services.*[9]

The focus upon employee satisfaction within these new approaches to employee management can largely be attributed to the fact that in the marketing of services much of what customers buy is labour, or human acts of performance. Consequently, attraction of the best personnel, their retention and motivation becomes of critical importance. Attraction, retention and motivation of high quality staff is especially critical in situations where the quality of the service is the only real differentiating factor between competitors. This situation occurs most frequently in service environments in which customers are highly demanding of employees, coupled with employees who in turn hold high expectations from their jobs as sources of self-actualization and self-development. Under these conditions it was thought that the effect of employing an IM approach would be to create more satisfied customer-contact employees who appreciate clearly the logic and benefit of courteous, empathetic behaviour when dealing with customers, and hence lead to greater customer satisfaction. Infused with this logic, the challenge of creating satisfied employees and hence customer satisfaction received a vigorous impetus. The fundamental tool for achieving employee satisfaction in this approach is the treatment of *employees as customers*. For instance, Berry and Parasuraman[10], who with a number of colleagues have carried out some of the most innovative research on service quality, state:

> *'Internal marketing is attracting, developing, motivating and retaining qualified employees through job-products that satisfy their needs. Internal marketing is the philosophy of treating employees as customers and it is the strategy of shaping job-products to fit human needs.*[11]

Notwithstanding the appeal of the *'employees as customers'* philosophy that underpins much of the logic of the first phase, there are a number of potential problems with this conceptualization of IM. Firstly, unlike the external marketing situation, the 'product' that employees are sold may in fact be unwanted by them or even possess negative utility. Secondly, unlike the external marketing situation, employees are unlikely to have a choice in the 'products' that they can select. Thirdly, because of the contractual nature of employment, employees can, in the final analysis, be 'coerced' into accepting 'products' they do not want. Fourthly, the financial cost of having satisfied employees could be considerable. And finally, the notion of 'employee as customer' also raises the question as to whether the needs of external customers have primacy over those of the employees. For instance, the proposition that personnel is the most important market of a service company accords primacy to the employee market and demotes the external customer to a secondary level. This would appear to invert one of the most fundamental axioms of marketing, namely that the external customer has primacy. This brings us on to the second phase.

Phase 2: customer orientation

The second major step in the development of the IM concept was undertaken by Christian Grönroos[12], whose starting point was the concern that because contact employees in services become involved in what he termed '*interactive marketing*' it is essential that they are responsive to customers' needs. Grönroos recognized that not only do buyer–seller interactions have an impact on purchasing and repeat purchasing decisions but also, crucially, that buyer–seller interactions provide a marketing opportunity for the organization. To take advantage of these opportunities requires *customer-oriented and sales-minded personnel*. Hence, the object of IM is, in his view, to '*get motivated and customer-conscious employees*'[13]. In this view, it is not sufficient that employees are motivated to perform better (as in the approach of Berry and his followers), but they must also be '*sales minded*'. Furthermore, effective service also requires effective co-ordination between contact staff and backroom support staff. Grönroos also views the IM concept as a means of integrating the different functions that are vital to the customer relations of service companies.

Grönroos extended his original definition of IM as a method of motivating personnel towards customer consciousness and sales mindedness, to include the use of *marketing-like activities* in this pursuit and redefining internal marketing as:

> '... *Holding that an organization's internal market of employees can be influenced most effectively and hence motivated to customer-consciousness, market orientation and sales-mindedness by a marketing-like internal approach and by applying marketing-like activities internally.*'[14]

George similarly accepts this position by asserting that IM holds that employees are 'best motivated for service-mindedness and customer-oriented behavior by an active marketing-like approach, where marketing-like activities are used internally'[15]. The addition of marketing-like techniques internally moves Grönroos' definition closer to that of Berry's definition, in that both sets of approaches stress the need to motivate employees, and advocate the use of 'marketing-like' techniques to do it. However, the critical difference between Grönroos' approach and that of Berry and collaborators is that employees are not treated as customers, as is the case in the latter conceptualization. Additionally, Grönroos' conceptualization focuses attention on creating customer orientation in employees through a process of influencing, rather than satisfying and motivating employees *per se*.

Phase 3: broadening the internal marketing concept – strategy implementation and change management

The beginning of the third phase is marked by insights drawn from a number of authors who explicitly began to recognize the role of IM as a vehicle for implementing strategy. Winter[16] was one of the earliest to bring to prominence the potential role of IM as a technique for managing employees towards the achievement of organizational goals. Winter emphasizes that the role of IM is that of:

> '*Aligning, educating and motivating staff towards institutional objectives the process by which personnel understand and recognize not only the value of the program but their place in it.*'[17]

This emphasis appears to have implanted the initial notions of IM as an implementation mechanism. The development of IM as an implementation vehicle was also aided by the growing belief that IM had potential as a *cross-functional* integration mechanism within the organization. For instance, George argued that IM is a philosophy for managing the organization's human resources '*as a holistic... management process to integrate the multiple functions*'[18]. This view is expressed more forcefully by Glassman and McAffee, who emphasize the role of IM in integrating marketing and personnel functions to the extent that *personnel becomes a resource for the marketing function*[19].

In this phase, the role of IM as an implementation tool/methodology is made more explicit. Initially, this viewpoint appeared in the context of services. Later, it was generalized to any type of marketing strategy by Piercy and Morgan, who showed that the tools and techniques of external marketing could be applied internally (see Figure 1.1)[20]. In addition, their model explicitly links internal marketing with external marketing programmes. A more generalized version of their model is presented in Figure 1.2. This model acknowledges the broader nature of external marketing efforts by incorporating relationship marketing and also integrates interactive marketing efforts into the model.

Broadly speaking, all of these approaches appear to be based upon the recognition that if strategies are to be implemented more effectively then there is a need to overcome inter-functional conflict and the need to achieve better internal communication. These extensions led IM to be advocated as a general tool for the implementation of *any* organizational

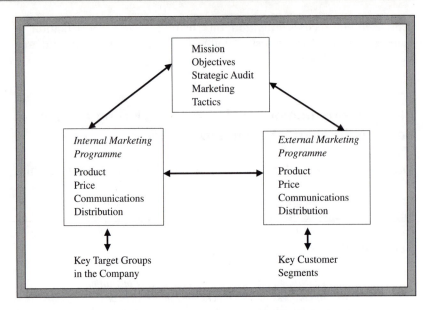

Figure 1.1 The link between internal and external marketing programmes. *Source*: Piercy, N. and Morgan, N. (1991). Internal marketing – the missing half of the marketing programme. *Long Range Planning*, 24 (2), 82–93.

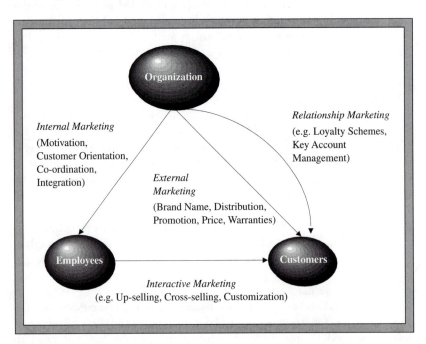

Figure 1.2 The relationship between internal marketing, external marketing, interactive marketing and relationship marketing.

strategy whether internal or external. In due course, IM has come to be seen as a mechanism for reducing departmental, reducing inter-functional friction and overcoming resistance to change. This has led to a widening of IM applications to any type of organization, not merely to services. For example, Harrell and Fors apply the concept to manufacturing firms, and Ahmed and Rafiq propose it as a change management implementation methodology suitable for a wide range of contexts[21].

The discussion of the third phase suggests that the scope of IM activity is much wider than motivation of employees towards customer consciousness. For instance, it can also be used to motivate non-contact employees towards behaving in a manner that enhances the service for end-customers. Taking these issues into account, in an earlier article, we defined internal marketing as '*planned effort to overcome organizational resistance to change and to align, motivate and integrate employees towards the effective implementation of corporate and functional strategies*'[22]. This definition incorporates the notion that any change in strategy is likely to require an IM effort to overcome organizational inertia and to motivate employees towards requisite behaviour. Furthermore, as some (including marketing) strategies are likely to span several functional areas, this is likely to require cross-functional integration. The above definition of IM appears capable of handling these issues within the remit of its boundary. Moreover, this definition also places less emphasis on the concept of employee as customer and more on the tasks and activities that need to be undertaken for the effective implementation of marketing and other programmes to achieve customer satisfaction, whilst recognizing the central role of employees.

Synthesis and definition of internal marketing

The review of work on IM indicates that there are a number of competing definitions and activities all claiming to address IM. From the analysis of the key conceptual and empirical literature, five main elements of internal marketing are identified. These are:

1 Employee motivation and satisfaction.
2 Customer orientation and customer satisfaction.
3 Inter-functional co-ordination and integration.
4 Marketing-like approach to the above.
5 Implementation of specific corporate or functional strategies.

From detailed examination of the literature, it is generally safe to say that in each of the different phases not all the elements of the criteria listed above are present. For instance, it was highlighted in the discussion earlier that employee motivation through employee satisfaction was the major concern during phase 1 of the development of the IM concept. During phase 2, customer orientation (or 'customer consciousness' as Grönroos puts it) and the use of marketing-like techniques received emphasis. In phase 3, the major emphasis was on inter-functional co-ordination and implementation.

Thus far, the definitions that come closest to fully satisfying the above criteria are those of Grönroos and Rafiq and Ahmed[23]. However, Grönroos' definition lacks an emphasis on inter-functional co-ordination, whilst Rafiq and Ahmed's definition fails to emphasize the use of a marketing-like approach. Hence, it is proposed that IM is defined either in the Grönroos sense, but suitably modified by incorporating inter-functional co-ordination and strategic dimension, or the definition of Rafiq and Ahmed is modified to incorporate the use of marketing techniques. Bearing in mind the weaknesses and strengths of existing definitions, as well as the need to generalize the conceptualization beyond the services context to a more widely relevant area of application, the following definition is proposed:

> *'Internal marketing is a planned effort using a marketing-like approach directed at motivating employees, for implementing and integrating organizational strategies towards customer orientation.'*

This definition incorporates the five requisite components of IM set out above. It emphasizes achieving customer satisfaction through the implementation of customer-orientated strategies by motivating employees and co-ordinating cross-functional efforts.

Summary

This chapter has traced the development of the IM concept over the last 20 years, and shown that there is still much discussion in the literature over its definition and scope. The chapter has also highlighted the fact that the IM conceptualization appears to have evolved through three distinct phases. From the synthesis of the ideas in each of the three phases, the chapter develops a list of essential components of an IM programme. These components are:

■ employee motivation and satisfaction;
■ customer orientation and customer satisfaction;

- inter-functional co-ordination and integration;
- marketing-like approach to the above;
- implementation of specific corporate or functional strategies.

These components are then integrated into a more rigorous definition of IM:

> 'Internal marketing is a planned effort using a marketing-like approach directed at motivating employees, for implementing and integrating organizational strategies towards customer orientation.'

The chapters that follow expand on this basic definition of internal marketing and the core elements that constitute it. They also elaborate on models of internal marketing showing how internal marketing works and can be implemented by managers.

References

1. Berry, L. L., Hensel, J. S. and Burke, M. C. (1976). Improving retailer capability for effective consumerism response. *Journal of Retailing*, **52** (3), Fall, 3–14, 94.
2. George, W. R. (1977). The retailing of services – a challenging future. *Journal of Retailing*, Fall, 85–98.
3. Thompson, T. W., Berry, L. L. and Davidson, P. H. (1978). *Banking Tomorrow: Managing Markets Through Planning*, p. 243. New York: Van Nostrand Reinhold.
4. Murray, J. G. (1979). The importance of internal marketing. *Bankers Magazine*, July/August, 38–40.
5. Sasser, W. E. and Arbeit, S. F. (1976). Selling jobs in the service sector. *Business Horizons*, June, 61–2.
6. Berry, L. L. (1981). The employee as customer. *Journal of Retail Banking*, **3** (March), 25–8.
7. George, W. R. (1977). Op. cit., p. 91.
8. Sasser, W. E. and Arbeit, S. F. (1976). Op. cit., p. 61.
9. Sasser, W. E. and Arbeit, S. F. (1976). Op. cit., p. 65.
10. Berry, L. L. and Parasuraman, A. (1991). *Marketing Services: Competing Through Quality*. New York: The Free Press.
11. Berry, L. L. and Parasuraman, A. (1991). Op. cit., p. 151.
12. Grönroos, C. (1981). Internal marketing – an integral part of marketing theory. In *Marketing of Services* (J. H. Donnelly and W. R. George, eds), pp. 236–8. American Marketing Association Proceedings Series.
13. Grönroos, C. (1981). Op. cit., p. 237.
14. Grönroos, C. (1985). Internal marketing – theory and practice. *American Marketing Association's Services Conference Proceedings*, pp. 41–7. Quotation from p. 42.

15. George, W. R. (1990). Internal marketing and organizational behavior: a partnership in developing customer-conscious employees at every level. *Journal of Business Research*, **20**, 63–70.
16. Winter, J. P. (1985). Getting your house in order with internal marketing: a marketing prerequisite. *Health Marketing Quarterly*, **3** (1), 69–77.
17. Winter, J. P. (1985). Op. cit., p. 69.
18. George, W. R. (1990). Op. cit., p. 64.
19. Glassman, M. and McAfee, B. (1992). Integrating the personnel and marketing functions. *Business Horizons*, **35** (3), May/June, 52–9.
20. Piercy, N. and Morgan, N. (1991). Internal marketing – the missing half of the marketing programme. *Long Range Planning*, **24** (2), 82–93.
21. Harrell, G. D. and Fors, M. F. (1992). Internal marketing of a service. *Industrial Marketing Management*, **21** (November), 299–306. Ahmed, P. K. and Rafiq, M. (1995). The role of internal marketing in the implementation of marketing strategies. *Journal of Marketing Practice: Applied Marketing Science*, **1** (4), 32–51.
22. Rafiq, M. and Ahmed, P. K. (1993). The scope of internal marketing: defining the boundary between marketing and human resource management. *Journal of Marketing Management*, **9**, 219–32.
23. Grönroos, C. (1985). Op. cit. Rafiq, M. and Ahmed, P. K. (1993). Op. cit.

chapter two

Models of internal marketing: how internal marketing works

Introduction

Despite the plethora of research, an examination of the literature shows that essentially there are two models of how IM works: one based on the work of Berry's concept of 'employees as customers' and the other based on Grönroos' idea of 'customer mindedness' and interactive marketing[1].

In the existing literature, most authors do not clearly distinguish between Berry's and Grönroos' models of IM. The major reason for this is the fact that both Berry and Grönroos do not spell out the exact components of their models and how they are connected with each other. An examination of Berry's and Grönroos' work (as well as their collaborators) on IM shows that both these authors are concerned with improving service quality. However, they differ in their methods for achieving it. A problem in examining the work of the two authors in this area is that they do not present systematic models of IM. Hence, what is presented below are the implicit models underlying the works of both Berry and Grönroos.

Berry's model of internal marketing

The distinguishing features of Leonard Berry's model are:

- The fundamental assertion that treating employees as customers will lead to changes in attitudes of employees; that is, employees becoming service minded, which leads to better service quality and competitive advantage in the marketplace.

- Treating employees as customers requires that jobs are treated as any other product of the company; that is, the needs and wants of the 'customer' are taken into account and an effort is made to make the product attractive to the 'customers'.

- Treating jobs as products requires a new approach from human resource management (HRM) and basically involves the application of marketing techniques internally both to attract and to retain customer-oriented employees.

The full model is presented in Figure 2.1.

Grönroos' model of internal marketing

Grönroos' original model is based on the premise that employees need to be customer conscious and sales minded so that they can take advantage of *interactive* marketing opportunities, leading to better service quality and higher sales, and consequently higher profits.

- The precursors of customer-conscious employees are supportive recruitment practices, requisite training and participative management style, which gives employees discretion in the service delivery process so that they can take advantage of resulting interactions

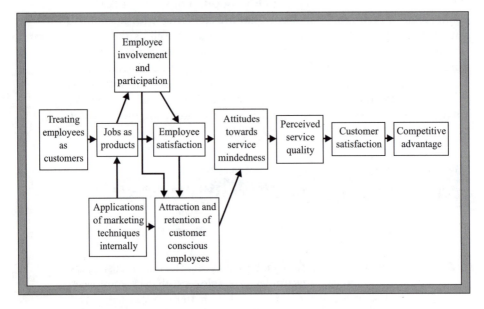

Figure 2.1 Berry's model of internal marketing.

between contact employees and customers. By giving employees discretion, that is by giving employees more control over their work, it is hoped that employee job satisfaction will increase and hence lead to more motivated and customer-conscious employees.

■ Additionally, employees need to be informed of any changes in marketing strategies and campaigns before they are launched on the external market. The idea behind this policy is that employees should thereby understand and realize the importance of their role in the service production and delivery process.

■ All this requires a supportive senior management.

The full Grönroos model is presented in Figure 2.2.

Whilst the objectives of the models are similar, it is clear that the mechanisms that they employ and their objectives are quite different. Moreover, the two models by themselves are incomplete in that the Berry model does not indicate the mechanisms that can be used to motivate employees other than a marketing approach. Similarly, the initial Grönroos model ignored a marketing-like approach to the motivation of employees. In order to provide a more comprehensive model of IM, both these approaches need to be combined.

A composite model of internal marketing in services

The new model of IM derived from the combination of the Berry and Grönroos models is presented in Figure 2.3. A number of additional features in the model include the elaboration of the relationship between customer satisfaction and customer loyalty and increased profits. Profits are also increased by word-of-mouth promotion by satisfied customers.

The model also suggests that the antecedents of employee satisfaction are a function of adequate training, employee discretion and participative management. The job also needs to meet the needs of the employees. In addition, good communication between marketing and contact employee is also essential.

The proposed model has a number of advantages:

■ The new model emphasizes the fact that the Grönroos and Berry models are not competing models but highlight different aspects of IM, and the new model uses these differences to build a more comprehensive conceptualization.

■ The model highlights a large number of implicit assumptions and relationships that need to be tested empirically.

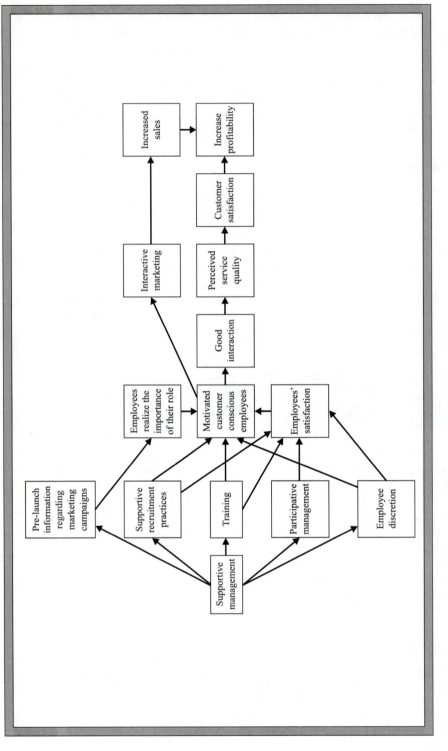

Figure 2.2 Grönroos' model of internal marketing.

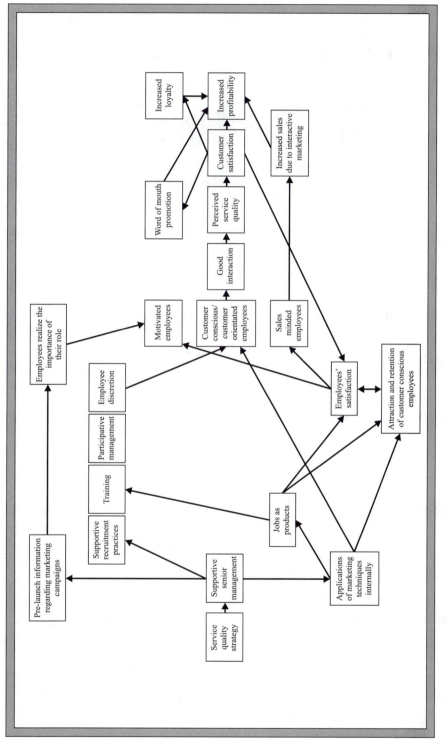

Figure 2.3 A meta-model of internal marketing.

- The model shows the mechanisms involved in the implementation of internal marketing.
- Whilst the model is somewhat more complex than the original models, it provides a more complete view of IM.

Basis of the model

A closer examination of the model also shows that it links together a number of major issues in the marketing field, namely customer orientation, customer satisfaction, customer loyalty, and the linkages between employee satisfaction, customer satisfaction and customer loyalty. In effect, the proposed model provides an integrating framework for these issues. The major elements of the proposed model are discussed in more detail below.

Job satisfaction and its antecedents

A considerable amount of empirical research already exists on the antecedents of job satisfaction in the marketing area, particularly relating to salespersons in industrial settings[2]. This literature is relevant to services marketing because the boundary spanning nature of salespeople is similar to that of contact employees in services in that they have to deal directly with customers and to resolve the conflicting demands of customers on the one hand, and the organization on the other.

Much of this research is concentrated on the impact of role conflict and role ambiguity on job satisfaction. The results of these studies are fairly consistent in showing that role conflict, role ambiguity and role stress negatively affect job satisfaction[3]. In fact, after conducting an analysis of 59 studies, Brown and Peterson concluded that role conflict and role ambiguity were the key antecedents of job satisfaction[4]. Jackson and Schuler, in their analysis of 96 reported organizational studies on role conflict and role ambiguity, found that the most frequent and significantly correlated organizational antecedents of role conflict and role ambiguity were autonomy, feedback from others, feedback from task, task identity, leader initiating structure, leader consideration, participation formalization and level[5].

Employees experience role ambiguity when they do not have the necessary information to do their job properly. Contact employees are more likely to experience role conflict because of the boundary spanning nature of their jobs as they attempt to reconcile the demands of the customers and the interests of the organization. The frequency, quality and accuracy of downward communication moderate role ambiguity. Role ambiguity can be reduced by training employees appropriately against the criteria used in the selection of employees[6].

Linking service quality and customer satisfaction

The basic thrust of the service quality literature is that service quality leads to increased customer satisfaction. This is supported by a considerable amount of empirical evidence for the proposition that service quality is antecedent of customer satisfaction in services. The effects of loyalty include lower price sensitivity, reduced costs of attracting new customers as a result of word-of-mouth promotion, higher reputation of the firm and reduced impact of competitor's activities. For instance, Churchill and Suprenant found that perceived service quality directly affected satisfaction for durables. Oliver and Desarbo also perceived service quality had direct impact on satisfaction[7].

Customer satisfaction, customer loyalty and profitability

In Berry's and Grönroos' models, there is little discussion of how customer satisfaction leads to profitability. However, the link between customer satisfaction and profitability has been proposed by a number of researchers[8]. For Heskett et al., customer satisfaction operates via customer loyalty through to profitability. Other authors have simply proposed a direct link between satisfaction and profitability. Empirically, in the retail banking sector, Hallowell has shown that there were positive relationships between customer satisfaction and loyalty and between loyalty and profitability, but did not find any conclusive evidence for the satisfaction–loyalty–profitability hypothesis.

The costs of implementing service quality are not usually discussed in the IM literature. In fact, the link between customer satisfaction and profitability is likely to display diminishing returns. That is, increasing investments in customer satisfaction will lead to decreasing returns after a point, which suggests that there exists an optimal level of satisfaction that the firm should be aiming for.

Developing a researchable internal marketing model

Whilst the model presented in Figure 2.3 shows how IM works, it is too complex. Figure 2.4 restates the relationships in the model in a more

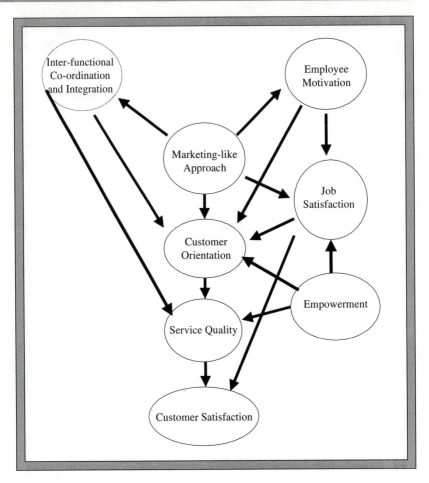

Figure 2.4 A framework for internal marketing of services.

tractable form. The relationships indicated in Figure 2.4 are derived directly from the IM literature. For instance, the motivation of employees via marketing-like activities is explicitly stated from the early literature onwards. Grönroos and others also recommend the marketing-like approach to improve the inter-functional co-ordination and hence customer orientation. Inter-functional co-ordination and integration are central to more recent IM literature. Improving customer orientation of the organization has been a central concern of the IM concept from its inception. More recently, the central reason for interest in IM has been the potential contribution of IM to effective implementation of strategies via increased inter-functional co-ordination and employee motivation.

At the centre of this framework is customer orientation, which is achieved through a marketing-like approach to the motivation of employees, and inter-functional co-ordination. The centrality of customer orientation reflects its importance in the marketing literature and its central role in achieving customer satisfaction and hence organizational goals. In fact, according to two sets of leading researchers in market orientation, inter-functional co-ordination is an essential facet of market orientation[9].

The inclusion of the empowerment variable is essential for the operationalization of Grönroos' interactive marketing concept. In order for interactive marketing to occur, front-line employees need to be empowered; that is, they require a degree of latitude of over the service task performance in order to be responsive to customer needs and be able to perform service recovery. The degree of empowerment given to service employees is contingent on the complexity/variability of customer needs and the degree of task complexity. Empowerment in our model impacts on job satisfaction, customer orientation and service quality.

The empirical evidence on the relationships in the model is fairly limited and somewhat mixed. For instance, Hoffman and Ingram found that there was a weak correlation between job satisfaction and customer orientation, and that role ambiguity, conflict and job satisfaction explained only 9 per cent of customer orientation[10]. Kelley's study of bank employees also found a weak correlation of customer orientation with job satisfaction and motivation[11]. However, when the effects of role clarity and motivation were held constant, job satisfaction was found not to be a significant predictor of customer orientation. Furthermore, although the study found that there was no significant difference in customer orientation among four groups of contact employees (managers, officers, customer service representatives and tellers), the tellers were significantly more dissatisfied with their jobs and significantly less motivated than the other groups of employees. What this suggests is that employees are quite capable of separating their feelings about their jobs (job satisfaction) from the actual performance of the job. Siguaw et al.[12] found that customer orientation was not related to job satisfaction; this is the inverse of the relationship proposed in IM models (i.e. job satisfaction leads to increased customer orientation). Herrington and Lomax[13], in their study of financial advisers of the UK, found no relationship between job satisfaction and customer perceptions of service quality. However, they did find a weak relationship between job satisfaction and customer intention to repurchase.

In view of the above, instead of regarding employee satisfaction as a major precursor to performance, it can be regarded as one of a number of factors, such as employee motivation, customer orientation and sales mindedness, simultaneously determining productivity and the quality of the service. Hence, in our model the impact of job satisfaction on service quality occurs indirectly via customer orientation rather than directly between job satisfaction and service quality. This may partially explain the ambiguity in the empirical research noted above.

Summary and managerial implications

The model outlined in this chapter highlights the importance of employee attitudes in service quality via their impact on customer orientation, employee motivation and job satisfaction. Furthermore, effective service quality also requires high levels of inter-functional co-ordination and integration. Central to ensuring that employees have the requisite attitudes and high levels of inter-functional co-ordination is a marketing-like approach by management to these tasks. In addition, employees need to be supported by requisite levels of empowerment to deliver the required levels of service quality. Empowerment is also a key to service recovery, a key component in perceptions of service quality.

For managerial purposes, Figure 2.3 details how IM can be put into practice. Examination of Figure 2.3 shows the following:

- Supportive senior management is fundamental to the success of IM, as it indicates to all employees the importance of IM initiatives and thereby facilitates inter-functional co-ordination.

- The importance of communicating marketing strategies and objectives to employees so that they understand their role and importance in the implementation of the strategies and achievement of marketing and organizational objectives.

- Employee satisfaction can be increased by treating 'jobs as products'; that is, designing jobs with features that prospective employees value.

- Ensuring that employees are highly motivated, customer oriented and sales minded requires recruitment practices that attract and select employees with the requisite attitudes, providing employees the right type and level of training to perform their jobs, a participative management style and a degree of discretion (contingent on the service strategy of the organization) to front-line employees so that they can meet customer expectations and take advantage of interactive marketing opportunities.

- The importance of explicitly managing the interactions of employees and customers or 'the moments of truth' by training employees for customer orientation and 'sales mindedness'.

- The importance of using a marketing-like approach to the motivation of employees, and inter-functional co-ordination.

Delivering high levels of service has its costs. For instance, service quality may be improved by providing employees with additional or better training. However, this has a consequence of increasing costs. Unless these costs are recovered by attracting extra customers, increase in repeat purchases or fewer service delivery mistakes, there will be a negative impact on profitability. Hence, this suggests that there is an optimal level of service quality that management should be aiming for, not necessarily the highest. The level of service quality that an organization offers is contingent on its positioning on service in the marketplace.

References

1. Berry, L. L. (1981). The employee as customer. *Journal of Retail Banking*, **3** (March), 25–8. Grönroos, C. (1985). Internal marketing – theory and practice. *American Marketing Association's Services Conference Proceedings*, pp. 41–7.

2. Churchill, G. A. Jr, Ford N. M. and Walker, O. C. Jr (1974). Measuring the job satisfaction of industrial salesmen. *Journal of Marketing Research*, **11** (August), 254–60. Churchill, G. A. Jr, Ford N. M. and Walker, O. C. Jr (1976). Organizational climate and job satisfaction in the salesforce. *Journal of Marketing Research*, **13** (November), 323–32. Rogers, J. D., Clow, K. E. and Kash, T. J. (1994). Increasing job satisfaction of service personnel. *The Journal of Services Marketing*, **8** (1), 14–26. Singh, J., Verbeke, W. and Rhoads, G. K. (1996). Do organizational practices matter in role stress processes? A study of direct and moderating effects for marketing-oriented boundary spanners. *Journal of Marketing*, **60** (3), 69–86.

3. Behrman, D. N. and Perreault, W. D. (1984). A role stress model of performance and satisfaction of industrial salespersons. *Journal of Marketing*, **48** (Fall), 9–12. Lysonski, S., Singer, A. and Wilemon, D. (1988). Coping with environmental uncertainty and boundary spanning in the product manager's role. *The Journal of Business and Industrial Marketing*, **3** (Winter), 5–16. Siguaw, J. A., Brown, G. and Widing, R. E. II (1994). The influence of the market orientation of the firm on sales force behaviour and attitudes. *Journal of Marketing Research*, **31** (1), 106–16. Teas, R. K. (1983). Supervisory behaviour, role stress, and the job satisfaction of industrial sales people. *Journal of Marketing Research*, **20** (February), 84–91.

4. Brown, S. P. and Peterson, R. A. (1993). Antecedents and consequences of salesperson job satisfaction: meta-analysis and causal effects. *Journal of Marketing Research*, **30** (February), 63–77.

5. Jackson, S. E. and Schuler, R. S. (1985). A meta-analysis and conceptual critique of research on role ambiguity and role conflict in work settings. *Organizational Behavior and Human Decision Processes*, **36** (1), 16–78.

6. Walker, O. C., Churchill, G. A. Jr and Ford, N. M. (1977). Motivation and performance in industrial selling: present knowledge and needed research. *Journal of Marketing Research*, **14** (May), 156–68. Walker, O. C., Churchill, G. A. Jr and Ford, N. M. (1975). Organizational determinants of the industrial salesman's role conflict and ambiguity. *Journal of Marketing*, **39** (January), 32–9. Zeithaml, V. A., Parasuraman, A. and Berry, L. L. (1990). *Delivering Quality Service*. New York: The Free Press.

7. Anderson, E. W. and Sullivan, M. (1993). The antecedents and consequences of customer satisfaction for firms. *Marketing Science*, **12** (Spring), 125–43.

Churchill, G. A. and Suprenant, C. F. (1982). An investigation into the determinants of customer satisfaction. *Journal of Marketing Research*, **19** (November), 491–504. Cronin, J. J. Jr and Taylor, S. A. (1992). Measuring service quality: a re-examination and extension. *Journal of Marketing*, **52** (3), July, 55–68. Fornell, C. (1992). A national customer satisfaction barometer: the Swedish experience. *Journal of Marketing*, **55** (January), 1–21. Oliver, R. L. and Desarbo, W. S. (1988). Response determinants in satisfaction judgements. *Journal of Consumer Research*, **14** (March), 495–507.

8. Anderson, E. W., Fornell, C. and Lehmann, D. R. (1994). Customer satisfaction, market share, and profitability: findings from Sweden. *Journal of Marketing*, **58** (3), 53–66. Gummesson, E. (1993). *Quality Management in Service Organizations: An Interpretation of the Service Quality Phenomenon and a Synthesis of International Research*. Karlstadt, Sweden: International Service Quality Association. Hallowell, R. (1996). The relationships of customer satisfaction, customer loyalty, and profitability: an empirical study. *International Journal of Service Industry Management*, **7** (4), 27–42. Heskett, J. L., Sasser, W. E. and Hart, C. W. L. (1990). *Breakthrough Service*. New York: The Free Press. Reicheld, F. F. and Sasser, W. E. Jr (1990). Zero defections comes to services. *Harvard Business Review*, **68** (September/October), 105–11. Rust, R. T., Zahorik, A. J. and Keiningham, T. L. (1995). Return on quality (ROQ): making service quality financially accountable. *Journal of Marketing*, **59** (2), 58–70. Schneider, B. and Bowen, D. E. (1995). *Winning the Service Game*. Boston, MA: HBS. Strobacka, K., Strandvik, T. and Grönroos, C. (1994). Managing customer relationships for profit: the dynamics of relationship quality. *International Journal of Service Industry Management*, **5** (5), 21–38.

9. Kohli, A. K. and Jaworski, B. J. (1990). Market orientation: the construct, research propositions, and managerial implications. *Journal of Marketing*, **54** (2), 35–58. Jaworski, B. J. and Kohli, A. K. (1993). Market orientation: antecedents and consequences. *Journal of Marketing*, **57** (3), 53–70. Narver, J. C. and Slater, S. F. (1990). The effect of a market orientation on business profitability. *Journal of Marketing*, **54** (5), 20–35.

10. Hoffman, D. K. and Ingram, T. N. (1991). Creating customer orientated employees: the case in home health care. *Journal of Health Care Marketing*, **11** (June), 24–32.

11. Kelley, S. W. (1990). Customer orientation of bank employees and culture. *International Journal of Bank Marketing*, **8** (6), 25–9.

12. Siguaw, J. A., Brown, G. and Widing, R. E. II (1994). The influence of the market orientation of the firm on sales force behavior and attitudes. *Journal of Marketing Research*, **31** (1), 106–16.

13. Herrington, G. and Lomax, W. (1999). Do satisfied employees make customers satisfied? An investigation into the relationship between service employee job satisfaction and customer perceived service quality. In *Marketing and Competition in the Information Age, Proceedings of the 28th EMAC Conference* (L. Hildebrandt, D. Annacker and Klapper, D., eds), 11–14 May, p. 110. Berlin: Humboldt University.

chapter three

The tools of internal marketing

As we have seen, a central plank of internal marketing is the use of marketing-like techniques to motivate employees. The question inevitably arises as to how useful are concepts techniques such as customers, segmentation, market research, and the marketing mix for developing customer-oriented behaviour and generally motivating employees? This is a pertinent question, as motivation of employees has traditionally been the realm of human resource management (HRM). In the following discussion, we examine how and the extent to which it is possible to use marketing techniques to motivate employees. This section takes up these questions, dealing firstly with application of the customer concept internally and then moving on to the various elements of the marketing mix, segmentation and market research techniques. The final section shows how IM was used to facilitate the implementation of a marketing strategy in the financial services sector.

Internal customers

Central to the marketing philosophy are the concepts of customer and exchange, namely that customers receive products they desire in exchange for payment of some kind (that is, a price). In the external marketing exchange situation, products are bought in order to derive some form of utility or satisfaction. Applying these concepts internally, as is implied by treating 'employees as customers', the concepts require some care.

Firstly, one of the main problems with this approach is that the 'products' that employees are being sold may be unwanted or may in fact have negative utility for them; that is, they may not want them (e.g. new methods of working). In normal marketing situations, customers do not *have to* buy products that they do not wish to buy. This is not true for employees, as they must either accept the 'product' or (in the final analysis) they can be 'forced' into acceptance under the threat of disciplinary action or dismissal. In normal marketing situations, the consequences of non-purchase are not so severe. Additionally, in normal marketing situations customers have a range of (competing) products to choose from; this is unlikely to be the case in an internal marketing situation, where one particular policy will be on offer. That is, the marketing approach consists of *non-coercive* actions to induce a response in another social unit[1]. Therefore, the use of force or formal authority is not considered to be a marketing solution to a problem.

Another problem with the notion of the employee as customer is the idea of customer sovereignty (that is the idea of customer is king, customer is always right and so forth). For, if employees were to behave like external customers, they would make impossible demands upon the organization and its resources. It is for this reason that in this approach employees *do not know* they are customers even though they are treated as such!

Moreover, the idea put forward by some that 'personnel is the first market of a service company' appears to suggest that the employee market has primacy[2]. This stands on its head the most fundamental axiom of marketing that the external customer has primacy. For it is the external customer that is the *raison d'être* of any company. For instance, many restaurant workers would prefer not to work late hours, but nevertheless have to because that is when the customers prefer to dine out. Accommodating employee preferences in this case would lead to commercial suicide.

Given the above caveats, the marketing principle of creating products that their internal customers want is rapidly gaining ground in all types of organizations. For instance, in the British National Health Service, human resource development trainers are increasingly shifting their practices away from product orientation to a market orientation. That is, instead of putting on courses that the trainers wanted to do or enrolling candidates on courses simply to achieve targets, they are now shifting toward providing training and courses that internal customers demand, whether they are senior management, line managers or other employees[3].

The problems associated with 'employees as customers' are largely avoided in the total quality management (TQM) concept of internal customers, as the emphasis is on relationships between employees themselves rather than between the organization and the employees. In the TQM approach, employees make demands upon each other rather than their organization. Furthermore, the types of demands that they can make upon each other are limited to ensuring that they, as suppliers, deliver 'products' that meet their 'customers' requirements and vice versa. If these requirements are met along the entire length of the production chain, then the quality of the final product will be assured.

The degree of customer orientation and co-ordination between different organizations depends on the degree and type of interdependence that exists between groups in organizations. Three types of interdependence can be distinguished, namely sequential interdependence, pooled interdependence and reciprocal interdependence[4]. For instance, in a manufacturing setting, where production largely progresses linearly, that is, where the output of one group is the input of another, and so on down the line, there is sequential interdependence between different groups or departments, similar to the TQM approach mentioned above. This situation is likely to be characterized by moderate levels of customer orientation and co-ordination between groups.

In situations of pooled interdependency, that is, cases where work does not flow between groups or departments, and they make separate and independent contributions to overall organizational or departmental goals (for instance, sales teams assigned to separate geographic areas of the target market), there is likely to be little concern for customer orientation or collaboration.

Reciprocal interdependence occurs where there is back and forth flow of work between groups. Such a situation requires a high level of collaboration between all the groups involved. Such a situation is typical in health care settings, where highly interdependent teamwork is required for complex patient treatment, frequently requiring multiple inputs from specialist teams and support services. In such a situation, the need for internal customer orientation is high and dominant, because the output of one group typically serves as the input for a second area, and the output of the second area might flow back as input for the first group again. In areas of high reciprocal interdependence, therefore, one would expect greater effort devoted by managers towards internal customer orientation. This is necessary in order to increase the sharing of expertise, the resolution of conflicts and priorities, and the sharing of the common goal of serving patient needs. Research evidence suggests that high level co-ordination of objectives increases both employee and patient satisfaction[5].

Developing an internal marketing mix

The idea behind the internal marketing mix concept is that a number of elements under the control of management are combined and integrated in order to produce the required response from the target market. Attempts at applying the marketing mix concept to internal marketing have been structured generally around the 4Ps marketing mix (Product, Promotion, Price and Place) framework[6]. However, because of the intangible nature of the product being 'marketed' in the internal marketing context (for instance, the idea of a customer-conscious employee), we propose that the extended marketing mix for services is used[7]. That is, it is proposed that in addition to the traditional 4Ps of product marketing (namely Product, Price, Promotion and Place), Physical Evidence, Process and Participants need to be added. This is because the extended 7Ps marketing mix (in particular the Process and Participants concepts) explicitly recognizes inter-functional interdependence and the need for an integrated effort for effective service (or product) delivery. An integrated effort is, after all, one of the major aims of an internal marketing programme. We begin the discussion of the application of the marketing mix to internal marketing with the product concept.

Product

At the strategic level, the product can refer to marketing strategies; what is sold is those values and attitudes needed to make a plan work. At the tactical level, the product could include new performance measures and new ways of handling customers. Product can also be used to refer to services and training courses provided by HRM. At a more fundamental level the product is the job[8]. In order to achieve acceptance of new initiatives, managers need to concentrate on the benefits of the product rather than its features. That is, managers should concentrate on explaining the benefits of new initiatives to the customers, to the organization, and consequently the employees themselves. Treating jobs as products means looking at jobs not only from the point of view of the tasks that need to be performed, but also from the perspective of the employees and the benefits they seek from the job. This means giving consideration not only to financial remuneration, but also to training needs, level of responsibility and involvement in decision making, career development opportunities, and the working environment, amongst other factors that employees value. Treating jobs in this way will facilitate the hiring retention and the motivation of employees. Also, treating jobs as products is a reminder that jobs need to be marketed well in order to recruit the best possible employees.

Price

Price can refer to the psychological cost of adopting to new methods of working, projects that have to be foregone in order to carry out new policies (i.e. the opportunity cost), or to transfer pricing and expense allocation between departments. As opportunity costs are difficult to measure precisely (unlike the monetary price of goods and services), employees may tend to overestimate the costs of undertaking new practices and hence be inclined to resist changes. In order to avoid this, the benefits of adopting the new policies need to be clearly explained and any fears allayed by providing employees with appropriate information.

Exhibit 3.1. Internal communications at Lloyds TSB

Large corporations are increasingly realizing the importance of using internal marketing for inculcating their corporate culture brand values. This is partly due to the increasing number of mergers, which create problems of integrating different corporate and brand cultures. Such situations require a planned programme of internal communications and just a speech or two from the new CEO. This is well illustrated by the Lloyds TSB merger in 1995 and its launch as a brand in its own right in 1999.

On 1 August 1995, Cheltenham & Gloucester (C&G) became part of the Lloyds Bank Group. In December of the same year, Lloyds Bank Group merged with TSB Group to form Lloyds TSB Group plc. In September 1996, Lloyds Abbey Life became a wholly owned subsidiary of Lloyds TSB Group. The merger created a single bank with around 77 000 employees and 15 million customers. However, Lloyds TSB needed to integrate its employees and offer its customers an integrated range of products and brand propositions that the customers understood. It was not until November 1998 that a full-scale pilot was launched in Norwich, with 13 branches offering a single branded service and product range to customers of both banks under the Lloyds TSB name. On 28 June 1999, Lloyds TSB was launched on the high street. The launch was accompanied by a new advertising campaign.

The bank realized that if it were to communicate its new brand values effectively to its customers it needed to communicate these values first to its employees and to motivate them to deliver the brand. Hence, prior to the full launch the bank instigated a comprehensive and sustained internal marketing programme. A key component of the programme was a live event at the NEC in Birmingham called 'Your Life. Your Bank', a month before the full launch. The objectives of the event were to reveal the new blue and green corporate identity, explain the values behind the brand, and gain commitment from the employees to new culture and the new methods of working required to deliver the brand.

(*continued*)

The problem that Lloyds TSB faced was how to get its entire workforce of 77 000 on message. The method that it hit on, with the help of the events organizer Caribiner, was to ask all its staff to nominate a 'pathfinder', or a brand ambassador, who would attend the event and then take the messages back to 15 of their colleagues.

A total of 5000 staff acted as pathfinders, about 2000 of whom were the senior people, with the remainder coming from all ranks.

The event comprised a 28-stand exhibition, representing all of the bank's departments. A number of presentations explored how Lloyds and TSB were coming together, whilst others focused on understanding the brand. There were contributions from all levels, from top management to the people who had put up the new signage. The event was compered by Carol Vorderman and climaxed with the arrival on stage of Irish pop band The Corrs, whose music featured in the new advertising campaign.

After the event, pathfinders passed on the knowledge that they had acquired about the new brand to their colleagues in prearranged meetings. They were equipped with packs containing summaries of key points, overhead transparencies and a video summary for this task. Research conducted among pathfinders before and after the live event showed that the pathfinders found that there was strong and positive change in their attitudes towards the impact of the changes on customers, employees and the excitement about the new company. The research also showed that the pathfinder approach had been successful in conveying the messages to staff who had not attended the event.

On the day of the full launch of the new brand, the bank's chief executive addressed the staff live on business TV and all staff received a letter welcoming them to their new bank.

Sources: Anonymous (2000). Internal communications. *Marketing*, 6 June, p. 19. Murphy, C. (2000). Instilling workers with brand values. *Marketing*, 27 January, pp. 31–2. Miller, R. (1999). Going live can put staff fears to rest. *Marketing*, 4 November, pp. 35–6. Anonymous (1999). Case study: Lloyds/TSB merger. *Marketing*, 4 November, p. 36. Lloyds TSB plc website (www.lloydstsb.com).

Internal communications/Promotion

Promotion in the context of the marketing mix refers to the use of advertising, publicity, personal selling (face-to-face presentations/communications) and sales promotions (incentives to purchase) in order to inform and to influence potential customers' attitudes towards a firm's products.

Motivating employees and influencing their attitudes is obviously an important aspect of internal marketing and hence the importance of getting the internal communications strategies right.

Human resource managers already use a wide variety of techniques and media to communicate with employees, ranging from oral briefings and company newspapers to corporate videos. However, for effective communication what is necessary is a co-ordinated use of these various media. Interest in new policies and training courses, for instance, can be generated by publicizing them in company newspapers and on company notice-boards. This needs to be followed up with setting up of contact points and leaflets and brochures giving further information.

Personal selling

Face-to-face presentations to individuals and groups can be even more effective than in external marketing, because the presenter (manager, supervisor) has implicit authority behind what he or she is saying and is evident from the fact that face-to-face communication is regarded as having far greater impact than other communications methods[9].

Incentives

It is clear from the notion of customer that employees must be offered some benefits in order to change their behaviour. The use of motivational incentives such as cash bonuses, awards, recognition programmes, prize draws and competitions directed at contact personnel in the services industry are very common. These can be used to overcome short-term resistance or to motivate employees toward consistent behaviour or to increase productivity.

Advertising

The use of mass media advertising (i.e. newspapers and television) to communicate with employees (in order to motivate them) is rare. It is only used in special circumstances such as strikes, where normal work-place methods of communications methods would be ineffective. This is because of the vast expense of these media and the fact that they are not narrowly targeted on a particular organization's employees. However, organizations need to take care of what image they are projecting of themselves and their workforce in their advertising aimed at external customers, as they are likely to be seen by their employees as well (see Exhibit 3.2). This can be turned into a positive advantage by portraying employees with positive customer-oriented attributes which employees can then attempt to emulate. An illustration of this is provided by the

Exhibit 3.2. Aligning internal and external communications at Sainsbury's

In the autumn of 1998, Sainsbury's launched a major advertising campaign with the strapline *'Value to shout about'*. The ad campaign showed the actor John Cleese talking to shop staff (played by actors) about low prices and urging them to be more positive about Sainsbury's offer. One advert showed him dressed in a brash checked jacket bellowing through a megaphone into the ear of a hapless sales assistant urging her to be more upbeat about the value of Sainsbury's offer. In an another advert, Cleese is seen promising that Sainsbury's will refund twice the difference if a customer buys a can of baked beans cheaper elsewhere.

The campaign created by the advertising agency Abbott Mead Vickers BBDO appeared to signal a significant shift in Sainsbury's pricing strategy. Previous TV campaigns had positioned Sainsbury's as a more sophisticated, top end of the market food retailer. This was exemplified by a series of adverts in the early 1990s showing a number of well-known television celebrities making their favourite recipes with Sainsbury's ingredients conveying an air of indulgence. The new campaign had been launched in a response to a survey by A. C. Nielsen that had rated Sainsbury's top in choice, quality and service, but not price. The adverts were designed to challenge consumer perceptions that Sainsbury's was more expensive than its rivals.

The adverts did not go down well with the customers or the employees. The employees complained that the adverts made them look stupid. Sales figures also showed that the customers had also been turned off. Even worse, in a survey of television viewers, the adverts were voted the most irritating adverts on TV in 1998. Sainsbury's could have easily avoided the error of alienating its staff by testing the adverts internally before airing them. Sainsbury's also failed to prepare its employees for the apparent shift in its price positioning strategy. However, Sainsbury's reacted quickly in response to staff complaints by editing the advert and taking the emphasis away from the employee.

The following year, Sainsbury's did not make the same mistake when it launched its new marketing campaign *'Making life taste better'*, designed to switch emphasis back on to quality. This time, the advertising campaign was preceded by an internal marketing programme.

The programme was aimed at educating and motivating staff as part of an attempt to revive confidence in the Sainsbury's brand. The programme, called 'One company, one agenda', was devised by M. & C. Saatchi. It was launched at a special conference by the then Marketing Director to give it added credence.

The Sainsbury's campaign included:

■ Posters placed at the back of shops and in corridors giving facts and figures about the changing customer using the strapline 'When we understand our customers we can make all our lives taste better.'

■ An obligatory induction video for all new employees showing how every staff member contributes to the chain, from the distribution warehouse to the checkout, using the theme of a little girl waiting for food for her birthday party.

■ The staff magazine was revamped with the new store identity.

■ Staff were also issued with company screen savers using the new 'living orange' logo and pictures of brightly coloured fruit.

The programme was a clear attempt to align internal communications with the external marketing campaign and to ensure that the brand promises were being delivered. The campaign was also designed to boost staff morale, as it coincided with the announcement of 1000 job losses. Sainsbury's main competitors, Tesco and Asda, already had successful staff motivation schemes and Wal-Mart, Asda's new owner, is well known for involving staff in company decisions.

Sources: Bainbridge, J. (1998). Are you marketing to your staff? *Marketing*, 8 October, pp. 20–21. Anonymous (1998). Cheesy John Cleese is top of the turn-offs. *The Times*, 18 December. Jardine, A. (1999). Sainsbury's motivating staff to revive image. *Marketing*, 17 June, p. 3. Witt, J. (2001). Are your staff and ads in tune? *Marketing*, 18 January, p. 21.

portrayal of enthusiastic and competent 'Kwik Fit Fitters' in Kwik Fit's advertisements on British television.

However, with the emergence of narrowcasting technology, organizations can now use live television to communicate with large numbers of employees simultaneously in diverse locations, in more targeted and cost-effective ways. Traditionally, large multi-sited organizations have communicated with their disparate workforce through newsletters, corporate videos and annual conferences. These are very costly methods, particularly conferences, which in addition to hotel bills and travel time, take employees away from their workplace. This is why, recently, instead of holding its biannual review meeting for officers and directors in Memphis, Federal Express, which has the largest corporate television network in the world with 1200 sites able to receive transmissions, transmitted a live 3-hour broadcast simultaneously to locations in the UK, Paris and Brussels, as well as the USA. All employees were able to watch the broadcast, with officers and directors participating in a phone-in session. The advantages of using such a medium for internal marketing are obvious.

Despite its potential, in the early 1990s only a handful of companies in the UK used business television and the market was worth only £3 million. In comparison, in the USA, the market for business television was estimated to be worth $350 million and estimated to be worth $1 billion by 1995. Business television was therefore predicted to be a growth area of employee communications because of the speed and reach of the medium[10]. However, with the widespread adoption of the Internet, business television is likely to be superseded by webcasting.

Place/distribution

Distribution refers to the place and the channels (or third parties) that are used to get products to customers. In the HRM context, place could mean meetings, conferences, etc. where policies are announced and channels could be used to refer to third parties (for example, consultants and training agencies) used to deliver training programmes.

Physical/tangible evidence

The physical evidence (also referred to as tangible evidence by some authors) refers to the environment in which a product is delivered and where interaction takes place between contact staff and customers, as well as any tangible goods that facilitate delivery or communication of the product. Physical evidence can be categorized as either essential or peripheral evidence. Peripheral evidence refers to tangible cues that a product has been delivered. Examples of peripheral evidence include such things as memos, guidelines, training manuals and so forth. Essential evidence, on the other hand, refers to the environment in which the product is delivered. In internal marketing situations, the environment in which the product is delivered is not as important as for services in general, because this will usually be the same as the normal work environment. However, special significance of particular policies may be signalled by holding conferences or by sending employees for special training to external agencies such as universities, for instance.

In contrast, tangible cues may be even more important in internal marketing than for the marketing of services in general. One of the more important tangible elements in internal marketing is documentation. Documentation of policies and changes in policies are important, because if employees are required to perform to certain standards then it is important that these standards are fully documented. Indeed, Quality Standards such as the British BS5750 and the International ISO 9000 put great emphasis on documentation in achieving quality. Other tangible elements may include training sessions to achieve required standards, for instance. The training sessions in themselves are a tangible manifestation of the commitment to the standards or particular policies.

Process

Process refers to how a 'customer' actually receives a product. In the internal marketing context, customer consciousness may be inculcated into employees by training (or retraining) staff. Structural changes such as the introduction of quality circles and new reporting methods may also be necessary. Process can also refer to whether new policies are introduced through negotiations with unions or imposed unilaterally. In the communications area, process can refer to the delivery method: for instance, whether circulars, videos or line managers are used to convey changes.

Participants

This refers both to people involved in delivering the product and those receiving the product who may influence the customer's perceptions. In an organizational context, communications need to be delivered by someone of the right level of authority if they are to be effective in achieving their implementation aims. Hence, in internal marketing the source of the internal marketing programmes plays a crucial role in their effectiveness.

Employees in general tend to be influenced most by their immediate superiors[11]. One implication implicit in this is that inter-departmental or inter-functional communications are likely to be least effective. This is because they have equal status; that is, no direct authority to enforce compliance. Of greater importance is the implication that if the performance of contact staff is to be improved then the most effective means of communication is through their immediate superiors, who in turn need to be motivated by strategic management. Direct communication between strategic management and contact staff, although helpful, would not by itself be sufficient for the implementation of internal marketing programmes.

Market segmentation here is the process of grouping employees with similar characteristics and needs and wants. In services, for instance, employees may be grouped on the basis of whether they are contact employees or not. Other bases for segmentation might include type of benefits that employees want, and roles and functions that they perform. The existence of complex grading systems, departmental, functional and other organizational structures, suggests that the use of segmentation is already widespread in the HRM area. It is suggested, however, that employees need to be segmented along motivational lines rather than departmental or other lines traditionally used in HRM.

Market research involves identifying the needs and wants of employees and monitoring the impact of HRM policies on employees. This type of research has a long history in the HRM area in the form of employee attitude surveys. In the UK, for instance, employee attitude surveys date back to the 1930s, when the National Institute of Industrial Psychology started using them to study labour turnover, but nowadays are used for a wide range of issues, including attitudes held on supervision, remuneration, working conditions, specific personnel practices, incentive schemes and so forth. The number of companies that use these types of surveys are relatively small and are estimated to be around 8 per cent[12]. However, some companies attach great importance to them. IBM, for instance, has been using them since 1962. It has now computerized the process to make it even more effective. Obviously, these market survey type techniques are much more likely to be used by larger firms for reasons of cost effectiveness.

Employee surveys need to be handled with care, even more so than consumer surveys, because of employees' fears of repercussions. Hence, it may be necessary to guarantee absolute confidentiality in order to ensure a good response. However, even if the response rates are high, the responses need to be interpreted carefully, as respondents are more likely to reply as they think the organization wishes them to respond rather than express their true views, because of the aforementioned fear of repercussions. Another important difference between employee and consumer surveys is that employee participation is not likely to be high if employees are not given feedback on the survey results. More importantly, management needs to show that action is taken over issues of concern uncovered by the surveys. Employees may also be suspicious of attitude surveys, as they have been used to weaken and deter unions[13].

The foregoing analysis highlights the fact that it is possible to apply marketing techniques and concepts in order to create a motivated workforce working towards the implementation of corporate goals. Great care needs to taken, however, as to how these concepts and techniques are applied.

A multi-level model of internal marketing

The model closely incorporates strategic elements by proposing a multi-level schema of how marketing tools and techniques can be used internally to generate commitment and effective implementation. Specifically, the model deploys six elements to constitute an internal marketing mix, as well as internal marketing research, internal segmentation, and positioning to operationalize the key parts of the model and stages. The combination of a multi-stage schema with a broader internal marketing mix provides a conceptualization able to highlight more clearly the role of segmentation and positioning in the internal context. By embedding the model within a strategic framework, it is also clearer in highlighting how implementation of strategy can be created.

The model is characterized by three strategic levels, namely Direction, Path and Action (see Figure 3.1). Level 1 is concerned with setting the general agenda of a particular mission or change, thus defining the direction in which organizational efforts are to be directed. This requires an evaluation of external opportunities and an understanding of organizational capabilities. Level 2, that of Path, requires specification of the route from the numerous alternative possibilities to achieve the set change or mission, which the organization opts to follow. Each of the alternatives needs to be examined closely. In particular, the types of barriers likely to be encountered and potential mechanisms for overcoming them need careful evaluation at this stage. The final level is that of Action. This requires a translation of a particular option into specific

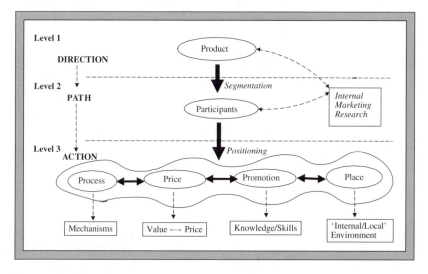

Figure 3.1 Multi-level model of internal marketing.

courses of action and activities. Detailed actions are necessary so as to make the undertaking as clear and trouble free as possible. The driving force at this level is dictated by decisions at level 2, which itself is defined by the direction set at level 1.

The interconnection between the strategic process and the internal marketing mix, marketing research, segmentation and positioning is depicted in Figure 3.1. The constituent activities of the internal marketing mix as defined by the internal context and how these relate to internal marketing research, segmentation and positioning are elaborated further in the discussion below.

Stage 1: Direction

At level 1 is the presence of the product element. In the internal context it is the product that sets direction. The product can be viewed as the definition and direction of change, which may simply be either in terms of changes in attitudes and behaviours of employees or in more tangible activities such as changed production activities or some other goal. Essentially, the product is any change in employee behaviour or attitudes that is required for the effective implementation of a particular corporate or functional strategy. In a strategic sense, the product dimension requires that the external environment and available opportunities are understood in relation to constraints upon the direction imposed by internal capabilities. Moreover, for true internal marketing to occur, the totality of the product package cannot solely be made up from a single vantage point, such as the owner/manager's viewpoint, but must incorporate aspects arising from the needs and requirements of employees. This is a necessary condition for efficient and effective implementation to occur. Two aspects of market research can be observed at this stage: external and internal research. External marketing research plays a role in identifying external opportunities and the changes necessary to take advantage of them, whereas internal marketing research, broadly speaking, can play a role in identifying capabilities and competencies through examination of the various sets of employees. Subsequently, this information can be fed into the process of specifying the 'product' for long-term success.

Stage 2: Path

Once a direction has been set by specifying the product, it leads onto the second level decision, namely that of Path. Here the general direction that has been taken needs to be broken into specific programme(s) that have to be delivered to particular groups of employees in order to achieve effective implementation. The Path level includes the Participants element, which examines ways of organizing individuals possessing particular needs against sets of organizational activities so as to facilitate the implementation process. At this level, the breakdown of the direction occurs, firstly by directing explicit attention to who (e.g. the individuals/Participants) is to be involved in the process of change and implementation, and secondly how they are to be involved. All participants, whether directly or indirectly involved, need to be explicitly defined in order to enhance effectiveness in the delivery process of the strategic change defined at level 1.

Internal segmentation

The next stage of the model's operationalization requires that internal marketing research is conducted so as to identify needs of the internal markets (e.g. employees). Numerous traditional marketing research techniques, ranging from simple surveys to indirect in-depth data collection techniques, can be usefully employed to capture a real sense of the motivations, potential fears and resistance of employees to the change programme. Once such needs and resistance have been explicated, then the next step is to examine the possibility of grouping these individuals upon their need requirements, as well as other characteristics such as demographics. Since a wealth of information, especially with respect to simple demographic information, is typically already resident in information stores such as personnel records, it can be easily complemented by further information, which may be of a psychographic nature. The first step in the internal segmentation process is to identify appropriate criteria for segmentation. It is important to note that extreme care needs to be exercised in the selection of segmentation criteria, since by definition these determine the usefulness and relevance of segments subsequently created. The second step is to apply the selected criteria to the relatively rich source of data to form segments.

The process of employee segmentation is necessary to identify whether participants form cohesive groups on the basis of some shared commonalties, by virtue of which it would be possible to create a specific package of activities that can then be directed at participant segments in order to facilitate implementation. The logic is that if specific needs and resistance can be associated with particular segments, then these needs and fears can be overcome by directing a specific package in a manner designed to satisfy employee needs and mediate their fears. As a process, this is much more effective than one that adopts a single approach for all employees, since neglecting employee differences diffuses implementation effort. Here, just as in external marketing research, a whole range of multivariate techniques such as clustering procedures, factor and conjoint analysis may be used to define needs and preferences in order to construct homogeneous groups (or segments). Moreover, given the relatively captive nature of the sampling population, it is possible to conduct depth and longitudinal studies with relative ease. At this stage, the whole process is strengthened if specific information with regard to resistance to change is explicitly incorporated into the process of grouping. This leads to a definition of homogeneous segments with regard to needs, resistances and actions required for a particular strategic course of action.

At this juncture, it is important to note that employee surveys need to be handled with care, even more so than consumer surveys, because of employees' fear of repercussions. Hence, it may be necessary to guarantee absolute confidentiality in order to ensure valid responses. Additionally, high response rates can potentially be elicited by employing external independent organizations such as consultants to conduct the research. However, even if the response rates are high, the responses need to be interpreted carefully, as respondents are more likely to reply as they think the organization wishes them to respond rather than express their true views, because of the aforementioned fears. Another important difference between employee and consumer surveys is that employee participation is not likely to be high if employees are not given feedback on the survey results. Importantly, management needs to show that action is taken over issues of concern uncovered by the surveys.

Stage 3: Action

Once participant segmentation has been completed, then it is possible to start thinking about positioning and targeting identified segments through construction and appropriate leverage of the remaining elements of the internal mix, namely Process, Price, Promotion and Place (i.e. those occurring at level 3).

Internal positioning

In the external context, positioning requires selecting those associations that are to be built upon and emphasized, and those which are to be removed and de-emphasized. The situation is the same in the internal context. Internal positioning aims to create a tactical package of actions so as to overcome identified barriers, as well as fulfilling employee needs. This may at times involve focusing upon changing the importance that employees accord to a particular benefit and/or identifying and emphasizing benefits not previously recognized. Internal positioning involves providing an appropriate mix of differentiated benefits to a specific employee segment that will motivate it to achieve effective implementation of marketing and other strategies. Just as in external market positioning, internal positioning is segment specific and involves the leverage of the marketing mix elements, particularly those specified at level 3 of the model, in order to attain pre-specified goals. However, it is as well to note that, since all the elements of the internal marketing programme can potentially affect position, all the elements of the internal mix, not just those at level 3, are consistent and supportive. Internal positioning, due to the fact that it constitutes the specific actions necessary to facilitate implementation, acts as the focal point in the tactical development of an effective internal marketing programme.

The process of internal positioning also serves to highlight that there exist numerous possible alternatives to reach a given end. Each alternative must be assessed for its benefits relative to costs. Such an economic perspective helps to highlight two aspects, namely activity costs and the relative nature of the implementation concept. In other words, strategy implementation firstly requires planned execution of activities that incur costs and secondly its effectiveness depends on the appropriateness of these activities to the specific context. On the positive side of such an economic balance, costs will be far outweighed by the benefits if the right types of activities/actions are selected, i.e. there is a match between the actions and the organizational context. On the negative side, inappropriate activities constituting positioning are likely to yield few benefits, yet are likely to inflict significant sink costs, much like failed or poor positioning in the external context. This highlights the importance of careful selection and planned execution of internal marketing efforts. Ad hoc, half-hearted and poorly executed attempts at internal marketing are doomed to failure at the outset. To make internal marketing work requires a high level of commitment as well as time for the effects of its effort to materialize.

It is also necessary to appreciate that internal marketing outcomes are time dependent. It is likely in most instances that there is a time lag between undertaking internal marketing actions and affecting desired outcomes. This means, particularly in the case of implementing marketing strategies, that internal marketing programmes need to take place well before the launch of external marketing programmes. This is also of particular importance in considering the metrics of assessment, which are needed to capture pertinent facets of the change programme. This indicates the necessity to conduct longitudinal internal and external research in order for correct judgement to be made with regard to the effectiveness of internal marketing actions. Moreover, continuous monitoring serves not only to provide diagnostic information regarding implementation effectiveness, but also provides insights to carry forward into future actions and strategies.

Clearly then, analogous to the situation in external marketing, segmentation and positioning to the internal market (that is employees) are of critical importance. Poor internal segmentation and positioning, even with very clearly defined and precise tactical actions, leads to few, if any, productive positive results in the internal context. This perhaps accounts for the failure of many change programmes in which detailed breakdowns of activities are undertaken but with little regard for the needs of participants and/or a clear understanding of how these may either be achieved or contradicted by the processes used to achieve them in the first place. The oft-quoted statement in many reported cases of change, 'the reward system did not encourage the change of activities', is a rather appropriate illustration of poor understanding of, as well as the failure to match process activities to, the needs of employees in the change programme. By virtue of detailing internal segments and then bundling a specific package of process activities via positioning to meet the needs of employees it becomes possible to strive for employee satisfaction and customer satisfaction whilst simultaneously reaching out for organizational aims.

The internal marketing effort to position against internal segments leads onto the third level of the model. The third level, denoted by the term Action, requires the specification of precise actions directed at various identified segments of participants at level 2 through specific processes and systems. The delivery of such actions is captured by the remaining elements of the internal mix, namely Process, Price, Promotion and Place.

Process

The Process element is closely interlinked with the Participants element, in that it defines the context and mechanisms through which the Price, Promotion and Place elements are structured. It includes under its remit mechanisms and systems involved in the structuring of issues such as power, authority and resources[14]. Essentially, it defines the nature and manner of involvement, in order to deliver upon requisite duties and goals. Items such as whether meetings are to be held, where they are to be held and who is designated to run them are included here.

The Process element requires that decisions regarding the appropriate mechanisms for the 'delivery' of the package of actions to a specific segment are carefully evaluated. In other words, it requires designing an appropriate delivery format. The types of factors that need to be scrutinized, generally, are likely to be items such as ensuring that an appropriate organizational structure, group/team structure, reward systems, power and responsibility and leadership are set in place requisite to the 'delivery' that needs to be undertaken.

Price

The element of Price can be operationalized within an internal context by viewing price not simply as a cost to the employee (as depicted by terms such as opportunity cost, psychological cost, etc.), which is the traditional way of looking at price. We propose that it is better to view the Price dimension in the internal context as a balance between utility/value against cost to both the organization and the individual. This way of operationalizing Price is preferred, since it directs attention not only to what the costs to the employees are (psychological or otherwise) of the courses of the required actions of change, but also to the value/utility that can be derived from these changes by the individual employee and the organization. For instance, a change may incur cost (price on the part of the employee) in terms of having to work harder, do a different type of job and learn something new, but at the same time some utility/value may intrinsically be attendant with the new activities. The new task(s) may provide the opportunity to increase pay, access bonuses, provide a chance to excel and shine, and thereby build a route to career promotion, or through acquisition of new skills strengthen their bargaining hand in the job market. Thus, the Price element is useful in fine-tuning activities defined in the Process element by addressing both gains and losses to employees involved in the process of change.

Promotion

With respect to the Promotion element, operationalization in the internal context can be achieved by examination of how the range of promotional devices can be used to increase knowledge, skills and awareness of strategic change issues. Promotion activities, whether communications such as internal advertising or other internally directed promotional devices to elicit a response, can be used to aid the 'buying into the programme' process by employees. Promotion, in this sense, can be viewed as a skills and knowledge generation function. Internal communications, presentations and training via demonstrations (an external comparison of which can be things like point of sales demonstrations in industrial or retail selling) can all be used to raise awareness and skills, and thus sensitize employees to the activities required of them. Thus, promotion can be an extremely effective vehicle for letting the employees know what to do, when to do it and exactly how to do it, and thereby serves to clarify their role in the enactment of strategy.

Place

The last remaining element, Place, contains activities that can be thought to affect or be affected by the local environment of the organization. The Place element in the external context is concerned with distribution channels and reaching targeted customers; its focus is predominantly centred around the actual exchange and its environmental setting. In the internal context, Place can be taken to represent the visible and tangible, as well as invisible and intangible, aspects of work and the work environment. In other words, it represents the setting within which transactions/exchange between parties occurs, namely between the organization and its employees. Taken in totality, it captures more than the physical aspects of the environment; it includes cultural, symbolic and metaphoric aspects of the organization, from and within which setting employees form allegiance to the organization[15]. As such, Place can be used to further fine-tune aspects of the process, such as with whom power resides, what is the level of power within particular groups or segments of people, and how this needs to be altered and/or adapted to allow for effective strategy implementation. The external analogy that can be drawn here is the importance of having correctly co-ordinated and dovetailed channel strategies, through apt steering and co-ordination via channel captaincy, structure and power manipulation[16].

The Place element can be used to draw attention to differences in culture and response arising from specific parts of the organization to the change programme. In fact, constituent activities of the Place element may be used to encourage certain types of behaviour, i.e. construct a culture change via mechanisms which alter the local environment by redistributing resources, power and responsibility away from some individuals to others more likely to champion the cause of change. This requires close scrutiny and understanding of current resources, work practices, the way the organization divides and factionalizes into groups and teams with their own identities and subcultures. Generally, we can say that the aim of the Place element is to attempt to devise an internal environment and atmosphere that is conducive to the achievement of particular goals. This may mean giving more resources, better support, changing or at least attempting to change and fine-tune organizational culture, as well as examining ways of empowering employees through structural and responsibility adjustments.

Relationship marketing and IM

The marketing mix reflects a marketing approach that is transaction based, that is, it is intended to maximize sales and profitability in the short term, and the marketing mix is used to influence consumer decision making and provide customer satisfaction. Direct contact with customers is minimal. Increasingly, however, the emphasis is away from transaction marketing and towards relationship marketing, which is regarded as more effective in today's environment.

Relationship marketing focuses not only on getting customers and generating transactions, but also on maintaining and enhancing relationships[17]. The emphasis is on continuous long-term relationships that lead to repeated market transaction, build loyalty and lead to profitability over the customer 'lifetime'. Relationship marketing is an inter-active approach to marketing. It relies on co-operation and trust rather than an adversarial approach. Building trust and commitment are crucial elements of relationship marketing. This requires delivering on promises and building financial, social and structural bonds between the firm and its customers. The relationship itself becomes the focus of marketing efforts rather than the product. In addition to the marketing mix vari-ables, customer care/customer service initiatives and interactive market-ing are central to relationship marketing. Key account management (or the designation of dedicated individuals or teams who deal specifically with key clients or accounts) is also central to developing and maintain-ing relationships with important customers. They are designed to foster co-operation and facilitate interaction so that the organization can respond quickly to the clients' needs.

In the relationship marketing approach, a transaction-oriented approach to marketing heavily reliant on the traditional marketing mix approach is just a special case where simple or non-personal relationships are sufficient to satisfy customer needs. This applies to many low value consumer packaged goods, whereas for services, industrial goods and consumer durables, relationship marketing of different levels of complex-ity is appropriate.

Given its interactive nature and the importance of customer service, the success of relationship marketing strategies is critically dependent on attitudes, commitment and performance of employees. Hence, relation-ship marketing is highly dependent on an ongoing internal marketing programme for its successful implementation.

At the same time, given the long-term nature of employment, and the need for commitment and trust between employees and the organizations (or different departments, functions, etc.), the foregoing suggests that the relationship marketing approach and techniques are also appropriate for internal marketing. And, just as with external customers, the relation-ships *per se* and process are central to the building of relationships in internal marketing. Trust and commitment are also generated by deliver-ing on promises. However, the marketing mix approach is likely to be more useful where a need for quick implementation is required, or high levels of employee turnover are common.

Barriers to implementation

New strategies inevitably require behavioural and/or attitudinal changes on the part of employees, which can also lead to some degree of resist-ance and barriers to effective implementation. In recognition of this fact, we suggest that internal marketing involves a planned effort to overcome organizational resistance to change and to align, motivate and integrate employees towards the effective implementation of corporate and functional strategies. These barriers can be identified by examining resistance to change by each employee segment. The existence of such barriers leads to the emergence of implementation gaps, which have to be closed for effective strategy implementation to occur. We classify the range of barriers into the following gaps: concept, people, mechanism, cost/utility, awareness/skills and local environment (see Figure 3.2). Although the barriers could have been grouped in a number of ways, we have chosen the classification in a manner that highlights elements of the internal marketing mix likely to predominate in the removal of the identified gap.

The implementation barriers are nested to highlight interdependency. Moving from the outer (level 1) to the inner (level 3) level, the barriers move from being broad and strategic to being specific and tactical in nature. The level and nature of the barriers exemplify the types of actions necessary to remove them. For instance, any shortcomings in the change programme itself (that is, the conceptualization), because of its strategic nature and thus diffuse effects, may lead to contradictions at levels 2 and 3 or fail to produce the desired outcomes in terms of marketplace success. In other words, problems at this level can, and often do, cascade downwards and outwards into the marketplace. We observe that flaws at this level lead to two types of error, which we will refer to as Type I and Type II. Type I errors are those in which *incorrect* strategic actions are *effectively* implemented and the outcome is that expected marketplace performance either fails to materialize or even declines. Type II errors are those in which the conceptualization fails to fully/adequately take into account the internal context and

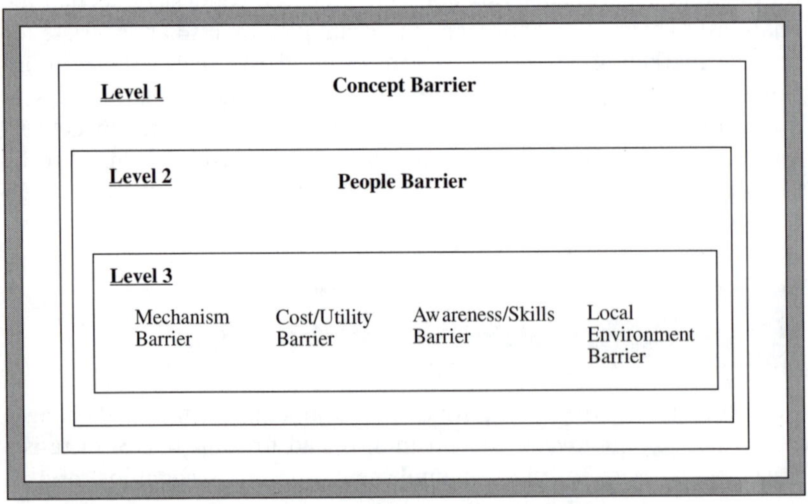

Figure 3.2 Barriers to implementation: a nested approach.

needs of various stakeholders, thereby creating internal contradictions and conflicts. These in turn manifest themselves by creating a certain level of organizational dysfunction and can lead to the appearance of implementation gaps at any one or even all the levels. If the shortcoming originates from level 2, for example in the way the segments were formed, then there will be ramifications at level 3, since it is likely that wrongly directed actions and activities will be set in place, i.e. relatively poor implementation is likely to follow. Instances of relatively poor implementation, even if the product conceptualization is appropriate to the specific context, we call Type III errors. Once again, we would observe that the problems at this level would cascade downward into level 3 actions. Problems originating at level 3 have a narrower effect in that no downward cascade exists. However, since each of the internal mix elements is interlinked, there are horizontal effects of one barrier leading to or compounding problems in another. Moreover, the interlinkage of the internal mix elements also indicates that it is not possible to preclude upward ripple effects. For instance, local environment changes involving adaptations at a broad level, such as attempting to modify organizational culture, have pervasive effects with important ramifications at the strategic product conceptualization level.

Finally, working through the three stages leads on to further diagnostic research that feeds back into the product, thus acting as a homeostatic monitoring mechanism, as well as creating cybernetic closure.

Case illustration of the multi-level internal marketing model

We use here a case to illustrate how the multi-level model of internal marketing can practically be used to direct attention to pertinent issues in the implementation of a change programme. The case is based on how Pearl Assurance dealt with the problem of changing the business mix of its products in face of opposition from some of its sales force. The case is an illustration of the model in directing managers' attention to factors that need to be addressed in generating effective implementation. The case information presented is based upon primary information as well as secondary sources.

Changing the business mix at Pearl Assurance

The background

In 1990, Pearl Assurance (PA) was acquired by Australia Mutual Provident (AMP). Until then, PA specialized in selling life assurance based on 'with-profits' policies. These policies guarantee to pay out a minimum sum assured on maturity of the policy or the death of the policyholder. The profits or bonuses are a share of the surplus that the company may make in excess of the guaranteed payout, as a result of its investments. These policies, also known as endowments, came into great demand in the late 1980s as a result of rising popularity of endowment mortgages in the housing market. A major disadvantage of the 'with-profits' product is that in order to provide these guaranteed payouts a substantial amount of the company's capital is tied up in reserves. However, this period also saw the development of 'unit-linked' products whose performance is tied to that of the stock market. With unit-linked products, policyholders are allocated a number of units in a life insurance fund, the value of which is published daily. In addition, AMP's experience in Australia had shown unit-linked products to be more profitable whilst tying up less capital in reserves. Hence, a decision was made to move the balance of products to be sold in favour of unit-linked business.

However, PA encountered opposition from its sales force when it attempted to pursue this policy. There were several reasons for this opposition. Firstly, the sales force had been 'turned off' unit-linked policies since the October 1987 stock market crash, which had graphically illustrated the high potential risks. Secondly, many of the sales force and the backroom staff were unfamiliar with unit-linked products. Moreover, the change in the policy was perceived to be as a direct consequence of change in ownership, which occurred with the AMP acquisition of PA, rather than a market-driven necessity.

Life assurance is a product that the majority of customers know very little about, as it is a complex and infrequently purchased product. The benefits of life assurance are such that they cannot be fully evaluated without first purchasing the product and then awaiting for the policy to reach maturity. Hence, sales personnel play a crucial role in the choice of products (that customers make), since customers are unlikely to be fully aware of the types of products available and their relative merit. Customers thus rely heavily on the advice of salespeople, who are regarded as experts. It was essential, therefore, that PA get its sales force behind the new policy.

Pearl Assurance has around 5000 salespeople, who are geographically dispersed across the UK. PA sensed resistance to the new policy was likely and took a decision to implement the change through the use of roadshows. The first roadshow, called Operation Sunrise, was used to highlight the benefits of all forms of equity-linked investments. Although effective in raising awareness of the market for unit-linked products, the increase in sales of these products was less than expected. What follows is an account of Operation High Noon, which was launched in October 1992, illustrated in a manner designed to highlight the practical role of the internal marketing model in directing attention to activities and actions necessary for effective implementation.

Product

The product in this case was the requirement to shift the emphasis of business away from with-profits policies towards unit-linked products (see Figure 3.3). The benefit of doing this was that unit-linked policies were a growth market. Moreover, unit-linked policies also had advantages for customers compared to with-profits, in that they were more flexible and allowed a reduction in the need to keep capital reserves, which could then be used to increase benefits to the customers and/or the organization. The executive believed that adoption of the policy would help PA increase competitiveness, improve performance and hence improve job security for everyone.

Market research

Before launching Operation High Noon, PA commissioned independent research on the attitudes of the salespeople to unit-linked policies. Interviews were conducted in two of the best and two of the worst performing divisions in terms of unit-linked policy sales. All grades of management were included as well as the sales force. Based on their attitudes to unit-linked and with-profits, respondents were classified as 'for' or 'against' change. This illustrates one way of segmenting 'the market' in an internal context.

We can see that, on the basis of information received from internal research, two segments appeared to emerge: an 'Enthusiastic' segment and a 'Resistant' segment. Investigation of the two segments highlighted that individuals for change tended to be enthusiastic managers and aspiring sales representatives. Those against change tended to be managers unwilling to impose change on those resisting the change and included among them many unambitious sales staff. The internal research also identified that those resisting change tended to be pre-1987 staff, who had received complaints from customers after the 1987 stock market crash, whereas the segment with a more favourable attitude (Enthusiastic segment) consisted predominantly of newer (post-1990) recruits. The logic of segmentation would indicate that different stratagems would be required to effect implementation because of differences in orientation of each segment. These differences in segment orientation were likely to manifest themselves in producing different gaps/barriers to the process of strategy implementation.

Participants

Participants in the process, as indicated in the above discussion, were identified to be two groups/segments with differing orientations. From the Enthusiastic segment, key individuals were selected on the basis of

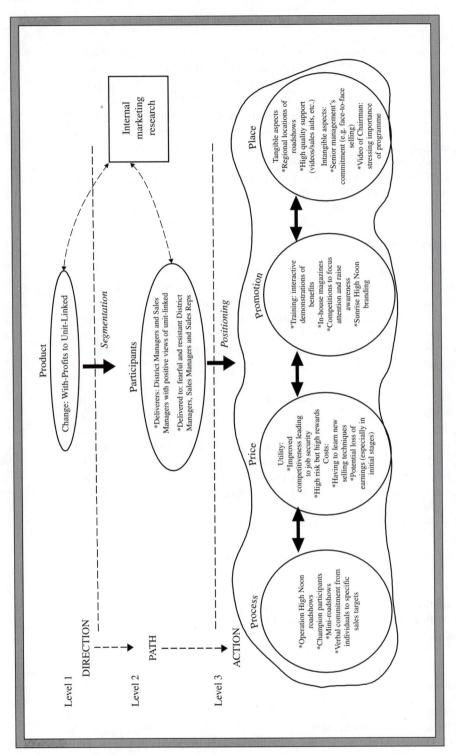

Figure 3.3 Case illustration of the multi-level model of internal marketing.

their enthusiasm and knowledge to run the Operation High Noon road-shows. These participants included both managers and sales representatives in order to ensure, and at the very least to convey an impression, that everybody's opinion was being taken into account. In other words, individuals from this segment of employees were used to drive the change to unit-linked policies (i.e. they were responsible for delivery).

Once created, the roadshows were targeted at District Managers, Sales Managers and Sales Representatives. Although all managers and representatives were included, the shows were particularly targeted at the more resistant segment of the audience. The process of segmentation was, in fact, carried one stage further, by forming sub-segments on a functional basis. And, in line with the logic of segmentation, separate seminars were designed for each of three different sub-segment groups (District Managers, Sales Mangers and Sales Representatives), with specifically targeted messages to each. On completion of internal segmentation, the next step is to move on to the third stage, which involves leverage of positioning actions and activities to facilitate tactical implementation.

Process

The mechanism through which the change was to be enacted (i.e. the Process) was the roadshow. Within this process, separate seminars were designed for delivery to different groups of people with different sets of needs. In fact, as noted above, segmentation was carried one stage further so as to create sub-segments of the initial Enthusiastic and Resistant segments on the basis of functional difference. This was deemed necessary because the functional category was considered an important parameter in defining segment needs.

The roadshows were used as a vehicle to explain the rationale behind unit-linked policies on a face-to-face basis by selected 'enthusiastic' managers. The enthusiastic managers themselves were provided with training for this purpose. The roadshow managers used these opportunities to point out that with-profits policies required PA to put aside capital reserves which could not be invested in the open market. Unit-linked products, on the other hand, free these reserves to be invested in the open market and thus serve their customers better than with-profits policies. The advantages of flexibility for customers of unit-linked policies were also highlighted, particularly the fact that they could alter options with their circumstances, without having to surrender their policies or drawing up new contracts, which either caused clients to be unhappy, because of losses incurred, or being levied extra charges, respectively. To reassure those representatives who were worried that the volatility of the stock market would lead to losses, it was pointed out that unit trusts were very safe because the risk was spread over numerous shares. It was further demonstrated that, whilst the stock market fluctuated in the short term, on a 15- or 20-year time horizon unit-linked policies out-performed with-profits policies. Another point made was that, due to an increased customer awareness of the advantages of unit-linked policies, there was a trend away from endowments towards unit-linked policies. Financial press reports were used to provide independent evidence of this.

At the sub-segment level, seminars were specifically developed to target and train particular audiences; seminars for District Managers were used to develop business plans in order to achieve targets set for unit-linked policies, seminars for Sales Managers were designed to help them motivate their sales representatives, and seminars for the sales representatives illustrated new sales techniques for unit-linked products. Moreover, in order to maintain momentum, each District Manager was asked to organize a mini-roadshow for his or her district. Within this process, each delegate was asked to state in writing how they would assign extra resources to achieve their unit-linked goals. For instance, Divisional Managers were asked, as a minimum, to give a verbal commitment of targets that they would set for their districts and how these would be achieved.

Price

The internal marketing operationalization here calls for an understanding of the costs incurred and the utility/value that is to be gained by the participants in each segment. Firstly, we consider the costs dimension. The fact was that unit-linked products were substantially different from with-profits policies and thus required time and effort, on the part of the sales representatives, to learn new selling techniques. This was additional to the psychological costs of change. Secondly, since the unit-linked products were new to them, it was possible that the sales representatives could suffer a potential loss of commissions. Furthermore, there was also a greater element of risk associated with unit-linked policies than with-profits policies. Thus, in order to convince the participants within each segment of the advantages of the change, it was necessary firstly to understand and secondly communicate effectively to each participant the value of the changeover. Facts, such as the unit-linked market being a rapidly growing market and that PA were getting into it early, and that the prospects for high commissions were good, needed to be stressed in order to overcome resistance. This was particularly relevant for the Resistant segment. Participants from the Enthusiastic segment selected for driving the roadshows were motivated by the prospect of promotion, if their efforts proved to be successful. Other benefits stressed were that involvement with unit-linked products would enhance and extend their skills. This would allow them not only to provide a better service to their customers, but would also boost future employment prospects.

Promotion

The promotion tool was used extensively to raise awareness, as well as build competence and confidence of the sales force in unit-linked policies. The initial mechanism to impart information and build skills was the roadshow demonstrations. This constituted a face-to-face communication, which capitalized on the advantages of an interactive medium to clarify and advance the cause of the change programme, as well as providing further opportunity to understand employee fears and resistance. Numerous other promotional techniques were used in addition to such face-to-face communications (or personal selling) by managers and senior staff to the sales force. For instance, in-house magazines were used to explain the rationale behind the changes, and competitions to incentivize individuals and rapidly heighten interest and awareness. Videos were also used at the roadshow, one of which featured the Chairman of PA to emphasize that the policy change had director level support for it. Another video showed sales managers overcoming objections to unit-linked policies. Further to this, in order to concentrate effort and focus the range of events, the roadshows were also 'branded' (the first roadshow was 'Sunrise' and the second 'High Noon').

An interesting point to emerge, with regard to who should actually be responsible for internal marketing, from the High Noon roadshow was that the marketing department had to take a less prominent role in the roadshows. Only then were the actions of change perceived to be acceptable to the sales force, who otherwise had been inclined to see it simply as a new sales gimmick from the marketing department. In fact, it was felt that the previous roadshow (Sunrise) had not been as successful as it could have been, because the thrust of all the literature had all originated from the marketing department. This indicates that a broader and more cross-sectional involvement is required in the use of internal marketing.

Place

As the sales force was widely dispersed geographically, the venues chosen were based on the regional locations of the sales force and roadshows were tailored to match each situation. Place in the internal marketing mix refers not only to the locations where products are provided to customers, but also other tangible and intangible aspects required to effectively carry out the task, such as back-up support material and personnel.

In this respect, the videos and high quality sales aids provided tangible evidence of the commitment of the organization to the change initiative. An example of one of these high quality sales aids was The ABC Risk/ Reward Presenter (where ABC stood for the Adventurous, Balanced and Cautious investor). The presenter illustrated how unit-linked products could be tailored for customers with different risk profiles, a feature not offered to with-profits customers. For instance, the adventurous customer could be sold a unit-linked product which had a high risk attached but had high potential rewards. The availability of the high quality support material and the associated training reduced the effort required from the sales force to change and therefore speeded up the support and acceptance of the unit-linked product. The sales literature was further supported by copies of speeches and overhead slides to act as a reminder and reinforcement of the principal message.

The second dimension of the Place element that requires attention is the role of intangible aspects in the implementation process. It is clearly necessary to examine the appropriateness of the organizational environment to the process of change, and if necessary amend it by effecting an appropriate cultural climate through transmission of appropriate cues. For example, the video featuring the Chairman emphasized the importance as well as the high level of commitment to the change programme. Without doubt, symbolic actions and metaphoric examples need to be carefully examined for their potential use in internal marketing. Regular exhortations as well as compliments on work well done were other simple devices to create and maintain a positive attitude to the programme.

Results

The degree of success of the programme of events can be ascertained from the fact that the Pearl Assurance 1993 Annual Report announced that whilst unit-linked business accounted for only 5 per cent in 1991, it had grown to 30 per cent by the end of 1993. The major problems encountered in this campaign were to maintain the momentum that was built up by the roadshows. The necessity of involving staff at different levels in the hierarchy led to a complicated cascading process of communication during the roadshows.

Summary

The purpose of this chapter has been to demonstrate how and to what extent marketing techniques such as segmentation, market research and the marketing mix can be used for developing customer-oriented behaviour and generally motivating employees.

The chapter began with a discussion of how the different elements of the traditional 4Ps marketing mix and the extended 7Ps services marketing can be applied to internal marketing. Application of segmentation and market research techniques are also discussed. This is followed by the elaboration of a multi-stage model which highlights how a marketing-like approach and techniques can be used internal to the organization. By expounding the concept of an internal marketing mix, internal market research, and the critical role of internal segmentation and internal positioning, we have advanced the notion that many of the concepts and frameworks which are critical in creating external marketplace success can be usefully employed, indeed need to be employed, albeit adapted to the internal context, to aid the process of strategy implementation. The model also serves to highlight the importance of an internal focus to complement an external marketplace focus. Without an effective internal focus capable of interlinking with an external focus, many potentially successful strategic visions are likely to remain just that: visions.

Another point of interest to emerge, particularly from case evidence, that needs to be highlighted is that the marketing department should not solely be charged with the responsibility of running internal marketing programmes. The dominance of a single functional department will have a tendency to lead to, in reality or simply in perception, to a sense of functional/departmental bias. The imposition, perceived or otherwise, of such a unitarist viewpoint is likely to create strong resistance. This strongly indicates the need to use cross-functional teams or task forces in the development and running of internal marketing programmes.

References

1. Kotler, P. (1972). A generic concept of marketing. *Journal of Marketing*, **36** (April), 346–54.
2. Sasser, W. E. and Arbeit, S. F. (1976). Selling jobs in the service sector. *Business Horizons*, June, 61–2.
3. Sambrook, S. (2001). HRD as an emergent and negotiated evolution: an ethnographic case study in the British National Health Service. *Human Resource Development Quarterly*, **12** (2), 169–93.
4. Carson, K. D., Carson P. P., Yallapragada, R. and Roe, C. W. (2001). Teamwork or interdepartmental cooperation: which is more important in the health care setting? *The Health Care Manager*, **19** (4), 39–46.
5. See Carson et al. above.
6. See, for instance, Piercy, N. and Morgan, N. (1991). Internal marketing: the missing half of the marketing programme. *Long Range Planning*, **24** (2), 82–93. Barnes, J. G. (1989). The role of internal marketing: if the staff won't buy it why should the customer? *Irish Marketing Review*, **4** (2), 11–21.
7. Booms, B. H. and Bitner, M. J. (1981). Marketing strategies and organisation structures for the service firms. In *Marketing of Services* (J. H. Donnelly and W. R. George, eds). Chicago: American Marketing Association, pp. 47–51.
8. Collins, B. and Payne, A. (1991). Internal marketing: a new perspective for HRM. *European Management Journal*, **9** (3), September, 261–70. Flipo, J.-P. (1986). Service firms: interdependence of external and internal marketing strategies. *Journal of European Marketing*, **20** (8), 5–14. Berry, L. L. and Parasuraman, A. (1991). *Marketing Services: Competing Through Quality*. New York: The Free Press.

9. Townley, B. (1989). Employee communications programmes. In *Personnel Management in Britain* (K. Sisson, ed.), pp. 329–55. Oxford: Basil Blackwell.

10. Button, K. (1991). Business television: management from outer space. *Management Week*, 20 November, pp. 46–9.

11. London, M. (1986). The boss's role in management development. *Journal of Management Development*, **5** (3), 25–35.

12. Millward, N. and Stevens, M. (1986). *The Second Workplace Industrial Relations Survey 1980–1984*, p. 153. Aldershot: Gower.

13. Jacoby, S. M. (1988). Employee attitude surveys in historical surveys. *Industrial Relations*, **27** (1), Winter, 74–93.

14. Giddens, A. (1979). *Central Problems in Social Theory*. London: Macmillan Press.

15. Smircich, L. (1983). Concepts of culture and organisational analysis. *Administrative Science Quarterly*, **28** (3), 339–58. Turner, B. (1986). Sociological aspects of organisational symbolism. *Organisation Studies*, **7**, 101–15.

16. Rosenbloom, B. (1991). *Marketing Channels: A Management View*. Orlando, FL: Harcourt Brace and Jovanovich College. Stern, L. W. and El-Ansary, A. I. (1992). *Marketing Channels*. Englewood Cliffs, NJ: Prentice-Hall.

17. For an excellent discussion of relationship marketing, see Grönroos, C. (1994). From marketing mix to relationship marketing: towards a paradigm shift in marketing. *Management Decision*, **32** (2), 4–20. Grönroos, C. (1996). Relationship marketing: strategic and tactical implications. *Management Decision*, **34** (3), 5–14. Gummesson, E. (1998). Implementation requires a relationship marketing paradigm. *Academy of Marketing Science Journal*, **26** (3), 242–9.

chapter four

Internal marketing and human resource management

Introduction

An examination of the internal marketing model proposed earlier shows that a number of mechanisms proposed in the model for the achievement of effective implementation of marketing and other strategies, namely inter-functional co-ordination, employee motivation, job satisfaction and empowerment, are functions that have been, in the past, mainly in the remit of the personnel or human resource management (HRM). This raises questions as to the respective roles of marketing and HRM in the achievement of implementation objectives. This chapter discusses the roles of HRM and marketing in IM, methods of increasing inter-functional co-ordination, and the implications of IM for management style and organizational culture. Issues relating to empowerment are discussed in Chapter 5.

The roles of marketing and HRM in internal marketing

There is, perhaps, an implicit assumption in discussions of internal marketing that effective use of inwardly directed marketing techniques can solve all employee-related quality and customer satisfaction problems. There are, however, limits to what can be achieved by marketing techniques alone and it is of crucial importance to note that internal marketing requires the involvement of a number of departments working in unison. This is illustrated by a case study reported by Richardson and Robinson[1].

Richardson and Robinson report a study on the implementation of internal marketing within a retail bank in which the effectiveness of the internal marketing programme is assessed by using groups of 'shoppers' to evaluate the service provided over a period of 3 months. Although the programme was generally a success, it is interesting to note how some of the problems that arose during the programme were solved. For instance, in one branch, three tellers were found to have performed particularly badly. Their weaknesses were pointed out to them. However, the performance of only one of them improved. Further investigation revealed that these two individuals did not enjoy the customer contact aspect of the job. That is, they were typical of task-oriented people doing people-oriented jobs[2]. They were therefore moved to back office positions and replaced with more suitable staff, and the subsequent performance ratings for the tellers improved markedly.

What this example illustrates is that, in certain circumstances, administrative action by the personnel function is much more likely to be effective than usage of marketing-like devices. The example also illustrates the importance of careful recruitment and selection for the motivation and effectiveness of staff.

Another branch suffered a loss in performance when some members were on training courses or on leave, and the replacement staff were from administrative (that is) task-oriented jobs and hence less skilled in dealing with people. Another branch, whilst showing a small improvement in performance, was well below the overall improvement levels achieved. On investigation, it was discovered that shortage of staff was leading to careless mistakes in one department and consequently lack of satisfaction on the part of customers. The employment of an extra member of staff led to increase in morale and a dramatic improvement in performance. These two examples illustrate the need for training and adequate staffing levels. The simple use of internally directed marketing efforts clearly cannot compensate for lack of training and inappropriate staffing levels.

We have dealt with this example at length to illustrate the differing roles of marketing and the personnel function, and the need for marketing and personnel to work together. Another purpose has been to show that the personnel function already has a wide array of techniques to improve performance and motivation techniques; for instance, job rotation, self-managing groups, career planning. Marketing techniques merely add to that array.

Boundary between marketing and HRM

The discussion above raises the question as to where the boundary between HRM and marketing lies, and inter-functional co-ordination can be achieved in the face of inter-functional conflict. This is important because some internal marketers have argued that activities that have traditionally been thought to be the preserve of the personnel functions should be undertaken by the marketing function. For example, Berry and Parasuraman extend the limits of internal marketing to include activities that are traditionally associated with the personnel function:

> 'Internal marketing is attracting, developing, motivating and retaining qualified employees through job-products that satisfy their needs. Internal marketing is the philosophy of treating employees as customers... and it is the strategy of shaping job-products to fit human needs.'[3]

Compare this with Willman's definition of human resource management:

> 'Human resource management is concerned with the set of decisions and policies through which the organizations attract, recruit and motivate, reward and develop their employees. In addition it is concerned with the ways in which employment is terminated.'[4]

In fact, George goes much further than Berry and Parasuraman and suggests that:

> 'It is time to replace the personnel department in service firms with product managers who can implement a marketing approach to service employment management.'[5]

The underlying reason for such an assertion is the fact that there is still relatively little recognition in the HRM literature that the nature of services requires different types of HRM practices to those required in the production of physical/manufactured goods. The services marketing literature has highlighted this and also the fact that it is imperative to have the right personnel at the point of delivery, because of their impact on the perception of the quality of service delivery and as it also provides a marketing opportunity, as well as the fact that the actions of the personnel themselves form part of the product that customers are buying.

Because of the nature of the service delivery process, it is essential that employees have the right training and attitudes. In particular, customer contact employees need to be more people oriented rather than task oriented. Furthermore, where the personnel and the services that they perform form a large part of the product being offered (high contact services), then marketing needs to be as closely involved as the HRM/personnel function in the recruitment, training and rewarding of employees. Motivation of these employees constitutes an essential element in the success of these services.

A useful definition of the boundary between marketing and HRM is provided by Kotler, who states that marketing consists of *non-coercive* actions to induce a response in another social unit[6]. That is, the use of force or formal authority is not considered to be a marketing solution to a problem. This is an important distinction, in that in many cases the persuasive tactics employed by internal marketing are likely to be unsuccessful, and in these instances 'formal' mechanisms that personnel management is empowered to use (by the contractual nature of employment) would need to be employed in order to achieve the implementation objectives.

Links between HRM and internal marketing

At the operational level, internal marketing implies the co-ordination of HRM and other functions so that the promises of the external marketing campaign are delivered. At the strategic level, the major objective of IM is to motivate employees towards customer orientation. This requires a supportive management style, recruitment policy, training and planning procedures[7].

Supportive senior management and management style is essential for the achievement of a motivated customer-oriented workforce. At a basic level, if senior managers are not customer oriented, then it is unlikely that the rest of the organization is likely to be customer oriented. This is because employees take their cues from senior management as to the types of behaviours and attitudes that are regarded as important to the organization. The management style also needs to be supportive. For example, where a product or service needs to be customized, employees need to be empowered to make the necessary decisions in order to satisfy customer needs (see Chapter 5 for a more detailed discussion). Such a situation requires a participative style of management. Centralized decision making in this context would lead to slow service, dissatisfied customers and frustrated employees.

A supportive personnel policy is also crucial in order to ensure that employees with the requisite skills, competencies and attitudes are recruited. Retention of good employees requires competitive remuneration policies and career progression paths. Remuneration policies need to reflect strategic objectives such as customer orientation and service orientation to achieve external and internal marketing objectives.

Training is essential to ensure that employees have the skills and competencies needed to produce the products and services at a level of quality expected by customers and to take advantage of marketing opportunities that arise. Training is also required to inculcate the core values of customer orientation and other attitudes (such as service orientation). The adoption of changes in policies and new ideas are generally more likely to be successful if the employees that are affected by the changes are involved in the planning process.

It is clear from the above that IM is very dependent on supporting HRM policies if it is to succeed. At the same time, the discussion above suggests that IM can be used by management to disseminate core organizational values throughout the firm. That is, IM can help to create a shared system of beliefs. For instance, for service firms, this may mean the implementation of a service orientation culture amongst employees. IM techniques together with HRM techniques could be used to achieve this objective. For instance, IM techniques could be used to communicate the importance of product quality, supported by training and incentives for appropriate behavioural outcomes.

Leadership and integration in internal marketing

Marketing management has long ascribed to itself the role of an integrative function, which is responsible for co-ordinating other company functions so that the performance of the company is customer oriented. The basis for this claim rests on the marketing function's direct contact with external customers. And in the case of services marketing, because of the importance of personnel in the delivery of service, some marketers have argued for supplanting of the personnel department so that a more marketing-like approach could be adopted for attracting, recruiting and managing service employees.

However, if such a policy were to be adopted, then it is bound to lead to conflict between marketing and HRM and operations management and other directly affected departments. This is because it may be seen as an attempt by the marketing function to increase its influence within the organization at the expense of other functional areas.

Inter-functional conflict can also arise because of differing priorities of functions. For instance, marketing may wish to increase sales via price promotions. The resulting increase in demand will have an impact on the production schedules, and may also increase the costs of the operations management department. If there is insufficient slack in production capacity, staff may have to accept more flexible working patterns. Inter-functional conflict can also arise due to different perspectives and approaches to problems. For instance, there is considerable evidence that conflict between the marketing and R&D department arises due to the fact that, whilst marketing's focus is on customer needs, R&D's focus is on exploiting new technologies.

Organizations, therefore, need to look at ways of increasing cross-functional co-ordination. For instance, in service marketing, where it is necessary to have friendly, customer-oriented personnel, the marketing department could have involvement in job specification, training and remuneration of contact employees. George goes even further and suggests that, for service-oriented firms, '*Policies for these two functional areas must be prepared simultaneously with each document containing ideas about the other*'[8].

Other methods of integrating the personnel and marketing functions include[9]:

- Involving representatives from personnel on marketing committees and vice versa.
- Creating liaison or boundary spanning roles. That is, appointing individuals within functions whose role is to communicate with other departments regarding any actions or policies that may impact on each other.
- Duplicating a personnel unit within marketing whilst maintaining a personnel department, or merging the personnel and marketing departments.
- Shared information systems. Such systems increase the speed and flow of information between functions, and help to build trust and thereby reduce the areas of inter-functional conflict.
- Cross-functional teams. Cross-functional teams have been found to be the most successful integrating mechanism. However, the teams need to have a clear focus and the composition of the teams needs careful consideration to ensure success.
- Matrix organizational structures in order to increase horizontal communication.

Many of these practices have been adopted already by firms in order to create knowledge in new ways, to increase sharing of information, and to respond more rapidly to changes in the market.

Given the nature of inter-functional rivalry and the potential for conflict, it is suggested that internal marketing cannot and should not be the sole responsibility of any department (i.e. marketing, HR or any other). Moreover, because of the very nature of internal marketing's function of motivating all employees towards the effective and integrated implementation of corporate and functional goals, the impetus for such a programme needs to come from strategic management. Such a policy avoids inter-departmental conflict and gives internal marketing the high level of managerial commitment that is necessary for its effective implementation and the achievement of high quality, customer-sensitive service delivery.

Internal marketing and organizational culture

Internal marketing is more than an instrument for disseminating organizational values. Given that the central aim of internal marketing is to develop customer-conscious employees, treating employees as customers and the use of marketing-like techniques to achieve these aims, IM itself constitutes a new cultural initiative. It requires that customer orientation is central to all the organization's activities and a core part of the organizational culture. This has a number of major implications for HRM function and the style of management (see Exhibit 4.1).

Having customer orientation at the centre of organization activities implies that HRM, like all other departments, needs to align its activities to the needs of the external market as envisioned by the marketing function. Such an alignment suggests a strategic approach to HRM. Alignment of human resources with the strategic requirements of the organization is widely accepted nowadays, and is the major thrust behind the emergence of strategic HRM concept and function. A strategic approach to HRM ensures that the requirements of implementation of strategies are taken into account at an early stage. It also ensures that the requisite competencies are developed within the organization, and the employees recruited have the requisite competencies and attitudes to perform tasks required to deliver products and services customers want and give the organization competitive advantage in the market. In such a climate, internal marketing programmes designed to support external marketing strategy or other corporate strategies are more likely to be accepted than in organizations where a strategic approach to HRM is lacking.

The treatment of employees as customers also implies a new approach to management. The underlying implication that organizations should attempt to understand the needs of their employees and then attempt to satisfy those needs implies a degree of consultation with employees and, hence, a management style that is participative to some extent. Whilst a participative management style is not strictly necessary for the implementation of specific internal marketing programmes, it is more likely to lead to their acceptance and efficient execution. For instance, a participative management style is likely to require less use of persuasive types of communications to employees, as consensus and agreement are an intrinsic part of the consultation process. As a minimum, this discussion implies that the existing style of management needs to be taken into account when designing internal marketing programmes. Internal marketing programmes based on the assumption of participative management are likely to fail in organizations dominated by a control-oriented centralized management style.

Exhibit 4.1. Turnaround: the role of HRM in the implementation of customer-focused management at Sears

The year 1992 was the worst financially in the history of the premier American retailer, Sears. It suffered a net loss $3.9 billion on sales of $52.3 billion. The losses were the culmination of years of poor performance by the retailer. Like many mass retailers, Sears had been slow to react to the changing needs of the consumer and had been losing market share to discount stores such as Wal-Mart, who were more focused in their activities. Sears' response of competing on price meant lower margins and consequently less expenditure on the hiring, training, motivating and remuneration of sales staff. The policy led to very high employee turnover and a dramatic fall in customer satisfaction levels.

In response to this situation, Sears instituted a turnaround strategy designed to narrow its focus on retailing. This led to the closure of its catalogue operations and divestment of its insurance and property subsidiaries – The Allstate Corp. and The Homart Development Co. By 1996, the company marked its first year of operations focused exclusively on retailing.

Sears also made changes to its retailing strategy. Realizing that 70 per cent of its customers were women, Sears launched 'the softer side of Sears' strategy and store refits that included installation of wider aisles, softer lighting and elaborate displays, emulating the more upmarket department stores. Service to customers was also increased and made more responsive to the needs of busy women. Sears also introduced new own-label lines in clothing and cosmetics. Over 100 stores were closed, reducing its mall-based stores portfolio. These changes increased sales by 9 per cent and generated a net income in 1993 of $750 million.

After returning to profitability in retailing, in 1994, under the direction of Arthur Martinez (who arrived to head the merchandising group in 1992 and later became CEO from 1995 to 2000), Sears grouped its top 120 executives into five task forces on the themes of customers, employees, financial performance, innovation and values. The task forces were charged with defining world class in each area and providing Sears with measures to track progress. They helped Sears arrive at a new vision for the business, namely to become 'a compelling place to shop, work and invest.' They became known as the three compellings or three Cs. The three Cs were supported by three core values – the three Ps – passion for the customer, our people add value and performance leadership. To support this strategy, the senior management set about transforming the HR function and the paternalistic command and control organizational culture.

Transforming human resource management at Sears

The design was a radical departure from the past, as the HR function was henceforth required to treat the internal organization as if it were the customer. That meant it had to identify the requirements of its customers before designing the new look HR function. Based on data derived from employee surveys, the HR transformation team went back and completely changed the HR function. Everyone in the HR function was reassessed according to the new standards of customer service orientation, responsiveness and so on. Then the department was completely restaffed using a 'zero-based' staffing approach. In addition, the reporting relationships of HR staff were also changed, so that instead of reporting to HR, they had to report to the businesses they supported and help colleagues in those businesses align with the company's new vision and strategy, thus helping HR to become a strategic business partner. The majority of the time of HR personnel was now spent making Sears a compelling place to work by developing a host of training, development and rewards strategies.

With over 800 full-line department stores, more than 2700 off-the-mall stores and over 300 000 employees, Sears needed a major drive to communicate the new vision and strategies to all its employees. Sears used a number of HR programmes to convey the new mission and inculcate the new Sears culture, including learning maps and monthly store meetings. Sears sales assistants now get much more training than before the turnaround began. For example, whereas no formal orientation existed before, an 8-week orientation process was introduced. Management education, which had been virtually non-existent before the turnaround,

(continued)

is given a high priority and the Sears University, which was established in 1995, was specifically set up to train managers.

The company developed new performance appraisal criteria and compensation systems for all its managers, emphasizing financial and non-financial performance. The annual performance appraisal is a 360-degree appraisal, including feedback from their supervisors, peers and subordinates, rating the managers on 12 leadership criteria, including customer service orientation, initiative and sense of urgency, business knowledge, problem solving, empowerment skills, team skills, and change leadership. The 12 criteria are also used for recruitment and training purposes. Thus, the company rewards managers who improve customer satisfaction and employee satisfaction levels by developing and supporting employees under their control. To further emphasize the importance of non-financial measures, from 1996, one-third of Sears' senior management's long-term incentives have been based on improvements in employee satisfaction as measured by the employee attitude surveys, one-third on improvements in customer satisfaction, and one-third sales and profitability measures. This was a big change from Sears' existing executive compensation programme, which rewarded executives for achieving sales and profit targets for their particular business units.

Measuring performance

The transformation team figured it was not sufficient to just have a vision, they had to determine exactly how to put that vision into action. They set out to come up with a business model and a set of indicators – the Sears Total Performance Indicators (TPI) – that would show how value is added in the retail operation and show the link between employee attitudes and profits. Using the data collected for the task forces and data routinely collected, a set of six indicators were refined to measure objectives in the areas of customer satisfaction (one indicator), employee satisfaction (two indicators) and financial performance (three indicators).

In addition, Sears also undertook a statistical modelling exercise to establish the relationship between the different variables in the TPI. Using data from 800 stores, Sears found that if positive employee attitudes (measured by 10 factors relating to their attitudes to the job and the organization)

(continued)

increase by 5 per cent, then customer satisfaction will increase by 1.3 per cent, leading to a 0.5 per cent increase in sales. On the current sales of over $40 billion, this translates to over $200 million annually.

A continuous process of data collection, analysis and modelling and experimentation, the Total Performance Indicators show Sears managers how well they are doing with customers, employees and financially. The model can also be used at a store or regional level to assess performance and indicate remedial action, if necessary.

Sears' customer satisfaction ratings began creeping upward in 1993 measured against their leading competitors. A *Fortune* magazine survey published in February 1997 showed more than twice as much customer satisfaction as any other retailer surveyed. In 1996 and 1997, its customer satisfaction scores rose two more percentage points, placing it at parity with its target competition.

Since March 1997, Sears cash tills have been randomly generating receipts that ask customers to call an automated toll-free number and respond to questions. The survey results show customer satisfaction has risen several per cent since 1996. This has been verified externally, for instance by a *Fortune* magazine survey in 1997, which showed that Sears' customer satisfaction increased by 5.6 per cent from 1995 to1996 and 2 per cent from 1996 to 1997.

Employee satisfaction scores have also increased. The employee satisfaction score was estimated to be 69.5 in 1999, having risen 1.5 per cent in the past year and a half alone. And what has been found is that stores that have higher employee satisfaction ratings generally perform better financially than those with lower ratings. Another measure of employee satisfaction is the fact that the company's turnover rate has plummeted from 100 per cent turnover when the turnaround project started to 66 per cent. This compares with an employee turnover rate of nearly 75 per cent a year for typical retail stores in the USA.

Sources: Laabs, J. (1999). The HR side of Sears' comeback. *Workforce*, **78** (3), March, 24–9. Sherman, S. (1997). Bringing Sears into the new world. *Fortune*, **136** (7), 13 October, 183–4. Martinez, A. (1999). Sears strategy for continuing renewal. *Chain Store Age*, July, 64–74. Rucci, R., Kirn, S. and Quinn, R. T. (1998). The employee–customer–profit chain at Sears. *Harvard Business Review*, January/February, 82–97.

The acceptance by the HRM function that marketing-like techniques can be used internally for the purposes of motivation and inter-functional integration is likely to transform the HRM function itself. For instance, if the customer orientation philosophy is adopted by HRM, then it will begin to market its services to its internal users rather than waiting to be approached or relying on formal mechanisms. In some instances, this is prompted by the need to compete with external suppliers. In these cases, internal marketing is acting as an agent of change and transforming the way the HRM function has traditionally operated.

Summary

Internal marketing programmes are not implemented in a vacuum. Effective implementation of IM programmes requires a supportive environment and structures. In particular, it requires close co-operation between the HRM and marketing functions in order to ensure that the requisite HRM policies are in place to support the external marketing strategies. A major role of IM is to increase inter-functional integration and to reduce inter-functional conflict, as this is a major barrier to effective implementation. Inter-functional conflict can arise for a number of reasons, including the perception that one function is trying to increase its power at the expense of the other. Greater inter-functional integration can be achieved in a number of ways including, amongst others, cross-functional teams, creating boundary spanning roles, and representation of marketing and HRM personnel on each other's committees.

Whilst closer co-operation and inter-functional integration are essential for the success of IM programmes, in the longer term IM also requires a culture shift in organizational values. Indeed, IM is a cultural initiative in itself. The acceptance of the central aim of internal marketing of developing customer-conscious employees, treating employees as customers and the use of marketing-like techniques to achieve these aims means that the organization is taking on board a new set of values. The IM approach also implies that a strategic human resource management approach and a participative style of management are more consistent with the implementation of internal marketing strategies. These values and approaches to management need to become part of organizational culture. The best way of transmitting these values through the organization is for senior management to buy into customer orientation and other values associated with internal marketing.

References

1. Richardson, B. A. and Robinson, G. C. (1986). The impact of internal marketing on customer service in a retail bank. *International Journal of Bank Marketing*, **4** (5), 3–30.
2. Blake, R. and Mouton, J. (1964). *The Management Grid.* Houston, TX: Gulf.
3. Berry, L. L. and Parasuraman, A. (1991). *Marketing Services: Competing Through Quality*, p. 151. New York: The Free Press.
4. Willman, P. (1989). Human resource management in the service sector. In *Management in Service Industries* (P. Jones, ed.), Chapter 14, pp. 209–22. London: Piton. Quotation from p. 210.
5. George, W. R. (1977). The retailing of services – a challenging future. *Journal of Retailing*, Fall, 85–98.
6. Kotler, P. (1972). A generic concept of marketing. *Journal of Marketing*, **36** (April), 346–54.
7. Grönroos, C. (1981). Internal marketing – an integral part of marketing theory. In *Marketing of Services* (J. H. Donnelly and W. R. George, eds), pp. 236–8. American Marketing Association Proceedings Series.
8. George, W. R. (1990). Internal marketing and organizational behaviour: a partnership in developing customer-conscious employees at every level. *Journal of Business Research*, **20**, 63–70. Quotation from p. 68.
9. Glassman, M. and McAfee, B. (1992). Integrating the personnel and marketing functions. *Business Horizons*, **35** (3), May/June, 52–9.

chapter five

A framework for empowering employees

Introduction

We saw in Chapter 2 that empowerment is an essential component of internal marketing, particularly in the area of services marketing. Whilst a great deal has been written on the subject of empowerment (also referred to as job involvement, and as employee participation) in the manufacturing industries, its application in the services area is surprisingly, as yet, still relatively underdeveloped. However, any rigorous examination of the literature shows that empowerment is not suitable for all occasions or all types of employees, as it can have both positive and negative consequences for employees and the organization. This chapter outlines a contingency framework for the empowerment of contact service employees. It is argued that the appropriate levels and the types of empowerment given to employees depend upon a combination of the complexity (or variability) of customer needs and the degree of task complexity (or variability) involved in delivering the services. It is also argued that, in any empowerment framework, it is essential that the degree and the type of empowerment be explicitly incorporated.

Background

The special nature of services, and in particular the simultaneity of production and consumption, is one of the major reasons that many services marketers argue that contact employees should be allowed a degree of discretion when dealing with customers. For instance, Grönroos argues that the interactive nature of services provides empowered employees an opportunity to rectify mistakes and an opportunity to increase sales:

'Ideally, the front-line employee... should have the authority to make prompt decisions. Otherwise, sales opportunities and opportunities to correct quality mistakes and avoid quality problems in these moments of truth are not used intelligently, and become truly wasted moments of opportunity to correct mistakes, recover critical situations and achieve re-sales and cross-sales.'[1]

However, other authors argue that service employees should have little or no discretion. For instance, Smith and Houston[2] propose a 'script-based' approach to managing customer and employee behaviour to control behaviour and process compliance. That is, Smith and Houston envisage little or no room for participation by employees. Levitt[3] forcefully argues for a 'production line' approach and the 'industrialization' of services in order to improve the productivity of services. One of the key elements in this approach to services is that it leaves little room for discretion for service employees.

Mills[4] argues that the degree of management control over service employees (or conversely the degree of employee empowerment) should depend on the structure of the service system: for low contact standardized services behaviour can be controlled by mechanistic means such as rules and regulations. For high contact, highly divergent services (that is, those requiring a high degree of customization), Mills suggests that employee self-management and peer-reference techniques are more successful. Even Grönroos recognizes that not all decision making can or should be decentralized as 'chaos may follow in an organization if strategic decisions, for example, concerning overall strategies, business missions and service concepts, are not made centrally'[5].

The foregoing suggests that the approach to participation is a contingent one. Before outlining the proposed framework, we begin with a discussion of the nature of empowerment, the rationale for it, and the differences in degree and types of empowerment that can be given to employees.

The nature of empowerment

Empowerment has been defined in numerous ways, but most authors agree that the core element of empowerment involves giving employees *discretion* (or latitude) over certain task-related activities[6]. Empowerment implies that front-line employees are allowed to exercise a degree of discretion during the service delivery process. Three types of discretion can be distinguished, namely routine, creative and deviant discretion[7]. Routine discretion is exercised where employees select an alternative from a list of possible actions in order to do their job (e.g. investment counsellors recommending a product from a list of the organization's products). Creative discretion is exercised where employees themselves have to develop alternative methods of performing a task (e.g. a professor's discretion over the content of a lecture). Creative behaviours are not specified by the organization, but are regarded positively by the organization. Deviant discretion, on the other hand, is negatively regarded by the organization, as it involves behaviours that are not part of the employee's formal job description and outside the area of the employee's authority.

Whilst discretion is regarded as perhaps the most important feature of employee empowerment, there are a number of other features of empowerment that are essential for the effective implementation of service delivery strategies. For instance, in addition to employee discretion, Bowen and Lawler[8] also include in their definition of empowerment the sharing of information regarding the organization's performance, rewards based on organizational performance, and knowledge that enables employees to understand and contribute to organizational performance. Berry goes further and argues that:

> 'Empowerment is a state of mind. An employee with an empowered state of mind experiences feelings of 1) control over how the job shall be performed, 2) awareness of the context in which the work is performed, 3) accountability for personal work output, 4) shared responsibility for unit and organizational performance, and 5) equity in the rewards based on individual and collective performance.'[9]

The important point to note is that both these sets of authors regard as important the sharing of information so that the employees understand the context in which they work. They also regard as important that empowered employees are remunerated appropriately and in the case of Berry that these rewards are based on individual and collective performance.

Reasons for empowering employees

It has already been intimated that one of the major reasons for empowering front-line service employees is so that they can take advantage of sales opportunities and cross-selling opportunities resulting from the interactive nature of the service delivery process. More generally, the reasons for empowering employees can be divided into those that improve the motivation and productivity of employees and those that improve service for the customer and market the service products more effectively.

In services marketing empowerment of the front-line can lead to both attitudinal and behavioural changes in employees. Attitudinal changes resulting from empowerment include increased job satisfaction, reduced role stress and less role ambiguity.

Empowerment also has important behavioural consequences. For instance, empowerment can increase the self-*efficacy* of employees as discretion allows them to decide the best way to perform a given task. Empowerment leads to employees becoming more adaptive. Empowerment also leads to quicker response by employees to the needs of customers, as less time is wasted in referring customer requests to line managers. In situations where customer needs are highly variable, empowerment is crucial in allowing employees to customize service delivery.

From a marketing perspective, because of the simultaneity of the production and consumption of services and the frequent involvement of the customer in the production process, there is far more scope and opportunity for customization of service products than manufactured products. Customization of the service during delivery can also be used as a source of differentiation and competitive advantage, and increase customer satisfaction. This, obviously, suggests the need to empower contact employees appropriately contingent upon the type of service product being provided.

Service recovery is another area where empowerment plays a vital role, as service failures are inevitable. Speedy service recovery is essential when service failures occur. Otherwise, if service failures are not rectified quickly and satisfactorily, customers may lose faith in the overall reliability of the service. Schlesinger and Heskett[10], for instance, note that empowerment of front-line employees is one of the key components in breaking the 'cycle of failure' in services. It is also a vital component in a service firm's strategy of maintaining customer satisfaction.

Degree and types of empowerment

Bowen and Lawler[11] suggest that the degree of empowerment varies from control oriented at one end and involvement orientation at the other. Control orientation is typified by the production line approach, where there is no empowerment of employees. Suggestion involvement is the next level of involvement in Bowen and Lawler's schema, followed by job involvement, and finally leading to high involvement.

Suggestion involvement need not involve any changes to the basic production line management approach, as it basically only allows employees to suggest changes in the service delivery and product changes, which may or may not be adopted. This type of involvement of employees includes activities such as employee attitude surveys, problem solving groups and quality circles (which have been widely used in the manufacturing sector). These techniques are designed basically to elicit information from employees. Other techniques, such as house journals and team briefing, are used to impart information to employees (in order to empower them) so that they are more effective in the performance of their jobs.

Job involvement involves a significant departure, as it gives employees discretion over various aspects of their jobs and how they organize their work. Such discretion can be given either to individuals or to groups of individuals (i.e. workgroups). Discretion given to workgroups may lead to them becoming semi-autonomous workgroups or self-managing teams. Self-managing teams are allowed to organize how they undertake tasks within the group.

Even higher levels of involvement occur where employees are involved not only in the performance of their jobs, but also in the organization's performance. According to Bowen and Lawler, *high involvement* occurs where:

> '*Business performance information is shared. Employees develop skills in teamwork, problem solving, and business operations. They participate in work unit management decisions. There is profit sharing and employee ownership.*'[12]

At the service delivery level, high involvement in the Bowen and Lawler sense is not relevant, as it does not *directly* empower contact service employees. High involvement in Bowen and Lawler's schema is an indirect method of empowering employees. Hence, in what follows *Low Empowerment* describes situations where employees are encouraged to make suggestions regarding the way in which services are delivered but management is not bound to act on the suggestions. *High Empowerment*, on the other hand, is used to describe situations where employees have a high degree of autonomy and discretion over the way in which they undertake service delivery tasks. Obviously, intermediate situations occur where moderate degrees of discretion are allowed to employees and thus are moderately empowered.

In any discussion of empowerment it is also important to distinguish between the types of discretion exercised. In fact, as mentioned above, the degree of empowerment that is appropriate for different types of services provided can be described by the level of creative and routine discretion exercised by employees. Clearly, a high degree of routine discretion is not the same as a high degree of creative discretion.

A framework for empowering service employees

Whilst the contingent nature of empowerment is implied by a number of authors, the only existing contingency framework for empowering service employees is that of Bowen and Lawler. According to Bowen and Lawler, there are five contingencies of empowerment, namely business strategy, tie to the customer, technology, business environment and types of employees. Before proposing an alternative framework, a brief discussion of these contingencies follows below.

- *Business strategy.* Firms undertaking a differentiation business strategy or a strategy that involves high degrees of customization and personalization of services should empower their employees. However, firms pursuing a low cost, high volume strategy should use a production line approach to managing employees.

- *Tie to the customer.* Where service delivery involves managing (long-term) relationships with customers rather than just performing a simple transaction, then empowerment is essential. This is particularly important in the case of industrial/organizational customers, where relationships are not only long term but the value of individual transactions is high.

- *Technology.* If the technology involved in service delivery simplifies and routinizes the task of service personnel, then a production line approach is more appropriate than empowerment. However, where the technology is non-routine or complex, then empowerment is more appropriate.

- *Business environment.* This relates to the relative predictability/variability of the business environment and that of customer needs. Bowen and Lawler illustrate this with examples of airlines who serve customers with a 'wide variety of special requests', which makes it impossible to anticipate many situations and therefore to 'program' employees to handle them. This is contrasted with a fast-food restaurant, where customer requirements are simpler and more predictable, and a production line approach is more appropriate.

- *Types of employees.* Bowen and Lawler recognize that empowerment and production line approaches require different types of employees. Employees most likely to respond positively to empowerment are those that have high growth needs and those that need to have their abilities tested at work. Where empowerment requires teamwork, employees need to have strong social and affiliative needs and good interpersonal and group skills. Empowerment requires Theory Y type managers, who allow employees to work independently to the benefit of the organization and its customers. The production line approach requires theory X type managers, who believe in close supervision of employees.

Whilst Bowen and Lawler's classification scheme is helpful in describing some of the situations in which service employees should be empowered, it is difficult to see what the underlying dimensions are behind these contingencies. The major weakness of Bowen and Lawler's contingency framework is that it does not distinguish between customer- and employee-related contingencies. Bowen and Lawler also seem to suggest that the decision to empower employees is, in part, a consequence of engaging employees with high growth, social and interpersonal needs, rather than vice versa. In fact, the type of employees is not a contingency but controllable factor in the delivery of services.

We propose that the appropriate levels and the types of empowerment given to employees depend upon a combination of the *complexity* (or variability) *of customer needs* and the *degree of task complexity* or variability involved in delivering the customer needs. The major reason for this is the fact that in services the degree and type of interaction between customer and contact employees can have a major impact on the degree of complexity of the task that a contact employee has to perform in order to satisfy customer needs. Complexity of customer needs includes, amongst other things, product complexity, complexity of relationship (tie to the customer) and variability in the needs of customers. Task complexity or variability is partly determined by, amongst other things, the type of technology employed and partly by the service product. Both of these are determined by the basic business strategy that is employed by the organization.

This is shown in the two-by-two matrix in Figure 5.1, together with the type of discretion exercised in each of the different situations. In Figure 5.1, Box A describes a situation where the variability in the needs of the customer is low and the complexity of the task performed is also low. An example of such a situation is the service provided by a checkout assistant in a supermarket. Employees in such situations have little or no routine or creative discretion in the way they perform their tasks or the service that they offer to customers. In some situations, customers may be allowed to customize the product by choosing from a limited amount of options. For instance, Burger King's 'Have It Your Way' allows customers to have their burgers with or without cheese. However, whilst option personalization increases the discretion of the customer, it does not affect the discretion that the employee has over the performance of his or her job.

Box B describes a situation where the task is still relatively simple, but the needs of the customer are more complex or variable. The situation is typical of one that is often faced by salespeople. The salesperson is allowed in this situation to offer different options to the customer in order to meet the needs of the customer. However, the options that the salesperson offers to the customer must be those that the salesperson has been authorized to offer and no other. The salesperson is not allowed to (or required to) create new options that may meet the customers needs. However, the options that the salesperson chooses to offer to the customer depend upon an assessment and an understanding of the needs of the customer and

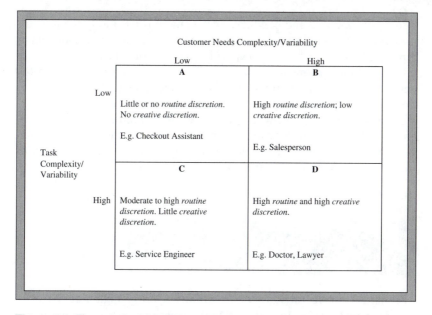

Figure 5.1 The relationship between customer needs, task complexity and discretion. *Source*: based on Willman, P. (1989). Human resource management in the service sector. In *Management in Service Industries* (P. Jones, ed.), Chapter 14, pp. 209–22. London: Pitman.

therefore requires a certain amount of creativity (or adaptiveness) on the part of the salesperson. Hence, salespeople may be allowed to exercise a small amount of creative discretion. Salespersons are also allowed a certain amount of discretion in how they perform their job. For instance, salespeople may be allowed to schedule their own calls on prospective customers rather than having to follow a prescribed routine. Salespersons also have discretion as to how they make the sales pitch.

Box C describes a situation where customer requirements are relatively simple, but the task is complex. An example of such a situation is where a service engineer is required to repair a photocopier, for instance. The task required to perform the service is complex in that it requires technical expertise. The organization therefore relies on the expert judgement of the employee to perform the task and allows the employee a high degree of discretion in how they perform the required tasks. However, this discretion is usually limited to alternative (usually approved) methods of working to provide the required service. The service engineers do not have any creative discretion. That is, they do not normally provide customized solutions to the customers. In any case, as the customer needs are fairly simple, creative discretion is not required.

Box D describes a situation where the needs of the customers are highly variable and the solutions required to meet the needs of the customer are

also highly variable and complex. Such situations inevitably require customized solutions. The relationship between a doctor and a patient is
typical of such a situation. Typically, the doctor has a great deal of
latitude in the treatment of patients. Even here, there are limits to the
degree of discretion, as the degree of latitude is limited to the area of
expertise of the doctor or, in more general terms, the expert.

In all the above cases, when employees go beyond the degree of discretion allowed them, they are exercising deviant discretion. Such behaviour can be detrimental to the organization and most organizations
would regard such behaviour as a disciplinary matter.

Dimensions of customer needs and task complexity

The matrix above provides organizations a fairly high level view of
empowerment issues. In order to make decisions regarding the degree
of empowerment that is appropriate for the specific context that an organization faces, it is necessary to specify more precisely the dimensions of
the contingencies of task complexity and customer needs complexity/
variability. For instance, in order to understand the degree of customer
needs complexity, the organization needs to examine its service product
from a customer perspective and identify the essential features that are
important to customers. Review of the literature suggests that the major
facets of customer needs complexity for services are service product complexity, customer needs complexity/variability, importance of speed of
service, customization and the importance of service quality (see Figure
5.2). The links between these features of service and empowerment are
discussed below.

1 *Service product complexity*. With complex products, customers
   expect a high level of expertise from contact employees. Hence,
   the greater the product complexity (from the customer's perspective), the greater the need to empower employees. High levels of
   empowerment give customers greater confidence in the ability of
   the contact employee (and the organization) to deliver the service.
   For instance, management consultancy and education are highly
   complex products, and customers of these products expect a high
   level of autonomy on the part of consultants and college professors
   in the delivery of the service.

2 *Customer needs complexity/variability*. The more complex or variable the needs of the customer, the greater the need for empowerment. Customers do not wish to be held up whilst the employee

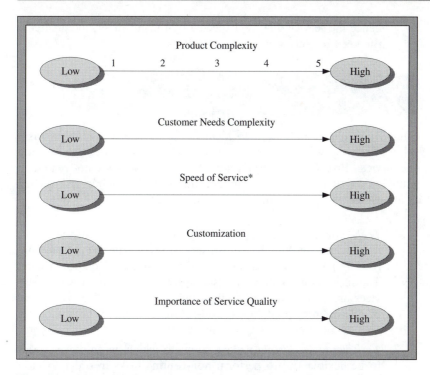

Figure 5.2 Features of customer needs complexity. *Speed of service is a reversed scored item. That is, the faster the speed of service needs to be, the more likely it is that a production line approach will be employed.

consults with a line manager, because the customer's needs vary from the standard service product.

3 *Importance of speed of service.* The speed with which customers expect a service delivery to be completed is an important aspect of any service product. The greater the importance of speed of service, the less appropriate is empowerment of contact employees, as speed is often gained by standardizing service delivery routines.

4 *Customization.* The degree to which customers expect products to be tailored to their specific needs. The greater the requirement for customization, the greater the need for empowerment.

5 *Importance of service quality.* Service quality is a complex area of service products. Berry et al.[13] have shown that customers assess service quality on five main dimensions, namely reliability, responsiveness, assurance, empathy and tangibles (in that order of importance). The responsiveness, assurance and empathy variables are obviously heavily dependent upon contact employees. Hence, the higher the level of responsiveness, empathy and assurance (and hence the service quality) expected by the customer, the greater is the need to empower contact employees.

Dimensions of task complexity

Similarly, organizations need to identify the key determinants of task-related activities which determine the features of the service product and the service delivery process (see Figure 5.3). The discussion above and an examination of the literature suggests the following major task-related contingencies for empowerment (see Figure 5.3).

1 *Technology (routine versus non-routine)*. This refers to the degree to which technology routinizes service tasks. The greater the non-routine nature of tasks, the greater the need for empowerment. The technology dimension also captures the extent to which services are equipment rather than people focused. The greater the people-oriented (and, hence, non-routine) nature of the service, the greater the need for empowerment.

2 *Task variety/uncertainty*. The extent to which an employee needs to be flexible and to perform non-routine tasks in order to meet non-routine needs of customers. This does not necessarily require the employee to be creative. That is, employees may be able to cope with task variety by being given routine discretion (rather than creative discretion). Generally, the greater the task variety, the greater is the need to empower employees. Otherwise, employees would need to constantly liaise with their line managers before undertaking the required tasks.

3 *Creativity*. The degree to which an employee is required to be creative (that is, required to generate specific solutions for specific customer needs) or innovative in order to meet customer needs. The greater the requirement for employees to be creative, the greater is the need for empowerment. In this case, it is obvious that employees need to be given creative discretion.

4 *Task complexity/difficulty*. The degree of complexity of the task depends on the number and sequence of steps required to perform the task or the knowledge intensity. Generally, the greater the complexity of the task, the greater will be the requirement for formal training of employees. The need for empowerment varies directly with task complexity.

5 *Process versus product focus*. The degree to which the service delivery process is important compared with the product itself. Process orientation requires greater empowerment, whereas product focus requires more of a production line orientation.

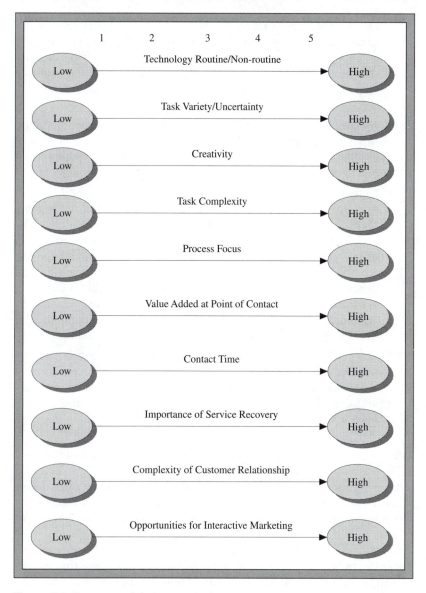

Figure 5.3 Features of task complexity.

6   *Value added at point of contact*. This refers to the proportion of value added by contact employees (front office) compared with back office employees. This is usually reflected in the relative proportion of front and back office employees. The greater the value added by contact employees, the greater is the need for empowerment.

7   *Contact time*. The duration of time per transaction spent by an employee in delivering a service compared with the total time spent

by the customer in receiving the service. The greater the contact time, the greater is the interaction between the customer and the contact employee. As a consequence, high contact services increase the uncertainty in the delivery process and, hence, the need for empowerment varies directly with the contact time between the service provider and the customer.

 8 *Importance of service recovery.* The degree of importance placed on rapid service recovery. The greater the need to recover service quickly, the greater the need to empower employees to take remedial action.

 9 *Complexity of customer relationship with the organization.* This refers to the extent to which transactions are part of an ongoing multi-faceted relationship rather than simple transactions. The longer the relationship and the greater the multi-faceted nature of the relationship, the greater is the complexity of the relationship (compare with Bowen and Lawler's 'tie to the customer' contingency). The greater the complexity of the relationship, the greater is the need to empower employees. Key account managers may be appointed where the particular relationships are complex and financially important in order to manage the relationship.

 10 *Opportunities for interactive marketing.* The extent to which opportunities exist for selling additional services to customers to meet their wider needs. The greater the extent of opportunities for interactive marketing, the greater is the need to empower employees to take advantage of the opportunities.

The schema above is partly based on Silvestro et al.'s[14] six-point service delivery process classification schema. The variables in Silvsetro et al.'s schema are equipment versus people focus, customer contact time, degree of customization, degree of discretion, value added by front office activities versus value added by back office activities, and product versus process focus.

Silvestro et al.'s equipment versus people focus variable is incorporated under the technology variable in our schema. The discretion (or empowerment) variable is excluded, as it is an outcome in our model and not an input variable as it is in the Silvestro et al. schema. Customization is excluded under the task complexity dimension, since it would involve double counting, as it already appears under the customer needs complexity dimension. It is also excluded because task variety, creativity and complexity are determined to a large extent by the degree of customization that employees are asked to perform. The business strategy variable has also been excluded, as its implementation should be reflected in all the variables that make up task complexity. Its inclusion would, therefore, involve double counting. The other variables in our schema are included as a result of the previous discussion on empowerment.

Developing indices of customer needs and task complexity

In order to make the determination of the level of task complexity and customer needs complexity more systematic, the identified attributes of each of these dimensions can be rated on a scale and all the ratings summed to give an index for the dimension. For instance, the attributes identified for customer needs complexity can be rated in terms of their importance to the customer and the individual ratings summed to give an index of the overall importance of all the identified attributes.

In Figure 5.2, for example, each attribute of customer needs complexity is rated on a scale of 1 to 5 (1 = Low, 5 = High) and the score on each attribute is used to form an index of complexity by summing across all the identified attributes. The total score (or index) can then be broken down into intervals which match the degree of empowerment. In the example above, with five identified attributes, the possible scores range from 5 to 25. Scores between 5 and 10 suggest a production line approach. Suggestion involvement is appropriate for scores between 11 and 15, job involvement with moderate degrees of routine and creative discretion for scores between 16 and 20, and job involvement with a high degree of creative discretion for scores between 21 and 25. The assumption above is that all attributes are equally important. If this is not the case, then appropriate weights need to be attached to each variable and the index recalculated. Also, each of the attributes above needs to be rated on the level of routine and creative discretion that is required to implement it. This information can then be used to help with the classification of the index scores.

Similarly, using a five-point scale system similar to that for customer needs complexity above, an index can be calculated for task complexity (see Figure 5.3) by summing across the variables and categorizing the scores into intervals, also similar to the above. The only difference is that, because of the different number of variables, the index ranges from 10 to 50 points rather than 5 to 25 points. As with the customer needs complexity variable above, each of the task complexity attributes needs to be rated on the level of routine and creative discretion that is required to implement it. This information can then be used to help with the classification of the index scores. Scores between 10 and 20 suggest a production line approach. Suggestion involvement is appropriate for scores between 21 and 30, job involvement with moderate degrees of routine and creative discretion for scores between 31 and 40, and job involvement with a high degree of creative discretion for scores between 41 and 50. Once again, the assumption above is that all attributes are equally important. This is unlikely in most cases and therefore appropriate weights will need to be attached to each variable and the index recalculated.

The final requirement is to plot the customer needs complexity scores against the task complexity scores to obtain the right degree of empowerment. The actual level of empowerment chosen will be a compromise between customer needs and task requirements. The scores on routine and creative discretion help to decide the type of empowerment that employees should be given.

The general application of the model outlined above may be illustrated by looking at two examples of highly successful organizations from the airline industry, namely Singapore Airlines and Southwest Airlines. Southwest Airlines specializes in short haul flights (less than 90 minutes) in the USA. It offers the lowest fares in specific markets. The airline provides a 'no-frills' service, that is, no meals, no assigned seats or baggage transfer between airlines. Southwest places a great deal of emphasis on cost reduction. For instance, Southwest can turn its aircraft around in 17 minutes compared with an average of 45 minutes for competing carriers. Southwest pays its employees average salaries plus profit sharing[15]. Budget airlines similar to Southwest Airlines, such as EasyJet and Go, have also emerged in Europe and follow roughly similar strategies and practices as the pioneer Southwest Airlines.

Singapore International Airlines (SIA), on the other hand, specializes in long haul flights, particularly for the business executive market. SIA is one of the most profitable international carriers. It is regularly nominated as best airline, particularly for service. In fact, it aims to be '*the* airline for fine service'. Its philosophy is that the customer comes first and that staff have to be flexible in dealing with customers. Employees are highly trained and paid above-average salaries.

From the limited information above, using the customer needs complexity and task complexity as outlined in Figures 5.2 and 5.3, one would expect the score for Southwest Airlines on the customer needs complexity to be between 5 and 10 (or perhaps slightly higher), and the score on task complexity to be between 10 and 20. That is, in the main, one would expect that Southwest Airlines would employ a production line approach in its people policies and that employees would be given very little discretion in their work.

In contrast, for SIA one would expect the score on the customer needs complexity to be between 31 and 40, and the score on task complexity to be between 41 and 50 (or lower). That is, in the main, one would expect that SIA would employ a human resource management (HRM) policy of job involvement with moderate to high levels of routine and creative discretion given to its employees.

The application of the model at the job level can be illustrated with the example of the different levels of empowerment given to different employees in hospitals when dealing with patients. The level of discretion given to receptionists and orderlies, for instance, is extremely low. This is because the customer needs and job requirements are relatively simple. However, the discretion given to nurses is higher because of the variability in the needs of customers, although the jobs that nurses are required to do are still relatively simple. On the other hand, the job of the radiographer may be complex, but the needs of the patient are relatively simple, that is, to be X-rayed. Hence, radiographers, because of their technical knowledge, are likely to have a high degree of routine discretion but little creative discretion. Doctors and consultants, on the other hand, because of their expertise and the complex nature of their patients' needs that they must deal with, have high levels of creative discretion.

Zones of empowerment

Within each of the quadrants of empowerment framework (Figure 5.1), there is a specific level of empowerment that is consistent with the specific task being performed. However, the multi-faceted nature of jobs that employees are asked to perform means that, whilst the majority of tasks fall within the parameters of the discretion allowed to them, there may be others where management wishes to limit the discretion allowed to employees.

To further enhance the operationalization of empowerment within organizations, employees need to be guided as to when they can exercise discretion and when they cannot. One simple method of doing this is to group tasks into empowerment zones[16]. Safe (Green) zones are situations where employees are allowed and expected to make decisions independently. Low-risk (Amber) zones are situations where the employee may consult their manager, and high-risk (Red) zones are situations where consultation with a manager is mandatory.

The zoning is determined by the degree of potential cost or loss the organization may incur as a result of a wrong decision being made by an employee. Hence, in the case of a doctor for instance, in the safe zone (for instance, prescribing medication for a cold), he or she is allowed full discretion. However, where surgery is involved, for instance, the doctor may be required to seek a second (or third) opinion from another colleague, or even to refer the patient to a specialist. In this particular case, there is also a high risk to the patient as well as the organization, hence the curtailment of discretion. In service recovery situations, a limit on the degree of discretion may be linked more directly to costs by placing a financial ceiling on the costs that can be incurred to rectify mistakes. For instance, Federal Express allows its employees to spend up to $100 to rectify customer-related problems[17].

Costs of empowerment

Empowerment is not without its costs. One of the consequences of empowerment is that it increases the scope of employees' jobs. This requires that employees are properly trained to cope with the wider range of tasks required of them. It also impacts on recruitment, as it is necessary to ensure that employees recruited have the requisite attitudinal characteristics and skills to cope with empowerment. Research conducted by Hartline and Ferrell[18] shows that empowerment can have both positive and negative outcomes for employees. They found that, although empowered employees gained confidence in their abilities (self-efficacy), they also experienced increased frustration (role conflict). This is because empowerment leads to employees taking on extra responsibilities. Additionally, the increased responsibilities and improved skills required from empowered employees often means that employees must be better compensated, thus adding to the labour costs.

Empowerment can also slow down the service delivery process as the empowered employee attempts to individualize the service for customers, thereby reducing the overall productivity of the service. This can be frustrating for customers waiting to be served. In addition, individualization of a service could potentially be perceived to be unfair in situations where employees are observed not to be adhering strictly to procedures. Another downside occurs in situations where employees are empowered to rectify service failures by give-aways. The obvious danger is that employees give too much away.

Another major dysfunctional aspect of empowerment is that employees may consciously or unconsciously use their discretion disproportionately to bestow a better service on customers who are similar to them. In other words, customers who are similar in terms of age, gender, ethnicity and other personal characteristics receive higher levels of service than those customers who do not share similar characteristics to the employee[19].

Summary

This chapter has outlined a framework for the empowerment of contact service employees based on customer needs complexity and task complexity. It has further outlined a methodology for determining the levels and type of empowerment that employees should be given. We believe that the distinction between creative and routine discretion is an important one and have, therefore, incorporated it into the model outlined. The chapter also suggests a system of grouping or zoning tasks, which defines the limits of employee discretion more precisely and guides employees in their day-to-day tasks. It must be emphasized here that the lessons learned with respect to services can be easily transferred to non-service environments.

The framework developed addresses three important elements in empowerment decisions, namely when to empower employees, how much discretion should be given and what type of discretion should be given to them. The indexing and zoning systems provide a practical methodology for operationalizing empowerment within organizations. Used correctly, empowerment can offer considerable competitive advantages to service firms.

The effective implantation of empowerment within an organization requires, in addition to discretion over service tasks, that employees have the requisite information to perform their tasks and understand their role in the service delivery process. Appropriate recruitment procedures and training are also necessary to ensure that the front-line employees have the requisite personal characteristics and skills to cope with empowerment, as not all employees can cope with the extra responsibilities associated with empowerment. It is also essential that empowered employees are remunerated according to the level of responsibility and skills required of them.

References

1. Grönroos, C. (1990). Service management: a management focus for service competition. *International Journal of Service Industry Management*, **1** (1), 6–14. Quotation from p. 9.
2. Smith, R. A. and Houston, M. J. (1983). Script-based evaluation of satisfaction with services. In *Emerging Perspectives on Services Marketing* (L. L. Berry et al., eds). Chicago: American Marketing Association, pp. 59–62.
3. Levitt, T. (1972). Production line approach to service. *Harvard Business Review*, September/October, 41–52. Levitt, T. (1976). The industrialization of service. *Harvard Business Review*, **54** (September/October), 63–74.
4. Mills, P. K. (1985). The control mechanisms of employees at the encounter of service organizations. In *The Service Encounter* (Czepiel, J. A. et al., eds). Lexington, MA: Lexington Books.
5. Grönroos, C. (1990). Op. cit., p.10.
6. Bowen, D. E. and Lawler, E. E. III (1992). The empowerment of service workers: what, why, when, and how. *Sloan Management Review*, Spring, 31–9. Conger, J. A. and Kanungo, R. N. (1988). The empowerment process: integrating theory and practice. *Academy of Management Review*, **13** (July), 471–82. Schlesinger, L. A. and Heskett, J. L. (1991). Breaking the cycle of failure in services. *Sloan Management Review*, 17–28.
7. Kelley, S. W. (1993). Discretion and the service employee. *Journal of Retailing*, **69** (1), Spring, 104–26.
8. Bowen, D. E. and Lawler, E. E. III (1992). Op. cit., p. 32.
9. Berry, L. L. (1995). *On Great Service*, p. 208. New York: The Free Press.

10. Schlesinger, L. A. and Heskett, J. L. (1991). Breaking the cycle of failure in services. *Sloan Management Review*, 17–28.
11. Bowen, D. E. and Lawler, E. E. III (1992). Op. cit.
12. Bowen, D. E. and Lawler, E. E. III (1992). Op. cit., p. 36.
13. Berry, L. L., Parasuraman, A. and Zeithamel, V. A. (1994). Improving service quality in America: lessons learned. *Academy of Management Executive*, **8** (2), 32–52.
14. Silvestro, R., Fitzgerald, L., Johnston, R. and Voss, C. (1992). Towards a classification of service processes. *International Journal of Service Industry Management*, **3** (3), 62–75.
15. Hallowell, R. (1996). Southwest Airlines: a case study linking employee needs satisfaction and organizational capabilities to competitive advantage. *Human Resource Management*, **35** (4), 513–34.
16. Berry, L. L. (1995). *On Great Service*. New York: The Free Press.
17. Berry, L. L. (1995). Op. cit.
18. Hartline, M. D. and Ferrell, O. C. (1996). The management of customer contact service employees: an empirical investigation. *Journal of Marketing*, **60** (October), 52–70.
19. Martin, C. L. (1996). Editorial: How powerful is empowerment. *The Journal of Services Marketing*, **10** (6), 4–5.

Section II

Internal Marketing Applications

chapter six

Total quality management (TQM) and internal marketing

Introduction

The rapid market share gains in world markets by far eastern competitors prompted many to examine how nations such as Japan have managed to build their success. The Japanese, over time, have come to represent a standard against which to measure manufacturing excellence. One of the most prominently mentioned issues in Japan's success is quality management.

Surviving in the new world of intense competition, companies have had to establish strategies that can cope with the turbulent changes in the environment. In this world, adding value is the hard work, but it is merely the entry-ticket in the battle for survival. Many companies spend their time figuring out how to provide high quality at low cost. But so do their competitors. This is the dynamic of competition. If others can mimic what you do, then what you do sums up to little differentiation value. The game-play of competition quickly erodes competitive advantage. To sustain competitive advantage, companies must build strong foundations that will not be blown away in competitive storms. This is not achievable over the long term, as the recent collapse of dotcoms illustrated, through a focus on hype and ceremony built by advertising and promotions. Rather, it requires organizational capabilities and competencies built on sound internal foundations. The foundations of competence are more important than short-term gains. Changes in the business environment can quickly alter cost structures, technologies and consumer preferences, but properly managed competencies can last a lifetime. Total quality management (TQM) in the modern world has become part of the fabric for organizational competence.

Total quality management successes

The use of TQM has, since the 1980s, become widespread. For instance, one survey found that 74 per cent of firms practise TQM[1]. Another survey found that 78 per cent of Fortune 1000 organizations plan to increase their use of TQM, while only 5 per cent plan to decrease their use of TQM[2]. There is also evidence that TQM positively impacts organizational performance, when practised correctly[3].

There are many success stories of how TQM has helped transform companies. For example:

- Ericsson Inc. of Lynchburg, Virginia, implemented a successful TQM programme. The TQM programme, named Winshare, saved the company approximately US $60 million over 10 years. Employees were divided into 63 teams, and each team elected a co-worker as a leader. Teams were used to develop improvement ideas and received US $6000 to implement them[4].

- AT&T Wireless Services used TQM to transform its call centre. The call centre, based in Austin, Texas, was growing in business volume by 40–50 per cent. This surge in service calls caused a decline in the quality of customer service, as well as employee development and training. Employee turnover rate rose to 25 per cent due to vague goals and expectations. Deploying TQM techniques, the company tackled the problem by installing a PC-based monitoring system and hiring extra personnel to help improve the process. With the PC system, calls could be stored during specific time periods and could be accessed from any touch-tone phone. Two call-quality monitors were hired to ease the load on supervisors and allow them to concentrate on other duties. Management implemented a grading system that directly linked performance with rewards and promotions. Individualized training resulted from the automation process, as employees began to review some of their own calls. The results led to an increase in employee performance, training and a better understanding of how pay is linked to performance. Employee turnover rate dropped to 11.0 per cent in 1995, showing that TQM worked for AT&T's call centre[5].

- Champion International Corporation's paper and wood pulp products plant operations were transformed through TQM. Total quality management enabled employees to break down compartmentalized departments into cross-functional teams to solve problems. Champion found that when personal satisfaction, derived from its quality efforts, increased it led to improvements in product consistency and reliability[6].

Many other companies, such as Xerox, Motorola, DuPont, Ford and General Motors, have used a range of TQM tools and methodologies, such as benchmarking, to improve product quality and operational efficiency. These improvements resulting from TQM have been real and significant. The question then is: what is TQM? And, how can the best results be derived from it?

Total quality management: the modern paradigm of organizational success

There are probably as many definitions of quality as there are writers. The notion of quality is as old as trade and exchange itself. In the modern day, quality is fundamentally about delivering customer satisfaction. According to quality guru W. E. Deming, competitiveness comes from delivering customer satisfaction, which is created by being responsive to the customer's views and needs, and constantly improving the fulfilment of these through continuous improvement of the product and service. The fundamental touchstone of the quality philosophy is fulfilling customer requirement[7].

Another quality guru, Ishikawa[8], suggests that quality means quality of:

- Work;
- Service;
- System;
- Information;
- People;
- Process; and
- Objectives.

The International Organization for Standardization (ISO), in its ISO 8402 charter, provides a series of quality definitions. According to the ISO 8402, quality is the totality of features and characteristics of a product or service that bear on its ability to satisfy stated or implied needs. Within this philosophy, quality control is an important function to ensure the fulfilment of given customer requirements. Ishikawa[9] states that quality control is carried out for the purpose of realizing the quality that conforms to customer requirements.

Total quality management derives from a business philosophy that focuses on customer satisfaction. It works through the integration and co-ordination of all activities in an organization, as well as on the continuous improvement of all activities in that organization. According to Deming[10], TQM is founded on three basic principles:

- empowered employees;
- continuous quality improvement; and
- quality improvement teams.

Total quality management involves designing organizations such that they are able to please customers day in, day out. Quality proposes two points of focus:

- careful *design* of the product or service;
- ensuring that the organization's *systems* can consistently produce the design.

These objectives can only be achieved if the whole organization is orientated towards them. Oakland[11] emphasizes the importance of integration and involvement, stating that:

> '... *everyone in the organization, from top to bottom, from offices to technical service, from headquarters to local sites, must play their part.*'

Product and service quality improvement is an essential and critical aspect of TQM, and quality is only that which holds value for the customers who are using the products or services[12]. Therefore, an organization must be able to identify the customer's needs, wishes and expectations. This means that a manager has to instil the idea of customer-driven quality throughout the organization and manage all employees in the different departments/functions so that there will be continuous improvement in quality.

Total quality management focuses externally on meeting customer requirements exactly, while internally it is driven by management commitment, employee training and education. The main objective of TQM programmes is to embed quality into processes, and thus into products and services. Total quality management stresses the involvement of everyone inside an organization and related persons outside the organization, such as customers and suppliers. Total quality management uses statistical techniques such as statistical process control (SPC) and pragmatic tools such as the Cause and Effect Fishbone to ensure improvement in the firm's quality. However, TQM entails much more than statistical tools. It requires top management commitment, leadership, training and teamwork. These are the key factors in a successful implementation of TQM. As Tobin[13] correctly notes, TQM is not mere techniques, it 'is the totally integrated effort for gaining competitive advantage by continuously improving every facet of organization culture'.

Total quality management principles

Total quality management in essence comprises of a set of quality principles and values that serve to build an organizational structure that supports effective quality improvement initiatives. These principles guide the development and implementation of quality concepts, tools and practices. For quality to get a foothold, it must be fully integrated into the managerial system of the company. Without integration with the mainstream managerial system quality programmes soon begin to lose energy and fade, and often fail to last long enough to produce significant improvements.

There are several individuals (Deming, Juran, Crosby, Feigenbaum), who have commented upon the general philosophy of TQM[14]. From these, several principles can be drawn:

- *TQM starts at the top.* In order to succeed, TQM must be part of a company's overall business strategy. An essential factor here is that absolute commitment by top management is a must. Additionally, this commitment has to be transparent to the whole company through adequate support and continuous monitoring.

- *TQM focuses on the customer.* Quality is based on the concept that everyone has a customer, and that the requirements, needs and expectations of all customers must be met every time. Therefore, both internal and external customers are important and should be the centre of attention.

- *TQM is process based.* Total quality management is basically a customer-oriented paradigm that occurs through processes. The emphasis on customer focus requires a company to be process based. A process organization is simply one that is conceived as a flow of interdependent processes, which must be understood and improved. Steward[15] notes:

'In the future, executive positions will not be defined in terms of collections of people like head of sales department, but in terms of process, like senior-VP-of-getting-stuff-to-customers,

*which is sales, shipping, billing. You'll no longer have a box on
an organization chart. You'll own part of a process map.'*

Scholtes and Hacquebord[16] explain how structural configuration
shapes employee priorities on the job as follows:

*'If you ask someone in your work,"who is important for you to
please?" and if he or she answers "my boss", that person
experiences the organisation as a chain of command. If the
answer is "the person in the next process, my internal
customer", that person has a systems perspective.'*

Numerous process improvement frameworks and methodologies
have been developed, such as the Taguchi methods[17] and quality
function deployment[18]. Complementing these are radical improvement methodologies such as Business Process Re-engineering.

■ *TQM uses teams.* Employee teams are part of the 'motivational
glue' within TQM. Total quality management uses teams as a
basic building block in its effort for continuous improvement. A
wide range of teams have been utilized within TQM, from quality
circles to self-managed autonomous teams. Collaboration in teams
is a fundamental necessity for TQM capability.

   Team building is one of the key tasks demanded of leadership in
a TQM organization. Indeed, process organization needs almost
by definition to be run cross-functionally. Cross-functional teams
work because they bring together people with different expertise
who might never cross paths in a function-led organization,
although their work might be highly interdependent.

■ *TQM requires training for everybody.* Quality is built through the
skills of the employees and their understanding of what is required.
Educating and training provides employees with the information
of what they need to do and informs them about the strategy and
direction of the organization. Training builds the skills they need
to secure quality improvement.

■ *TQM uses tools to measure and follow progress.* In TQM culture
there is an emphasis toward 'what gets measured gets done'.
Measurement and feedback are the basis for improvement
activities.

■ *TQM requires continuous improvement.* The concept of continuous
improvement is built on the premise that 'work' is the result of a
series of interrelated steps and activities that result in an output.
Continuous attention to each of these steps in the work process is
necessary to improve the reliability of the process and, hence, the
output quality.

Kanji[19] proposes a pyramid model of Quality Management, which is based on the proposition that to achieve a high customer satisfaction level (*delight the customer*), the organization has to improve continuously all aspects of its operation (*continuous improvement*). This needs leadership to make decisions on objective evidence of what is actually happening (*management by fact*), through involvement of all employees in quality improvement activities (people-based management), leading ultimately to business excellence. Kanji's model is made up of four principles: delight the customer; management by fact, people-based management and continuous improvement (see Figure 6.1).

- *Delight the customer*. Delight means being best at what matters most to customers, and this changes over time. Understanding these changes and delighting the customer now and in the future is an integral part of TQM.

- *People-based management*. Knowing what to do, how to do it and getting feedback on performance is one way of encouraging people to take responsibility for the quality of their work. Involvement and commitment to customer satisfaction are ways to generate this.

- *Continuous improvement*. Continuous improvement or incremental change, not major breakthroughs, is the aim of all who wish to move towards total quality.

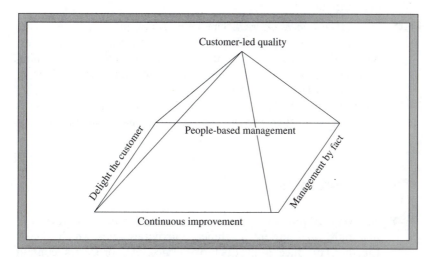

Figure 6.1 Total quality management. *Source*: adapted from Kanji, G. K. (1996). Implementation and pitfalls of quality management. *Total Quality Management*, 7, 331–43.

■ *Management by fact*. Knowing the current performance levels of the products or services in the customers' hands and of all employees is the first stage of being able to improve. Management must have the facts necessary to manage business at all levels. Giving that information to people so that decisions are based upon facts rather than 'gut feelings' is essential to continuous improvement.

Leadership features as a prime mover in this model. It is through leadership effort that all the principles and core concepts are resourced and communicated for business excellence. The development and implementation of quality strategies require fundamental changes in corporate culture and organizational behaviour and therefore can only be achieved through active leadership from top management. The biggest role of leadership is to motivate people.

Each of the above principles is subdivided into two core concepts, namely customer satisfaction and internal customers are real; all work is process and measurement based; teamwork and people make quality; continuous improvement cycle and prevention (Figure 6.1).

Delight the customer

■ *Customer satisfaction*. Companies must uncover what is important for their customers and measure their own performance against customer targets.

■ *Internal customers are real*. The definition of quality (i.e. satisfying agreed customer requirements) relates to internal as well as external customers. This is encapsulated in the customer/supplier chain and highlights the need to get internal relationships working in order to satisfy the external customer. Whether it is supplying information, products or a service, the people you supply internally depend on their internal suppliers for quality work.

Management by fact

■ *All work is process*. A process is a combination of methods, materials, manpower, machinery, activities, etc. which, taken together, produce a product or service. All processes contain inherent variability. The approach in quality improvement is progressively to reduce variation. This is the basis of quality control.

■ *Measurement.* Having a measure of how the organization is doing provides guidance for improvement. Measures can focus internally or externally, i.e. on employee satisfaction, or meeting external customer needs.

People

■ *Teamwork.* When people are able to perceive commonality in goals, then it becomes easier to communicate over departmental or functional walls. Teams, by working towards a common collaborative goal, help in breaking down barriers and act as agents for change.

■ *People make quality.* The role of managers within an organization is to ensure that everything necessary is in place to allow people to make quality products. This in turn starts to create the environment where people are willing to take responsibility for the quality of their own work.

Continuous improvement

■ *The continuous improvement cycle.* The continuous cycle of establishing customer requirements, meeting the requirements, measuring success and continuing to improve can be used internally to fuel the engine of external and continuous improvement. By continually checking customers' requirements, a company can find areas in which improvements can be made.

■ *Prevention.* Prevention means causing problems not to happen. The continual process of driving possible failure out of the system breeds a culture of continuous improvement over time.

Total quality management is an evolving concept. Over time, the scope of its application has expanded and with this evolution there have been changes in perspective and a growth in the tool-bag of techniques. Garvin[20] has suggested that quality has evolved across four distinct historical stages: inspection, statistical quality control, quality assurance and strategic quality management.

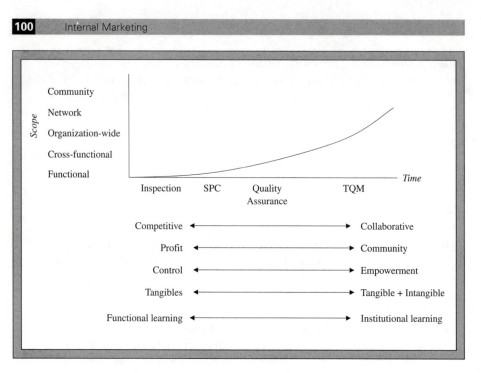

Figure 6.2 Evolution of the quality concept.

Stage 1. Inspection stage

In its initial phase of evolution, quality was simply about inspection, sorting and counting. The orientation was one of defect detection.

Stage 2. Statistical process control

In the next phase, statistical quality control tools and techniques were applied to narrow areas of manufacturing and engineering. During this phase, quality was confined to engineering departments. After this point, the range of involvement and application of quality control techniques expanded hugely.

Stage 3. Quality assurance

In the next phase, quality moved from a narrow manufacturing engineering activity to cover the entire production chain, from design to market. It began to involve all functional groups within the company except top management participation. Accompanying the concept's scope expansion, the range of quality techniques also expanded to include quality measurements, systems audit, quality planning, quality costs, seven basic quality control tools and programme design. The role of all these additions was to 'assure quality'.

Stage 4. TQM

In the TQM era, the quality notion was expanded to encompass an even broader remit. In this period, quality was adapted as a management tool, and the entire system of an organization as well as the external environment became part of quality. Quality management became 'the tool' for *all* people involved in a company. Vertically, it involved all people from top to bottom and from bottom to top, and horizontally it involved all related departments as well as external organizations. Policy deployment, quality function deployment, performance measurements, the seven management and planning tools, people management and benchmarking were added as quality techniques. In this phase, quality was linked to strategy. For the first time, quality was appreciated to be part of everyone's job and everyone's responsibility.

Each of these stages of evolution represents an expansion of the scope of quality. Hand in hand with the broadening of scope was deepening of application. As the discipline of quality matured, so more techniques were developed or adopted. Additional techniques were adopted to tackle the relevant problems being faced, over time, by the organization. In line with the diversity and greater difficulty of problems faced, richer and more sophisticated techniques were adopted. These changes can be captured as paradigmatic shifts. Dahlgaard Su Mi Park[21] captured these shifts as being:

■ *Shifts in the meaning of quality as concept and philosophy*. In its early stage of development, quality was related to products and the degree of conformity to specified standards was the major concern. Gradually, Juran's term 'fitness for use' became more important, and later on quality began to encompass 'meeting requirements' of customers. Subsequently, meeting requirements changed to satisfying the customers and finally this itself changed to delight the customers. With the changing meaning of quality, there was an accompanying shift from perceiving products as tangibles to include both tangible and intangible aspects and thereby capturing almost everything supplied to the customer.

■ *Shift in the understanding of the concept of quality 'control'*. In the first stages of the quality evolution, the meaning of control was understood as inspection, detection or test of the final products. In later stages, control came to represent 'maintenance' and latterly it has also started to include improvement. The meaning of the concept of control moved from checking products to building in quality. With these developments the concept changed from backward-looking activities to forward-looking activities, from passive and reactive to proactive, and from focusing on the results only to focusing on the processes and the interrelationships. Of significant note was the shift from 'control' to 'management'.

- *Shift in the concept of managing people.* The basic principle for people management has been changed from 'control' aspects to a building aspect. The scientific management model of people management, where people were controlled and ordered, has changed to empowerment. This corresponds to the movement from a backward-looking attitude to a forward-looking attitude, and from a preventing attitude to a creating attitude.

- *Shift in the understanding of the boundary and role of the organization.* In the early phases of the quality evolution, an organization was mainly regarded as an economic entity or a profit-making 'machine'. Gradually this changed to embrace a social function of an organization, as more and more research highlighted the importance of human aspects. In the modern TQM era, the role of an organization has become even more encompassing. Today, an organization is not just regarded as a profit-making social entity, but as an integral part of society. Under this perspective, a company must be operated as a small community within society, and it is responsible not just for its own members, but also for wider societal concerns.

- *Shift in the understanding of motivation.* The evolution phases of the human motivation factors are closely allied to the evolution of the concept of an organization. In the early phases of organizational development, there was a tendency to see the organization as an economic entity, and the focus was mainly on the tangible aspects of human motivation. It was believed that people were motivated and satisfied by material rewards. However, over time, social aspects have come to be emphasized as important drivers of motivation, together with material rewards. In the TQM era, where organizations have come to be regarded as a community, the motivation aspects have embraced deeper intangible motivation factors, such as self-actualization, self-development, recognition, learning and creativity. The change from a focus on tangible aspects to intangible aspects corresponds to the movement from focusing on extrinsic motivation to intrinsic motivational factors.

- *Shift in the appreciation of feedback and measurement.* A similar phenomenon is observed in measurement areas. In the initial stages, quality was measured in defect rates, complaint rates, returns, etc. In the TQM era, two new important measurements have been introduced. These two measurements are customer satisfaction measurements and employee satisfaction measurements.

■ *Shift in the understanding of continuous improvement and learning.* In the first wave of quality, the primary focus was on improving tangible work processes and changes made by front-line workers. In this stage, the initial tools were derived from statistics and other related methods for diagramming, analysing and redesigning work processes to reduce variability and to enable systematic improvements. In the second wave of quality, the focus shifted from improving work processes to improving how we work. The second wave was initiated in Japan; as early as the 1960s, leading Japanese companies began to mass deploy quality tools. Furthermore, with quality control circle activities everybody participated in quality improvements. In the third wave of quality, the learning aspects become institutionalized as an inescapable way of life for managers as well as for workers. Peter Senge[22], analysing the quality movement from the learning aspects, claims that the second wave is well under way in Japan, driven by their seven new tools for management. In his opinion, with a few exceptions, the US is still in the first wave, because the basic behaviour of US managers, especially senior managers, has not really changed much.

The history of quality movement shows that it has been able to adapt to new circumstances continuously, and in this way it was able to integrate new ideas, tools and methods. At the same time, the history of the quality movement shows that it has also been able to reach a deeper level in each relevant area regarding its conceptual development and implementation aspects. A point of note with this evolutionary trajectory is that it can be divided into two different dimensions: the quality evolution history of implementation and the quality evolution history of TQM's conceptual development. As quality has matured conceptually, the major weakness explaining many of the failures that we are still witnessing can be said to originate mainly from weaknesses in its implementation.

The factor for TQM success: implementation

Like any programme or effort, TQM's success is affected by how well it is implemented. Gurnani[23] suggests that eight essential ingredients can be discerned in TQM implementation:

1 *Quality policy*. It is almost a statement of human nature that people follow policy, good or bad. A clear and concise policy on quality needs to be stated to ensure that all employees understand what behaviour is expected of them from top management. For instance, in times of conflict in objectives (quantity versus quality of output), managers should not violate their commitment to quality and succumb to the temptation of delivering low quality products simply to achieve a one-off on-time delivery.

2 *Senior management commitment*. Strong commitment from the management is an essential ingredient. Support must be made transparent to the whole company through adequate resources, monitoring, coherence and absolute top priority to quality improvement programmes. Top management must create a 'climate' for quality improvement by their personal attitude if they are to encourage employees to respond favourably towards quality improvement efforts.

3 *Steering committee*. Steering committee members act out dual roles of 'quality leaders' and 'quality guardians'. It takes deep appreciation and conviction to make the quality improvement effort sustainable over time. This means that steering committee members themselves must first become educated about the quality philosophy: its history, concepts and tools. They need not be involved in the minutiae of the effort, but it is essential that they lead and champion the effort. During the implementation stage of the TQM programmes, the role of the steering committee is to detect any deviation from the planned trajectories and to redirect everything back on track.

4 *Employee commitment and involvement*. Quality improvement is impossible unless it enlists the commitment of all employees at all levels in the organizational hierarchy. The ingredients for this to happen include frequent participation, enthusiasm and total involvement. Employee involvement is a process of empowering members of the organization to make decisions and to solve problems appropriate to their levels in the organization.

5 *Training and problem-solving tools*. Training provides a common language and a common set of tools to be used in the firm. Like quality improvement, training education about quality improvement is an ongoing process. Management must consider who must learn what, how and by when.

6 *Communication*. Effective and efficient two-way communication channels are a prerequisite of any quality improvement programme. Communications signal change from the top management, as well as transmit important messages up and down the vertical and horizontal implementation chain.

7 *Standards and measurement*. It is essential to have criteria for measuring progress towards the overall aims of the company. Standards serve to stipulate expected performance levels. To reap full benefits, standards must be complemented by other activities such as benchmarking, which help set the improvement direction and targets.

8 *Reward and recognition*. Recognizing people means informing individuals that their efforts are being appreciated. Teams and individuals who successfully apply the quality process must be recognized and possibly rewarded so that the rest of the organization begins to understand what is expected of them. Without clear feedback, employees tend not to adjust their performance and even become de-motivated because 'no one seems to notice their efforts'.

To have a successful TQM effort, it is important to have solid managerial techniques in place before the programme is initiated. Employee involvement is a necessity for quality. Managers must be able to identify weak performing areas for improvement and recognize the areas that a company is performing well, so their strength can be enhanced. The summary ingredient in a successful TQM programme is the effective rewarding of employees for quality initiatives and hard work.

Successful implementations of TQM have resulted in dramatic improvements in profits and other tangible measurements. A study conducted by Tatikonda and Tatikonda[24], looking at winners of the Malcolm Baldridge Quality Award, revealed that on average these companies achieved a 70 per cent increase in return on sales and a 50 per cent increase in return on assets.

Problems causing TQM failures

While there have been many corporate success stories of quality management, equally there has been an abundance of failures. A survey conducted by Arthur D. Little of 500 manufacturing and service companies found that approximately one-third felt the TQM programme had a 'significant impact' on their competitiveness. Surprisingly, the remaining two-thirds felt that the TQM programmes did not impact their organization positively. Also, a study conducted by A. T. Kearney of 100 British organizations revealed that only one-fifth felt positive results occurred as a result of the TQM programme[25].

A variety of factors impedes effective implementation of TQM programmes. These are:

- TQM has been implemented reactively, as a quick fix, blindly
  following a fad, or simply to boost some individual's ego.
  Accordingly, it is nothing more than a 'technique' that managers
  feel they must use because it has been adopted in one form or
  another in a significant number of other organizations.

- TQM creates and develops a cumbersome bureaucracy. Many
  programmes require a significant increase in paperwork and
  other bureaucratic requirements that supposedly are necessary to
  track the programme's benefits. Many organizations appear to
  have created a plethora of mechanisms that demoralize employees
  who are trying to implement the TQM programme.

- About two-thirds of companies fail in implementing TQM programmes because they create dual structures. Total quality management companies often build new structures of committees and
  teams in addition to the real organization structure. However, to
  work the TQM programme must be integrated into the way the
  business is run on a day-to-day basis.

- TQM is implemented using an off-the-shelf approach. Pre-pack-
  aged programmes fail to consider the unique aspects of the company trying to implement the programme.

- Many TQM efforts have tended to ignore the importance and role
  of measurement in the quality process. They simply jump on the
  'doing' because it is much sexier rather than reflect adequately on
  the feedback and measurement process. Measurement and feedback are long-term drivers of improvement and have very important bearing in directing behaviour. It is questionable whether
  adequate measurement processes, techniques and metrics have
  even been devised. *What* you measure and *how* you measure things
  reflects what you get.

- Lack of proper training is another major pitfall of TQM programmes. A lot of the training has tended to be vague, diffuse
  and not specifically directed to create specific competences for
  TQM. Additionally, there is an emphasis towards mass training
  of shop floor employees without the training and involvement of
  all levels of management. Without a deep appreciation by middle
  and senior management of all aspects of quality, TQM programmes soon falter and grind to a halt.

The above examples represent a few of the possible reasons for failure of
TQM programmes.

Examples of TQM failures

Despite its successes, many companies have experienced that simply having a quality programme does not guarantee business success. Several high profile TQM companies have fallen victim to this condition. Among them have been recipients of prestigious quality awards, such as the Baldridge, Deming Prize and EFQM award. These failures include Douglas Aircraft (a subsidiary of McDonnell Douglas Corporation), Florida Power and Light, Wallace Co., Bell Helicopter Textron, Modicon, and British Telecom.

- *Douglas Aircraft.* The company started its TQM programme by training 8000 employees using a 2-week programme and spent additional time preparing the workplace for the implementation of a TQM programme. Two years later, the company found it was no better off than before the programme.
- *Florida Power and Light* halted its TQ programme due to extensive complaints about excessive paperwork from employees. This decision was made in spite of the fact that Florida Power and Light had won Japan's Deming Prize for quality management in 1989. The decision was made when the company's chairman found that many employees believed the quality improvement process had become a tyrannical bureaucracy. Employees believed that the mechanics of the programme were overemphasized. While there were some improvements in the quality of services, the improvements were insignificant compared with the scale of the TQM programme.
- *Wallace Co.*, an oil field supply company, filed for bankruptcy protection shortly after it had won the Malcolm Baldridge National Quality Award. According to CEO John W. Wallace[26], many of the personnel within the organization were too busy making quality presentations after winning the 1990 award, and were not able to devote the necessary time to generate new sales.
- *Bell Helicopter Textron* held a 36 per cent share of the new helicopter sales market worldwide. The company recognized the increasing need for quality and trained over 3000 people in TQM during the next few years. By July 1992, Bell had not realized any benefits from the programme. In fact, the company's share of new helicopter sales declined to 20 per cent.
- *Modicon*, a producer of industrial automation systems, began its TQM programme in the late 1980s. Modicon's senior managers expected near instant results. Needless to say, the quick results did not materialize and it was not long before resistance to the total

quality management programme arose from the senior ranks, who measured the firm's quality programme against short-term financial performance.

■ *British Telecom* launched a quality programme in the late 1980s. The company is still attempting to recover from being bogged down in quality processes and bureaucracy. The company failed to focus on customers and began to dismantle most of its quality bureaucracy[27].

As we noted earlier, there are many roadblocks to successful implementation of a TQM programme. The most common obstacle is lack of management commitment to the TQM concept. Top management often shift responsibility to middle management for finding solutions to central business problems. Gordon et al.[28] describe the seven 'sins' of TQM that cause the erosion of confidence of employees and management alike:

■ Reorganization with no real reason, causing damage to people, processes and profit.

■ Obsessing over winning a quality award is always the wrong goal.

■ Collecting data on every piece of the processes is wasteful and expensive.

■ Customer satisfaction measurement is often overdone.

■ Wasting time, effort and money when all employees are trained in SPC.

■ Workers solve non-consequential problems, thus productivity suffers because TQM places all employees above management.

■ When management is removed from the process of TQM, the sole focus shifts to the process.

It is clear that while TQM has proven to be of tremendous value for some companies, for others, approximately two-thirds of companies attempting it, TQM efforts have failed to either produce results or have stalled[29]. Gordon et al.[30] report in a survey that 26 per cent of Fortune 500 CEOs were either 'disappointed' or 'very disappointed' in their returns on investments in TQM. Many of these programmes are currently being cancelled or have been cancelled due to the negative impact on profits. In fact, TQM is one of few managerial initiatives that began to show declines in the late 1990s[31].

This raises the question of effective implementation of quality programmes. Internal marketing plays a role in facilitating the implementation of effective quality programmes. This role and importance of IM is elaborated in the discussion that follows.

Total quality management, marketing and internal marketing

The traditional organizational approach, particularly within marketing, focuses on external customers and markets, with an emphasis upon attracting and retaining customers at a profit. However, marketing has been slow in incorporating a more encompassing interpretation of the 'customer', such as that employed in quality management. In quality, there has long been recognition of the importance of both external and internal customers. Indeed, Deming's famous 'chain reaction' portrays the organization as a system and receives its impetus from the end-consumer. The system is arranged as a process chain of customer–supplier that encapsulates within itself the external customer. The TQM concept, by adopting a systemic view, is able to shows how an internal focus can lead to positive external outcomes. This works only as long as the internal production system assigns a clear position for the external customer within its chain.

In quality management there is insistence upon the overriding importance of the customer. W. E. Deming conceptualized quality as that which attracts and captures the customer. This view persists in modern conceptualizations of TQM. What is notable in the quality conceptualization is the customer–supplier transposition, whose interlinkages connect to form the production process system. From this, it is clear that any supplier affects all subsequent customers. Initially the impact is upon internal customers, but eventually the effect will extend to external customers. Such thinking is slowly permeating into marketing, especially in the marketing practitioners' thought-world. As we noted earlier, the internal customer is not a figment of imagination, he or she is real. With the help of TQM thinking, the concept of the internal customer is

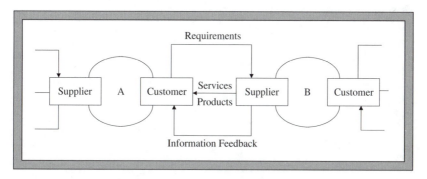

Figure 6.3 The internal customer in the customer–supplier chain.

becoming increasingly accepted and established. This has helped increase the visibility to the practice of internal marketing.

Companies are steadily coming to see the linkages that exist between quality, productivity, employee satisfaction and customer satisfaction. Mitchell[32] notes: 'You can't make happy customers with unhappy employees... if the internal customers are satisfied they will love their jobs and feel a sense of pride.' And as Neave reminds us: '... the whole quality of our work is... affected by what is supplied to us... Awareness of the substantial and involved interleaving customer–supplier structure makes us begin to realize how serious any mistake or any poorly-designed part of the productive system can be...'[33].

In contrast, unfortunately, many of the conceptualizations of quality by marketers have been generally unhelpful. For example, the distinction of quality by the marketing academics[34] into two main categories – 'technical quality' and 'functional quality' – in which technical quality provides the customer with a technical solution and functional quality represents those additional elements that have an impact on customer experiences during the customer–supplier interface process, is generally unhelpful, if not misleading. This is evidenced by the failure of the terms to enter mainstream TQM vocabulary and TQM practice.

Just like external customers, internal customers want to have their needs satisfied. Fulfilling these needs enhances employee motivation and retention. Utilizing the supplier–customer logic, internal marketing

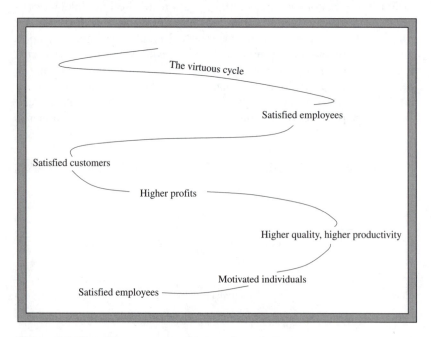

Figure 6.4 The virtuous cycle of internal marketing.

through its internal focus serves the cause for external customer orientation.

The internal marketing logic is simple: satisfied employees → motivated individuals → higher quality, higher productivity → satisfied customers → higher profits (virtuous cycle).

Internal marketing asks management to view the organization as a market, where there exists an internal supply chain consisting of internal suppliers and customers. The logic of internal marketing is that by satisfying the needs of internal customers, an organization should be in a better position to deliver the quality desired to satisfy external customers. The activation of the interaction processes between internal supplier and customer with each iteration moves the product/service along the supply chain and closer to the end-customer. The higher the degree of employee satisfaction, the higher the possibility of generating external satisfaction and loyalty. Satisfying and delighting customers triggers several bottom line and associated benefits.

Internal marketing as integrator: role of internal marketing in TQM and marketing

A persistent remnant of traditional organizational structuring is that companies continue to live in functional silos. Activities such as quality and marketing are so fundamental that they cannot be considered as separate functions. They are in fact the whole business seen from the point of view of its outcome, that is, from the customer's point of view. In this sense, marketing and quality are all pervasive and are part of everyone's job description. More than this, if we can combine marketing with quality then we are able to integrate the customer into the design of the product/service and develop a systematic process for delivering to these needs. This integration occurs through the enactment and interaction of a set of internal relationships. Companies must gain an understanding of how to develop and manage these internal relationships, with individuals and groups of individuals. This extends not just to employees, but also others who fall within the boundary of internal markets, such as suppliers and distributors. It is the management of these organizational sets of relationships that allows the 'delivery' to what marketing has promised externally.

A key question is how the company can develop an effective process for structuring and managing internal relationships. Our answer is that they have to install internal marketing activities. Internal marketing enables this because it is the interface between the internal process of quality and the external customer. By focusing on the management of internal processes and structuring and aligning relationships, internal marketing acts as the driving force in achieving the primary objectives of quality, efficiency, effectiveness, loyalty and profitability.

Total quality management and marketing derive from a common business philosophy that focuses on customer satisfaction for long-term profitability. Internal marketing helps bring the two together by systematically integrating activities. Internal marketing by facilitating employee motivation toward quality consciousness, and hence customer consciousness, can have a major impact upon an organization. By aligning and improving internal relationships and satisfaction, the company can reduce costs, increase profits and build a platform for competitive success.

In a well-managed company, all functions will have a clear understanding of what defines their contribution to the overall mission and objectives. In such companies, customers' needs and wishes are not seen as the responsibility solely of the organization's marketing function or efforts. Marketing is essential, but it is not the only custodian of the customer. Marketing must co-operate with other people in the organization who perform non-marketing tasks. The case is the same for the quality function. In a large organization, for example, manufacturing, engineering, purchasing, accounting and finance are all jigsaw parts of the internal structure. For the corporate entity, no single management function is effective if it operates in isolation. Multiple operations and people with different skill-sets have to be actively involved in creating and delivering products and services. These cross-functional activities and the people who perform them all have a major influence upon the final outcome. The implication of this is that today's managers must ensure that every employee in all parts of the organization places top priority on the delivery of quality throughout the whole of the customer–supplier chain.

Whilst TQM's focus is on quality of product and service and marketing's focus is on the marketplace, IM is based on a more inclusive and broader perspective because it considers the 'totality' of internal and external functions and relationships necessary to get things done. When companies look at their business through their customers' eyes and measure their performance against their customers' expectations, then it is not possible to view quality narrowly, as something that the manufacturing department achieves by inspecting products for compliance with specifications and eliminating defective ones. Internal marketing helps TQM in its search for quality improvement by motivating employees toward continuous improvement. Marketing when combined with TQM also means that everyone in all parts of the organization places top priority on customer-led continuous quality improvement. This requires managing all internal and external relationships and processes. Internal marketing structures and enables the effective management of such relationships by facilitating an effective delivery process. Internal marketing is the interface between TQM and marketing (i.e. TQM is the internal

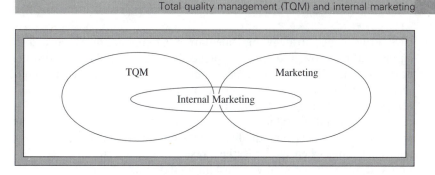

Figure 6.5 Internal marketing as interface agency.

delivery agency, whereas marketing is the external delivery agency, and IM is the facilitating interface agency).

Internal marketing generates involvement and commitment to quality. Involvement concerns not only people, but also includes all organizational resources, such as systems, equipment and information. One primary aim of internal marketing is to assess and help put in place processes to improve effort toward quality and meet the customers' requirements and needs. To satisfy the needs of the external customers, the company has first to satisfy its internal customers. When this philosophy is applied, the barriers between departments and functions are broken down and removed. Internal marketing includes all individual and organizational functions, activities, communications and elements that a firm uses to create, develop and maintain appropriate interlinkages that result in the delivery of high quality to the final customer. Internal marketing, by helping to focus on integrating marketing with quality, leads to cost savings (i.e. machinery, inspection, testing, rework and complaints costs), which in turn leads to higher productivity through employee motivation.

Internal marketing's role is to help create, interpret, maintain and enhance positive, sustainable and close relationships within the company, thereby facilitating implementation of strategies that engender high levels of satisfaction in the external marketplace. Internal marketing focuses on and is concerned with all integrated activities within the organization (internal relationships). Whilst the focus is to manage the internal marketplace relationships, these internal marketplace relationships influence and enhance external marketplace relationships. Internal marketing complements quality management and external marketing. It melds the internal quality process to external market needs. It is through these actions, not plans and thoughts, that real sustainable competitive advantage is built. In this sense, internal marketing is emerging as a way of raising quality levels in organizations and stimulating corporate effectiveness.

Combining TQM with marketing through internal marketing can lead to optimal co-ordination and integration of operations, activities and efforts for aligned strategy implementation. Combined, the three lead to an integration between quality, employee loyalty, productivity and profits. Internal marketing's co-ordination or integration of operations, activities and efforts is merely an operational means to an end: customer orientation. Internal marketing helps focus the organization toward a customer orientation, which works internally by facilitating the process and behaviours to deliver a quality orientation. Internal marketing, TQM and marketing, when used together, result in greater customer satisfaction and allow the company to sustain a competitive edge.

Thus, the success of a quality programme is mediated by the partnership between the employee and the company. Internal marketing works on getting quality by paying attention to:

- ■ *Quality of processes*. Internal marketing plays a role in examining the activities of work and ensuring that the processes are effective in delivering maximum value for customer needs. Internal marketing does this by examining the process for overall aims, assessing and aligning these to strategic goals and then communicating the existence of the process, and informing how the process functions. By raising the awareness of aims and function, internal marketing improves the operational quality of the process.

- ■ *Quality of infrastructure*. Internal marketing assesses the quality of the internal structures and internal resources and activities. It examines how well these processes and activities are managed and co-ordinated.

- ■ *Quality of interaction*. Internal marketing assesses and improves the quality of information exchange, financial exchange and social exchange. As a direct consequence of high 'quality' exchange, internal relationships can be improved and more effectively aligned to desired aims.

- ■ *Quality of environment*. Internal marketing assesses the relationship and interaction process between the parties, and the impact of the environment within which the interactions occurs. The quality of the environment determines how well people co-operate and operate. The organizational atmosphere can be described as an artefact of organizational culture, and depicts its reality along dimensions such as level of dependence versus interdependence, conflict as opposed to co-operation, expectations and reciprocity, communication, trust and commitment. A high 'quality' environment involves high trust, commitment and reciprocity between involved business parties.

- ■ *Quality of people*. Internal marketing assesses current capabilities and competencies of people, and identifies the gaps that need to be filled to make strategies happen. Internal marketing assesses the competence, experience, know-how, internal relationships, motivation and attitudes necessary for embedding the quality philosophy throughout the organization. It examines for these and formulates plans to generate appropriate reflexes.

■ *Quality of plans*. Internal marketing examines and helps the translation of strategies into tactical plans for operations. In the translation process, internal marketing considers what benefits individuals can derive from implementing these strategies, in the long as well as the short term, and then develops appropriate internal marketing strategies to engender buy-in.

Effective co-ordination and integration of these results in:

■ *Quality of product/service*. This is what the customers receive. From product/service quality comes customer satisfaction, which is the primary reason for initiating the TQM programme or any other effort.

The internal marketing philosophy builds an interrelationship between quality and external marketing. This it does by structuring appropriate exchanges and building employee relationships. Using internal marketing, companies can effectively interweave the customer's perspective into the quality process. Internal marketing helps build cross-functionalism, where different functions inside and outside an organization work together in teams.

Internal marketing understands that there are links and interdependencies between product/service quality, customer satisfaction, employee relationship and profitability. From this appreciation, internal marketing aids the process of helping everyone in the organization see the linkage between what they do and its impact on the eventual customer relationship. Co-ordinating the internal and external activities in a harmonious manner is essential to establish and quantify the requirements of internal customers (employees), and aids the delivery of external customer satisfaction. This is the key role of internal marketing.

In short, IM focuses on:

■ integrating and co-ordinating activities within the organization (*integrative focus*) by

■ facilitating interlinkage between external customers (*market-led focus*) with

■ internal quality and continuous improvement of the products/services and processes (*efficiency and effectiveness focus*),

■ through a focus on employees in the organization, who are responsible for the execution of strategies of continuous improvement (*internal focus* via internal relationships).

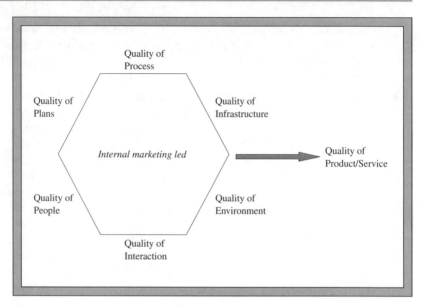

Figure 6.6 The internal marketing-led quality diamond.

Internal marketing as strategy and internal marketing as philosophy

Internal marketing is a co-ordinating philosophy because it considers and co-ordinates 'all' activities – including internal and external relationships, network interactions and collaborations – by examining all activities involved in satisfying customers throughout the quality supply chain. It is a philosophy because it focuses attention on customer satisfaction and organizational productivity through continuous attention and improvement of the 'jobs' that employees execute and the environment in which they execute them. Internal marketing communicates the idea that a major goal of management is to plan and build appropriate close and flexible relationships with internal parties to continuously improve quality.

Internal marketing is a strategy because it triggers appropriate actions to occur, such that strategic words become translated into actions that deliver quality-led customer satisfaction. Internal marketing therefore helps guide the overall thinking in the organization and plays a role in decision making, as well as in the execution of predetermined plans.

The main role behind internal marketing within a TQ setting is to structure and enhance appropriate internal relationships with employees and collaborators. By bringing together quality and marketing, internal marketing's main goal is to produce and deliver customer satisfaction. This allows the company to realize strategies for sustainable competitive advantage.

Internal marketing is an interaction process between the organization and its employees within a given company context. Internal marketing works at the level of creating precisely the right type of atmosphere and environment in which employees are encouraged to create, co-ordinate and improve the whole business. This means that internal marketing works towards actions, interactions and adaptations that enhance customer satisfaction. This is engendered by creating an environment in which quality-enhancing behaviours become a reflexive part of employee action. This environment and the accompanying quality-enhancing behaviours by employees determine the ultimate source of competitive advantage in a dynamic environment.

Internal marketing guides all people, functions and departments of an organization (e.g. the production department, the service department and the marketing department) by its systematic appreciation of the needs, aspirations and costs of each. This underpins the internal customer supply chain, which must be understood and accepted by every single employee, from top management to middle managers, all the way down to shop-floor workers. Organizationally, this hierarchy results in a network of relationships within which different collaborations evolve as a consequence of a multiplicity of interaction episodes. Each of these relationships and interactions can be managed, where appropriate, with a formal internal marketing strategy and internal marketing plan.

Co-ordinating a web of customer–supplier relationships is certainly not an easy task. In the new world, companies can no longer afford to maintain barriers between functions and departments. Success is driven by integrating related functions within the organization – production, sales and distribution, services, advertising, sales promotion, product planning and market research – to achieve the organization's business and marketing objectives. Internal marketing examines and manages the total set of relationships and interactions that bring about additional value. It is important that everyone in the organization can see the linkage between what she or he does and its impact on the external customer. Therefore, creating and aligning internal relationships between departments, functions and employees inside the organization is necessary to improve the performance of the company and its employees. The main challenge is how the different internal and external parts of a business can be co-ordinated in an efficient and flexible manner[35]. Internal marketing fulfils this challenge. By managing and structuring for integrated action, internal marketing creates managerial value that eventually culminates in competitive advantage.

To implement TQM, managers must gain a full understanding of how the different parts of a whole business can be co-ordinated in a holistic way that is simultaneously efficient, flexible and conducive to continuous improvement. Becoming a quality organization is not just a matter of practising new management techniques and methodologies, though these may certainly help. It is also about becoming more integrated and co-ordinated in action. Understanding and managing all these internal relationships, functions and interactions in an effective and profitable manner is an essential condition to gain long-term competitive advantages. The only solution for an organization to reach the ultimate competitive edge and advantage is to adopt a strategic approach to internal marketing. Most employee perceptions of corporate programmes, such as quality, are affected by their perceptions of other elements of the corporate package. Employee motivation to do as the organization bids is driven by what they are being offered, not just from the programmes they are being asked to implement, but also their perception of the whole corporate package. This means that the company must establish a 'high contract partnership' between the employee along multiple dimensions. Tools of internal marketing help co-ordinate this. Internal marketing is about structuring and creating the action.

Good internal marketing identifies and removes barriers that divide employees and factionalize organizational action. Internal marketing, by building a deeper and clearer understanding of the inside of the organization, is a key capability to respond to the challenges of a hyper-competitive world. Internal marketing harmonizes the bits into a whole. Only in this way can quality be delivered. The internal marketing approach provides strategic guidance on how to leverage business performance and profitability in an increasingly competitive environment. Strategic internal marketing is more than just a written plan. For instance, a formal quality programme is of little value if employees are not motivated and empowered to deliver the type and level of effort required. Internal marketing works by formally assimilating strategy into a plan of internal actions necessary for motivated internal implementation.

Internal marketing fundamentals for TQM success

Organizations wishing to successfully implement internal marketing need to focus upon a select number of areas over which they have control: human resources, training, organizational structures and processes, plans and procedures. By examining these elements, the company can design job products to motivate employees toward quality consciousness, and hence customer satisfaction. Internal marketing is concerned with employee motivation and loyalty, and suggests that retaining talented employees contributes to enhanced profitability. Employee motivation calls for perfect supplier chain performance and companies must deliver on their promises to their internal markets. The tools and techniques from IM aid the strategic implementation of marketing-led TQM. Internal marketing initiates efforts and selected behaviours, such as quality, customer consciousness and continuous improvement. Profitability is higher due to efficiencies achieved through better use of internal resources (e.g. reduction of costs and working capital). Organizations that practise an internal marketing orientation can help the company become a leader in total quality.

It is imperative that a company:

- understands employee needs
- considers employees as partners; and
- ensures that employees are driven/aligned in ways to satisfy customers' needs.

According to the internal marketing perspective, companies must consider the management of all relationships with which a business is involved. This means managing all contacts that a company has with employees who have the potential to influence and motivate customer satisfaction. Many companies face adversarial relations between management and workers within the workplace. Internal marketing's aim is to get competitive collaboration. Competitive collaboration is an effort that seeks to continuously improve through collaborative alignment. This implies supplying employees with the highest possible quality with respect to their individual requirements within the internal customer–supplier chain.

Internal marketing works by establishing, developing and maintaining successful exchange relationships within the organization. Within the internal marketplace such internal exchange is based upon:

- understanding and intimacy;
- trust;
- commitment.

Internal marketing helps builds intimacy between suppliers and their customers. Internal marketing works in the organization by managing interactions and connectivity to ensure that the full talent and creativity of all employees is incorporated into the organizational system.

Internal marketing is built on 'trust'. When people trust the organization will do what it says, then it encourages behaviours within the organization that allow for quality to be embedded through the entire supply chain process. This enables internal customers to receive the right resources to do the right jobs at the right time in the right way. By systematically aligning interactions through explicit considerations to a full set of stakeholder needs, internal marketing helps in the development and growth of trust and commitment among parties. This underpins perfect delivery of quality each and every time to the specifications that attract and appeal to the consumer. This in turn motivates customer retention. By looking after the needs of the employees, internal marketing provides a clear signal to the internal market that the company values its employees. This begins the circle of reciprocity: when the company can demonstrate that it is committed to its employees, its employees respond in kind and become committed to its success.

Unsuccessful implementation of strategies is caused by an inability to harmonize interactions and failure to build inter-connections between departments. The role of internal marketing is to help marketing, not just simply to connect with external customers through the marketing mix, but also to facilitate a process whereby external information is effectively disseminated to employees within the company. This allows the company to become more proactive in its product/service design and delivery process activities.

Internal marketing is therefore a management philosophy for both motivation and support towards market-led TQM. Employees experience the business as part of their lived reality, and how this experience unfolds on a day-to-day basis determines individual actions. Positive experience leads to behaviours befitting an organizational quality orientation. Negative experience creates tensions and divides the organization into 'us and them' factions. Internal marketing is very valuable in nurturing internal environments, which are conducive to quality creation through development of common values and behaviours.

Internal marketing helps the quality effort by:

- Attracting, developing, motivating and retaining employees who are capable and willing to give excellent service by treating them well and making them feel important.
- Aligning employees to the mission, goals, strategies and processes of the company.
- Creating thematic coherence by placing stress on the critical few issues, so that employees will be able to 'do the right things right' (effectiveness) rather than just 'do many things' (efficiency).
- Cascading consistent decision making and action through appropriate communication, tracking and feedback.
- Emphasizing the internal customer–supplier chain as an enabler of good (external) customer service by paying explicit attention to the management of internal exchanges.
- Motivating and training employees to recognize the external and internal customer by 'thinking backwards to the customer' and then driving forwards with actions for continuous improvement.

- Building employee competencies necessary for long-term competitive success.
- Acting as an interface between employees and management, and between departments.
- Shifting the workforce from a production orientation toward customer-led process orientation.
- Enhancing customer orientation by information exchange on customer needs. Internal marketing works toward customer orientation and quality culture by familiarizing all employees with their own customer–supplier relationships. This it does by ensuring that appropriate information is packaged and relayed. The end result is a better integration of work activities between people and across departments.
- Retaining employees by helping them identify with the norms, values and culture of the organization. If individuals buy into and share organizational values, then they are less inclined to leave. Values compatibility creates a sense of belonging and unconsciously motivates behaviours toward higher customer consciousness.
- Developing a stronger quality-led customer culture by emphasizing a desirable set of corporate values, that synthesize the company's identity. Internal marketing, via the process of 'selling' the concept of quality, enables the company to get its employees to internalize an appropriate set of values. Its aim is to influence and change attitudes and behaviour.
- Enhancing internal linkages by altering employee attitudes and associated behaviour in their interactions with internal customers.

Summary

Actively involving people is a basic requisite of total quality management. Internal marketing plays an extremely useful role in identifying and clarifying each individual's role, and then providing information and training to enable them to fulfil the tasks they have responsibility over. In helping companies to implement TQM, it is necessary to emphasize that quality should not be managed just as the interface between customer and supplier, but instead should encompass all relationships within the organization. Internal marketing plays a central role in the management of these interfaces and relationships. This is crucial because, as Oakland[36] notes: 'For an organization to be truly effective, every single part must work properly together, failure to meet the requirements in one part or area creates problems elsewhere'. Atkinson[37] clarifies further by expressing the

Figure 6.7 The internal marketing onion for quality and customer consciousness.

view that 'emphasis should be on the internal dynamics of the organization, recognizing that meeting the requirements of the internal customer is as important as meeting the needs of the external customer'. Such beliefs have led to the thinking that departments must consider themselves as members of a 'customer chain'[38]. Internal marketing works exactly on this recognition. By placing the internal customer at centre stage, internal marketing works to generate quality for marketplace success.

References

1. Moran, L., Hogeveen, J., Latham, J. and Ross-Eft, D. (1994). *Winning Competitive Advantage: A Blended Strategy Works Best*. Cupertino, CA: Zenger-Miller.
2. Lawler, E. E. III, Mohrman, S. A. and Ledford, G. E. Jr (1995). *Creating High Performance Organisations: Practices and Results of Employee Involvement and Total Quality Management in Fortune 1000 Companies*. San Francisco, CA: Jossey-Bass.
3. General Accounting Office (1991). *Management Practices: US Companies Improve Performance Through Quality Efforts*. Washington, DC: US General Accounting Office. Hendricks, K. B. and Singhal, V. R. (1996).

Quality awards and the market value of the firm: an empirical investigation. *Management Science*, **42** (3), 415–36. Lawler, E. E. III et al. (1995). Op cit.

4. Caldwell, K. (1996). Will vendors reintroduce Total Quality Management? *Electrical World*, November, 68–9.

5. Nelson, M. (1996). How to keep that personal touch. *Telephony*, **231**, 38–9.

6. Cruz, C. (1996). Quality program softens boundaries at Champion. *Purchasing*, **12**, 73–6.

7. Deming, W. E. (1986). *Out of the Crisis*. Cambridge: Cambridge University Press.

8. Ishikawa, K. (1985). *What is Total Quality Control, The Japanese Way*. Englewood Cliffs, NJ: Prentice-Hall.

9. Ibid.

10. Deming, W. E. (1986). Op.cit.

11. Oakland, J. S. (1992), *Total Quality Management*. Pitman.

12. Ishikawa, K. (1985). Op. cit.

13. Tobin, L. M. (1990). The new quality landscape: Total Quality Management. *Journal of System Management*, **41**, 10–14.

14. Crosby, P. B. (1979). *Quality is Free*. New York: McGraw-Hill. Deming, W. E. (1986). *Out of the Crisis*. Cambridge: Cambridge University Press. Feigenbaum, A. V. (1991). *Total Quality Control*. New York: McGraw-Hill. Hakes, C. (1991). *Total Quality Management: A Key to Business Improvement*. London: Chapman & Hall. Juran, J. M. (1974). *The Quality Control Handbook*, 3rd edn. New York: McGraw-Hill. Kanji, G. K. (1990). Total Quality Management: the second Industrial Revolution. *Total Quality Management*, **1**, 3–12.

15. Steward, T. A. (1992). The search for the organisation of tomorrow. *Fortune*, 18 May, pp. 92–8.

16. Scholtes, P. and Hacquebord, H. (1988). Beginning the quality transformation, parts 1 and 2. *Quality Progress*, July, 28–33.

17. Taguchi, G. (1979). *Introducing the Off Line Quality Control*. Japanese Standard Association.

18. Akao, Y. (1990). *Quality Function Deployment*. Cambridge, MA: Productivity Press.

19. Kanji, G. K. (1996). Implementation and pitfalls of quality management. *Total Quality Management*, **7**, 331–43.

20. Garvin, D. (1988). *Managing Quality: The Strategies and Competitive Edge*. New York: The Free Press.

21. Dahlgaard Su Mi Park (1999). The evolution patterns of quality management: some reflections on the quality movement. *Total Quality Management*, July, S473–81.

22. Senge, P., cited in Costin, H. (1994). *Readings in Total Quality Management*. Orlando, FL: Dryden Press.

23. Gurnani, H. (1999). Pitfalls in total quality management implementation; the case of Hong Kong. *Total Quality Management*, **10** (2), 209–28.

24. Tatikonda, L. U. and Tatikonda, R. J. (1996). Top ten reasons your TQM effort is failing to improve profit. *Production and Inventory Management Journal*, **37**, 5–9.

25. *The Economist* (1992). The cracks in quality. 18 April, pp. 67–8. Katz, A. (1993). Eight TQM pitfalls. *Journal for Quality and Participation*, **16** (4), July/August, 24–7.

26. *Training and Development* (1992). The downside of quality. March, p. 11.
27. *The Economist* (1992). Op. cit.
28. Gordon, G., Lee, C., Picard, M. and Stamps, D. (1996). The seven deadly sins of TQM. *Training*, **33**, 16–19.
29. Hubiak, W. A. and O'Donnell, S. J. (1996). Do Americans have their minds set against TQM? *National Productivity Review,* **IS** (3), 19–20.
30. Gordon, G., Lee, C., Picard, M. and Stamps, D. (1996). Op. cit.
31. Anonymous (1996). Industry report: trends. *Training*, **33**, 67–71.
32. Mitchell, V. W. (1992). Organisational homeostasis: a role for internal marketing. *Management Decisions*, **30**, 3–7.
33. Neave, H. R. (1990). *The Deming Dimension*. Knoxville, TN: SPC Press.
34. Grönroos, C. (1982). *Strategic Management & Marketing in the Service Sector*. Helsingfors, Finland: Swedish School of Economics and Business Administration. Gummesson, E. (1993). *Quality Management in Service Organisations*. New York: International Service Quality Association.
35. Jarillo, J. C. (1993). *Strategic Networks: Creating the Borderless Organisation*. Stoneham, MA: Butterworth-Heinemann.
36. Oakland, J. S. (1992). Op. cit.
37. Atkinson, P. E. (1990). *Creating Culture Change: The Key to Successful Total Quality Management*. Bedford: IFS Publications.
38. Schonberger, R. J. (1990). *Building a Chain of Customers*. London: Hutchinson.

chapter seven

Innovation and internal marketing

Introduction

New products are central to corporate growth and prosperity. An estimated 40 per cent of sales come from new products[1]. Providing value and winning customers has, over time, remained the major challenge. To do this, companies must quickly and accurately identify changing customer needs and wants, develop more complex products to satisfy those needs, provide higher levels of customer support and service, while also utilizing the power of information technology in providing greater functionality, performance and reliability. Improved innovation is one of the major strategic ways of making this happen.

Unfortunately, as Cooper et al.[2] note:

- one product concept out of seven becomes a commercial success, and only one project in four results in a winner;
- roughly half of the resources that industry devotes to product innovation is spent on failures and killed projects;
- 63 per cent of executives are 'somewhat' or 'very disappointed' in the results of their firms' new product development (NPD) efforts;
- new products face a 35 per cent failure rate at launch.

This highlights the need to take great care when attempting to implement a product development system within an organization. It is important to ensure that the NPD framework interfaces well with existing processes and that it is designed to meet the objectives for which it is being implemented. Also, as organizations evolve, it is imperative that their NPD framework also evolves in a manner that continues to support strategic repositioning and growth objectives.

Notwithstanding the problems, the potential for large benefits from innovation has led it to be increasingly perceived as one of the most important processes within organizations[3]. For many companies, success in innovation is through development of a superior NPD framework[4]. This reliance and focus on a strong innovation capacity is reinforced by research that shows a strong correlation between new product success and a company's health[5]. Indeed, NPD frameworks are increasingly seen as an important source of competitive advantage[6]. However, the development and implementation of an NPD framework is by no means simple, nor a guarantee for new product success. In fact, no one best way has been found to organize innovation[7], so it comes as no surprise that the causes of new product success and failure often can be traced back to the NPD framework.

Research studies[8] have found that:

- the technical knowledge, motivational abilities and skills of the project manager are correlated with NPD success and failure;
- project manager styles and authority patterns (degree of delegation, formality, etc.) affect product success and failure;
- proficiencies in executing the various stages of NPD processes (concept, development, prototyping, etc.) frequently affect outcomes;
- the amount and quality of the technical, marketing and management skill applied to the NPD process are also important;
- the degree of 'integration' between the commercial and technical entities is correlated with new product success and failure.

Further clarification around success factors in NPD was offered by Cooper[9] and is summarized below:

- a strong market orientation;
- an in-depth understanding of user needs and wants;
- a unique or superior product, i.e. a product with a high performance to cost ratio;
- a strong market launch, backed by significant resources devoted to the selling/promotion effort;
- an attractive market – a high demand and a large growing market;
- synergy in a number of areas, including technology and marketing;
- top management support;
- good internal and external communications.

In a more recent analysis, Griffin[10] identified successful firms from lower performers in their:

- execution of a commonly agreed to and disciplined NPD process;
- cultivation of a supportive organization and infrastructure for NPD;
- setting of a clear innovation agenda and management of the portfolio of projects in aggregate.

Proficiency in the performance of NPD activities increases the likelihood of new product success. Proficiency in development and marketing produces the largest increase in project success. By improving performance of key NPD activities under hostile environmental conditions, a company greatly increases the likelihood of success for a new launch.

Benefits of managing for improved innovation

Three major benefits are derived from improving the new product development process. These are outlined below.

Reduced product development costs

Over the course of a new product development project, costs generally increase at an accelerated rate as the product moves towards commercialization[11]. Due to accelerating costs over the NPD process, it is important to eliminate failures early before they lead to a major loss in investment[12].

It is estimated that, between the design and manufacturing stage, about 85 per cent of a product's costs can be determined at a point when only 10 per cent of the cost is expended[13]. This corresponds closely with the work by Pawar et al.[14], who found that 80 per cent of a product's cost is committed during the design phase, whereas design itself only absorbs 8 per cent of incurred costs. Managing this process properly means ensuring only those products that stand a reasonable chance of being commercially successful will receive funding. This capability was demonstrated by Colgate-Palmolive, who saw a drop in the number of products that reached the prototype stage from 50 to 20 per cent once an NPD framework had been adopted and implemented. Consequently, the levels of funding applied to programmes which are killed later is reduced, resulting in an improved return on the overall R&D available.

The likelihood of missing key steps, which may require expensive rework or have an impact on cycle time, can also be avoided by providing a roadmap defining tasks and deliverables. With improved clarity of purpose comes the ability to more effectively plan activities and allocate resources. This helps in identifying and allowing opportunities for concurrent activity, while also avoiding any potential functional bottlenecks. The introduction of significant functional improvements offering operational efficiencies (such as DFX techniques) also helps in this effort.

New product development frameworks also contribute to improved levels of planning and decision making by encouraging information to be gathered from all key functions and forcing an evaluation at key milestones within the project to focus the attention on the quality of execution.

The whole focus of the reduction in product development cost is to drive out any unnecessary cost of quality. This is achieved primarily through improved execution, achieved by providing greater stability to the organizational linkages or offering accurate information to guide planning and decision making. Additionally, improved product development productivity is achieved through shorter development cycles and reduced levels of waste. As a consequence, projects with a decreased development lead-time are less expensive (−33 per cent), while those products with higher development lead-time are more expensive to develop (+400 per cent)[15].

Time to market

Product development, if accelerated, can give rise to benefits such as establishing dominant designs, jumping ahead of the learning curve, realizing higher profit margins, incorporating new technical advances sooner, or influencing and setting industry standards[16].

The time employed in new product development is determined by the efficiency of the information process, the levels of uncertainty in development and the amount of effort needed to combine all information elements[17]. It is therefore not enough to automate the shop floor. For effective NPD, the entire design–manufacturing process must be addressed. A faster but inefficient organization is likely to produce a large volume of wastage with defective goods and poor service, resulting in a devastating effect on the bottom line of the organization[18].

Apart from the external advantages, companies adopting NPD frameworks can realize a number of internal benefits[19]:

- rapid generation of economies of learning with lower overhead and labour costs;
- more information sharing and problem solving across the organization;
- higher quality of goods and services;
- lower requirements of working capital;

■ less need for engineering and design changes due to environmental variations.

New product advantages

The ability to satisfy identified customer needs and wants, by definition, requires an organization to be capable of developing new products effectively and efficiently. Regardless of the types of new products introduced by a company, one thing is clear: the rewards for the development and successful launch of a new product can be significant. For example:

■ Seven hundred US organizations between 1976 and 1981 stated that 22 per cent of profits and 28 per cent sales growth came from new products.

■ Fifty-six per cent of all products that actually get launched are still on the market 5 years later. Other studies estimate the long-term success rate of new products at 65 per cent.

■ The companies that lead their industries in profitability and sales growth get 49 per cent of their revenues from products developed over the past 5 years. The least successful get only 11 per cent from new products.

■ According to a 1982 study by Booz, Allen & Hamilton, successful organizations are likely to derive one-third of their profits from new products[20].

Those firms that do not keep their NPD practices up to date suffer marked competitive disadvantage. To remain competitive, 'Best In Class' firms employ the basic attributes of an effective NPD framework, but continue to show evolutionary improvements on multiple fronts to retain their lead. Consequently, the following advantages can be gained:

■ improved productivity through upgrades and advancements in technology;

■ improved competitive positioning (allowing a thought leadership profile);

■ improved ability to penetrate new markets, set rules for existing markets and adjust segmentation criteria, thus adversely affecting competitive reaction;

■ improved defence against competitive attacks (shoring up defences through offering flexible configurations or a full product family, thus preventing weaker opponents building up a distribution capability);

- ensuring a highly skilled work force is retained and motivated to proceed;
- reducing business risks by having less dependence for revenue and margins on outdated components;
- stimulating an environment of creativity and innovation that allows companies to compete;
- reduced inventory required (and costs) due to the ability to apply new technology (replace rather than fix).

Evolution of innovation process management systems

Diverse approaches to managing innovation have been attempted over the years, beginning with rudimentary efforts to grapple with technology to sophisticated and encapsulating complex systems of management. Fortunately, these approaches can be categorized into fairly distinct evolutionary phases or generations of development. Rothwell[21] distinguishes five generations in the evolutionary development of innovation systems. These development phases are informative in that they help to define the likely trajectory for future progress in the management of innovation.

The first-generation innovation process (1950s to mid 1960s)

This first generation, or technology push, concept of innovation (Figure 7.1) assumed that 'more R&D in' resulted in 'more successful new products out'. With one or two notable exceptions, little attention was paid to the transformation process itself or the role of the marketplace in the process.

Figure 7.1 Technology push (first generation). *Source*: Rothwell, R. (1994). Towards the fifth-generation innovation process. *International Marketing Review*, 11 (1), 7–31.

The second-generation innovation process (mid 1960s to early 1970s)

Perceptions of the innovation process began to change as the business environment began to move toward emphasizing demand side factors, i.e. the marketplace. This resulted in the emergence of the second generation or 'market pull' (sometimes referred to as the 'need pull') model of innovation shown in Figure 7.2. This is a simple sequential model, in which the market is the source of ideas for directing R&D. R&D merely plays a reactive role in the process.

One of the primary dangers of following this model was that it could easily lead companies to neglect long-term R&D programmes and become locked in to a regime of technological incrementalism. Companies using this approach were being directed to adapt existing products to meet changing user requirements along maturing performance trajectories. By doing so, they ran the risk of being outstripped by radical innovators.

The third-generation innovation process (early 1970s to mid 1980s)

The technology push and need pull models of innovation are polar examples of a more general process. This led to the development of a third interactive or 'coupling' generation. The coupling model (Figure 7.3), according to Rothwell, can be regarded as:

> 'A logically sequential, though not necessarily continuous process, that can be divided into a series of functionally distinct but interacting and interdependent stages. The overall pattern of the innovation process can be thought of as a complex net of communication paths, both intra-organisational and extra-organisational, linking together the various in-house functions and linking the firm to the broader scientific and technological community and to the marketplace. In other words the process of innovation represents the confluence of technological capabilities and market-needs within the framework of the innovating firm.[22]

The third-generation innovation model was seen by most western companies, certainly up to the mid 1980s or so, as presenting best practice. It was still essentially a sequential process, but with feedback loops.

Rothwell[23] notes two sets of issues for success, namely project execution and corporate level factors:

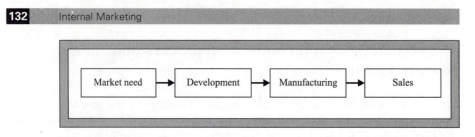

Figure 7.2 Market pull (second generation). *Source*: Rothwell, R. (1994). Towards the fifth-generation innovation process. *International Marketing Review*, 11 (1), 7–31.

Project execution factors

- good internal and external communication – accessing external know-how;
- treating innovation as a corporate-wide task – effective inter-functional co-ordination, good balance of functions;
- implementing careful planning and project control procedures – high equality up-front analysis;
- efficiency in development work and high quality production;
- strong marketing orientation – emphasis on satisfying user needs, development emphasis on creating user value;
- providing a good technical and spares service to customers – effective user education;
- effective product champions and technological gatekeepers;

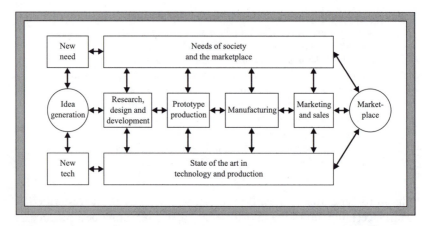

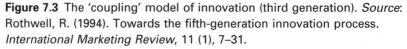

Figure 7.3 The 'coupling' model of innovation (third generation). *Source*: Rothwell, R. (1994). Towards the fifth-generation innovation process. *International Marketing Review*, 11 (1), 7–31.

■ high quality, open-minded management – commitment to the development of human capital;

■ attaining cross-project synergies and inter-project learning.

Corporate level factors

■ top management commitment and visible support for innovation;

■ long-term corporate strategy with associated technology strategy;

■ long-term commitment to major projects (patient money);

■ corporate flexibility and responsiveness to change;

■ top management acceptance of risk;

■ innovation-accepting, entrepreneurship-accommodating culture.

These factors show that success or failure can rarely be explained in terms of one or two factors only. Rather, explanations are usually multi-faceted. In other words, success is rarely associated with performing one or two tasks brilliantly, but with doing most tasks competently and in a balanced and well co-ordinated manner. At the very heart of the successful innovation process are 'key individuals' of high quality and ability, people with individual flair and a strong commitment to innovation.

Fourth-generation innovation process (early 1980s to early 1990s)

With shortening product life cycles, speed of development became an increasingly important weapon in competitive battles. It was during this period that Western companies began to notice the remarkable per-formance of Japanese innovators in world markets. It soon transpired that the Japanese innovators possessed system characteristics that enabled them to innovate more rapidly and efficiently than their Western counterparts. Two striking features of Japanese innovation (the basis of the fourth-generation innovation model) were *integration* and *parallel development*. The Japanese not only integrated suppliers into the new product development process at an early stage, but also were able to simultaneously integrate the activities of the different func-tional parties, working on the innovation (in parallel) rather than sequen-tially (in series). This came to be called the 'rugby' approach to new product development. An illustrative example of the fourth generation as practised in Nissan is given in Figure 7.4. Many leading Western companies are even today grappling to come to terms with the essential features of this fourth-generation process.

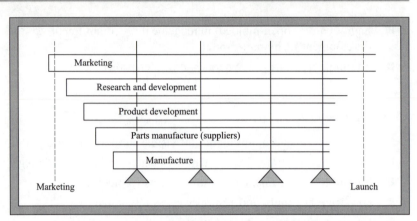

Figure 7.4 Example of the integrated (fourth-generation) innovation process. *Source*: Rothwell, R. (1994). Towards the fifth-generation innovation process. *International Marketing Review*, 11 (1), 7–31.

The fifth-generation innovation process

By the late 1990s, there was a strong trend toward the practice of speed to market. Organizationally faster development speed and greater efficiency mean creating tighter internal and external linkages and using a higher level of sophisticated electronic toolkits to facilitate the innovation process. Taken together, these changes of practice represent a shift towards the fifth-generation innovation process. The fifth generation involves enhanced systems integration and networking. It is essentially a development of the fourth-generation (parallel, integrated) process via higher utilization of technology to induce integrated and networked product development.

The characteristics of the fifth generation (5G), in terms both of underlying strategic elements and the primary enabling factors, are:

Underlying strategy elements

- time-based strategy (faster, more efficient product development);
- development focus on quality and other non-price factors;
- emphasis on corporate flexibility and responsiveness;
- customer focus at the forefront of strategy;
- strategic integration with primary suppliers;
- strategies for horizontal technological collaboration;
- electronic data processing strategies;
- policy of total quality control.

Primary enabling features

- greater overall organization and systems integration:

  - parallel and integrated (cross-functional) development process;
  - early supplier involvement in product development;
  - involvement of leading-edge users in product development;
  - establishing horizontal technological collaboration where appropriate;

- flatter, more flexible organizational structures for rapid and effective decision making:

  - greater empowerment of managers at lower levels;
  - empowered product champions/project leaders/teams;

- fully developed internal databases:

  - effective data sharing systems;
  - product development metrics, computer-based heuristics, expert systems;
  - electronically assisted product development using 3D-CAD systems and simulation modelling;
  - linked CAD/CAE systems to enhance product development flexibility and product manufacturability;

- effective external data link:

  - co-development with suppliers using linked CAD systems;
  - use of CAD at the customer interface;
  - effective data links with R&D collaborators.

The most radical feature of 5G is that it represents a more comprehensive process of electronification of innovation across the whole innovation system. The electronification process has a positive side-effect: it increases the potential for know-how accumulation and learning (Figure 7.5). Electronic product development tools allow efficient real-time handling of information across the whole system of innovation. In sum, 5G is a process of parallel information processing, which brings together the traditional informal face-to-face human interaction with electronic information processing and interaction. In general, electronic systems help to leverage knowledge.

Whatever the outcome, it seems probable that it is those companies that invest in mastering the 5G process today who will be the leading-edge innovators of tomorrow.

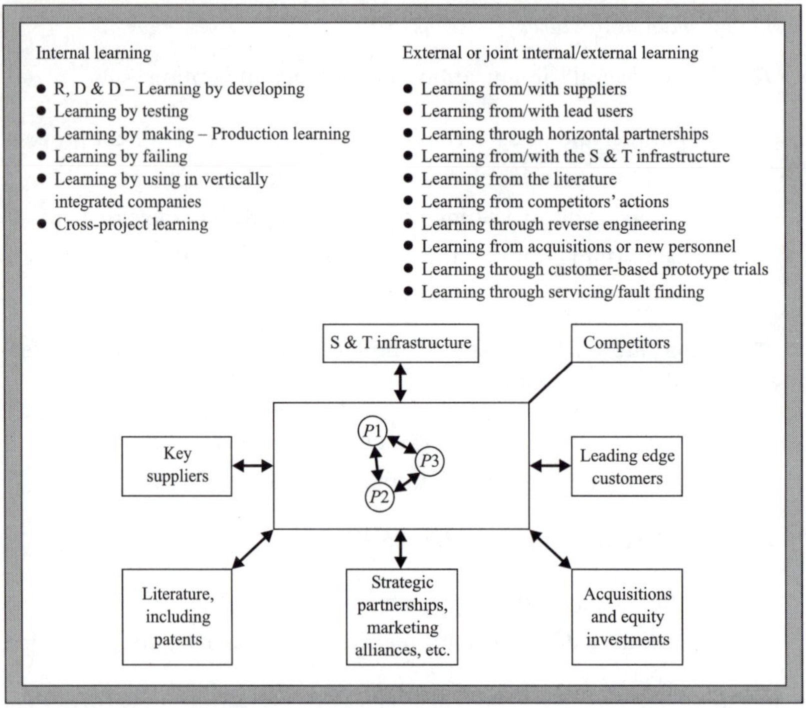
Internal learning
• R, D & D – Learning by developing
• Learning by testing
• Learning by making – Production learning
• Learning by failing
• Learning by using in vertically integrated companies
• Cross-project learning
External or joint internal/external learning
• Learning from/with suppliers
• Learning from/with lead users
• Learning through horizontal partnerships
• Learning from/with the S & T infrastructure
• Learning from the literature
• Learning from competitors' actions
• Learning through reverse engineering
• Learning from acquisitions or new personnel
• Learning through customer-based prototype trials
• Learning through servicing/fault finding
S & T infrastructure
Competitors
P1
P3
P2
Key suppliers
Leading edge customers
Literature, including patents
Strategic partnerships, marketing alliances, etc.
Acquisitions and equity investments

Figure 7.5 Innovation as a process of know-how accumulation. *Source*: Rothwell, R. (1992). Successful industrial innovation: critical factors for the 1990s. *R&D Management*, 22 (3), 221–38.

New product development – a generic framework

Having sketched the evolutionary trajectories, we present a detailed discussion of a generic model that constitutes the foundation of modern day practice.

A number of NPD frameworks have been developed to satisfy the needs of different organizations operating in different markets. Their goal is to bring products to market on time, to optimize business results by reducing cycle-times and costs, and to manage the programmes according to agreed business plans over the products' life cycle. The majority of these NPD frameworks possess a number of similar important characteristics, which when executed in a balanced and effective manner can significantly improve NPD performance. These characteristics generally include:

- Use of a '*Structured Development Process*', providing the 'rules of the game' and describing entry and exit criteria between key programme milestones, primary tasks, schedules and resource assignments.

- A team of senior executives, called a '*Review Board*', who provide oversight of the programmes by resolving cross-project issues, setting project priorities, resolving issues and make GO/KILL decisions.

- Use of '*Realization Teams*' (cross-functional execution teams), operating under a product 'champion' and reporting to the assigned senior management oversight board.

- '*Phase or Stage/Gate Reviews*' at major development milestones, when funding, resources and project schedules are approved or rejected by the Review Board.

The activities are generally organized into distinct phases that are carried out sequentially by the Realization Teams and separated by 'Stage/Gate' reviews held by the Review Board. This is illustrated below using a 'Best in Class' NPD Framework called 'PACE' (Product And Cycle-time Excellence) devised by the consultants PRTM[24] (see Figure 7.6).

Each component is discussed in more detail next.

Structured Product Development Process (SDP)

In many companies, the way products are developed is completely unstructured. There is no consistent terminology; each project team uniquely defines its activities, even though many are similar. This need for additional structure is demonstrated by an associated high cost of quality demonstrated by the following symptoms[25]:

- Inconsistent terminology and definitions, leading to garbled or confused hand-offs (up to 39 per cent has been estimated), causing wasted effort, misdirected work and demanding increased numbers of clarification meetings.

- Inability to estimate resource requirements and schedules, resulting in sub-optimal planning and execution in support of programmes considered vital to the company.

- Excessive task interdependence, resulting in complex and inefficient communication channels, and plans being made disjointedly between groups and a poor understanding of responsibilities. In some instances, 42 per cent of work has been repeated because of upstream changes, which have occurred due to late customer input, something being overlooked or errors in specifications.

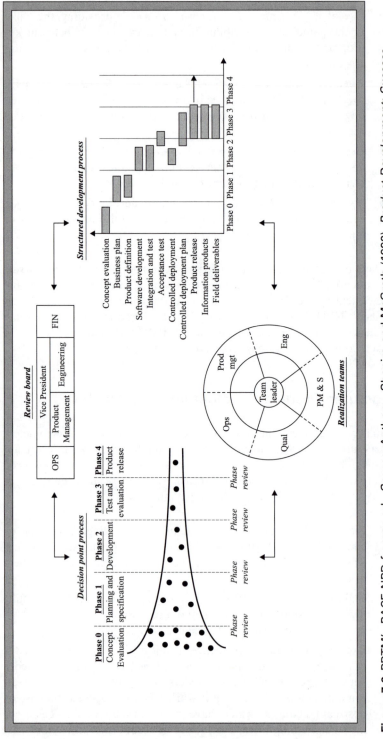

Figure 7.6 PRTM's PACE NPD framework. *Source:* Anthony, Shapiro and McGrath (1992). *Product Development: Success Through Product & Cycle-time Excellence (PACE).* London: Butterworth-Heinemann.

■ Attention focused on fire fighting. In some cases, at least 48 per cent of development work has been identified as fire fighting and caused by unplanned work, which appears unexpectedly but requires immediate attention.

Structured Development Processes (SDP) offers a framework consisting of terms that describe what needs to be done in development and allows them to be consistently applied across all projects. For this, the SDP must be used uniformly across the company and compliance must be mandatory. In this way, it forms part of the organizational culture. 'Best in Class' companies create guidelines around the SDP to ensure major tasks are performed across all projects and ensure mistakes, once identified, are not repeated. The clarity offered in these documents concerning key cross-functional linkages and responsibilities ensures an effective overlap of activities, improved hand-offs between functional groups, setting of realistic and more achievable schedules, and improved planning and control.

The major activities commonly seen to be executed within a typical NPD framework, after the original idea has been screened and accepted by management, are to:

■ develop and test the product concept;
■ formulate a marketing strategy;
■ analyse the impact on the business in terms of sales, cost and profit projections;
■ develop the concept into a product;
■ market test the product and time its design and market strategy;
■ build and launch the product.

The SDP offers the guidance to execute these activities in the company in an effective and co-ordinated fashion.

Realization Teams

The secret to successful product development teams lies in organizing them to achieve effective *communication, co-ordination* and *decision making*. Many different organization structures exist in support of different companies' business objectives. Predominantly, organizations employ hierarchical and bureaucratic structures to implement. Unfortunately, with extensive rules and procedures in place, many of the different departments operate almost independently of each other. With the increased importance placed in better developing new products, many companies attempt to impose their functional organization onto the

NPD framework, resulting in such models as the serial 'Relay Race', iterative 'Ping-Pong' and parallel 'Rugby' approaches – with varying degrees of success.

A number of studies have been conducted to identify the most effective team structure to support NPD activities, resulting in the identification of many different approaches to team composition and the associated authority which can be employed (see Figure 7.7).

Work by Corey and Starr[26], in their survey of 500 manufacturing firms, reported that core teams or autonomous (Realization) teams operating in a matrix organization were most successful amongst all other alternatives. Use of traditional functional teams produces the lowest success in controlling cost, meeting schedules, achieving technical performance and overall results[27]. The value in using empowered senior cross-functional teams to drive such programmes is one that is not lost on the majority of companies. Trygg[28] found '96 per cent of all groups who had halved product development times employed the use of cross-functional teams'. A further contributing factor to the success of these teams was the extent to which leadership is provided by a 'product champion'[29].

These teams are key enablers of the NPD framework. They facilitate a change in focus within the company away from functional and towards project-specific goals – something which is supported by the high level of

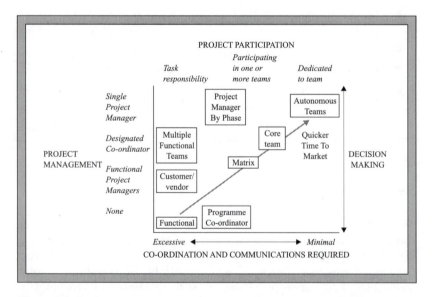

Figure 7.7 Project team construction: empowerment and effectiveness. *Source*: Anthony, Shapiro and McGrath (1992). *Product Development: Success Through Product & Cycle-time Excellence (PACE)*. London: Butterworth-Heinemann.

budget control they are assigned. Their accountability and responsibility for project-related goals fosters a greater sense of ownership and commitment, and the improved communications result in a highly effective and dedicated team.

The important message to take from this is that team approaches produce lower production and labour costs and more committed employees. Indeed, self-managed cross-functional teams are seen as the keystone to leaner and more flexible organizations capable of managing intensifying competitive pressures and the inexorable acceleration of technology. This is also seen as the logical means to generate more creative, less problem-riddled solutions, faster.

Review Boards

Senior management involvement is generally channelled through formally designated Review Boards. These bodies can also be referred to as Product Approval Committees (PAC), Resource Boards or New Product Executive Groups. This group is designated within the company to approve and prioritize new product development investments. Specifically, it has the authority and responsibility to:

- initiate new product development projects;
- cancel and re-prioritize projects;
- ensure that products being developed fit the company's strategy;
- allocate development resources.

Because this is a decision-making group, it should remain small, and typically include the 'Chief Executive Officer' (CEO), 'Chief Operating Officer' (COO) or General Manager, and the Heads of the Marketing, Engineering, Finance and Operations areas. In this capacity, each would be expected to dedicate around 10–15 per cent of their time on oversight-related activities. The specific roles expected to be performed by these members generally include:

- *Establish the vision*. Setting strategy by establishing a vision for their company's products. With this clear vision, the entire company can execute development activities to achieve it.
- *Make decisions*. Senior management needs to review the right information at the right time to make the right decisions.
- *Cultivate the product development process*. A superior process can be a source of competitive advantage. Supporting a common process smoothens the execution of product development activities.

- *Motivate.* Successful motivation and leadership in product development require that senior management has already achieved respect in the three previous roles.
- *Recruit the best development staff.* This is especially important when trying to secure individuals with specific technical skill or expertise.

It is important that the balance is achieved between the Review team's authority and the empowerment exercised by the Realization Teams. This is a view supported by Anthony and McKay[30], who state: 'the foundation for leadership in NPD is based on balancing product development and process control and its associated information needs between top management (responsible for the strategic direction and resource allocation) and the development teams (responsible for conceptualizing, designing, testing, manufacturing, launching and screening new products)'. The issue of project and resource management in NPD is an important one and can lead to the control of an NPD framework being unbalanced (being either insufficient), overbearing, inappropriate or based on incomplete information. Two dimensions in determining this balance are:

- locus of control between top management and cross-functional execution teams;
- degree to which the control is exercised.

The symptoms that can be expected from an unbalanced NPD framework, by applying these two dimensions, are shown in Figure 7.8.

Anthony and McKay found that improvements due to balancing the NPD framework can be dramatic – frequently a 50 per cent reduction in cycle-time can be achieved within the first year. Other benefits include better products, lower development costs, improved predictability and the ability to handle more development projects concurrently.

Phase review process

All companies have a decision-making process for new products, although some may not recognize it as an explicitly defined process. In this instance, decision making can become unreliable and consequently introduce significant delays to product development programmes. This can be overcome by applying a well-defined and effective phase review process.

The phase review process drives the other product development processes. It is the process whereby the Review Board:

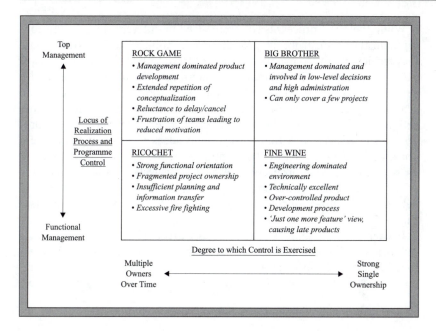

Figure 7.8 New product development balance (locus of control and degree to which it is exercised. *Source*: Anthony, M. T. and McKay, J. (1992). 'FROM EXPERIENCE: balancing the product development process: achieving Product and Cycle-time Excellence in high technology industries. *Journal of Product Innovation Management*, 9, 140–7.

- makes the difficult strategic-level product decisions;
- allocates resources to product development efforts;
- provides direction and leadership to the project teams; and
- empowers the Realization Teams to develop the programme on a phase-by-phase basis.

These decisions are made through approval at the conclusion of specific phases in the development effort, and are generally guided by a list of deliverables and milestones that are expected to be completed in support of a GO/NO-GO decision.

The phase review process is intended to cover all significant product development efforts, including all major new product development opportunities. In addition, projects that have a significant impact on multiple functional areas, such as manufacturing, support, sales and marketing, should be included in this process. Very small projects such as minor enhancements are usually managed by a simpler process or grouped and managed as a package.

While the NPD process is conceptualized in different ways, many conceptualizations incorporate project review points. Review Boards use these review points to examine projected technical, marketing and financial performance of programmes to determine whether to proceed with developing the new product or to terminate it prior to commercialization. The stage/gate model shown in Figure 7.9 has five stages, although more or less may be employed by different companies. The phase review process can be viewed as a funnel with many ideas entering at the concept phase and, through a series of screenings over the course of development, narrowed to a few appropriately resourced projects with high likelihood of market success. At the conclusion of each phase, a review is held to determine the direction of the project: proceed, cancel or redirect (see Figure 7.9).

In each phase, a number of activities are executed concurrently across a number of different functions. At specific points, these are brought together in the form of specific phase review deliverables that are presented to the Review Board. On the basis of the information provided,

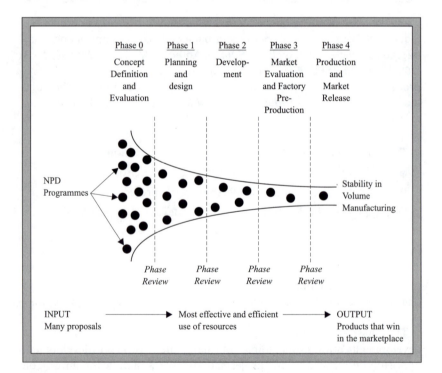

Figure 7.9 Funnel approach of new product development frameworks. *Source*: Anthony, Shapiro and McGrath (1992). *Product Development: Success Through Product & Cycle-time Excellence (PACE).* London: Butterworth-Heinemann.

the innovation programme will be permitted to proceed to the next phase (with commitments in funding and resources given), given instructions to refocus, or cancelled. This review activity ensures that funded programmes are consistent with the company's strategic and financial goals, and are supported and resourced in a manner that increases the likelihood of success.

Clearly, at the front of this funnel, very little may be known about a concept or the target market to which it is to be applied. As a result, the information to support the opportunity is somewhat rough and incomplete. However, over time and as the programme moves through the funnel, the levels of completeness and accuracy of the supporting information improve. As a result, the Review Board will be able to approve increasing levels of resource to support an opportunity as the quality of information improves over time (see Figure 7.10).

This ability to review programmes and commit resources based on increasing understanding of the opportunity offers an important risk abatement mechanism by allowing undesirable programmes to be cancelled prior to the development phase, when most resources are expended. This is supported by the finding that 80 per cent of a product's cost is committed during the design phase, whereas design only absorbs 8 per cent of incurred costs[31].

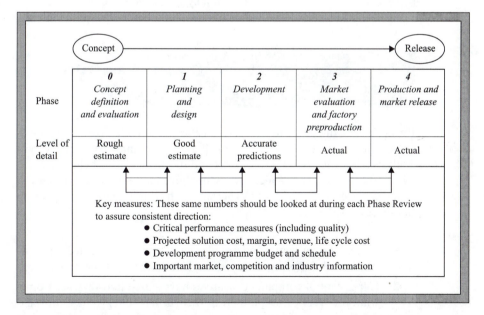

Figure 7.10 Risk abatement in NPD decision points. *Source*: Pittiglio, Raban, Todd and McGrath (1992). *Product and Cycle-time Excellence (PACE) – Revision C*, NCR SSSD, February.

Clearly, the contribution NPD frameworks can make to a company is determined by the effectiveness of its decision-making process to identify what opportunities to pursue. This also requires some insight into the interdependencies between programmes and the associated resource allocations. As a result, the definition and application of an effective phase review process should exhibit the following major characteristics:

- provide a clear and consistent process for making major decisions on new products and enhancements;
- empower project teams to execute a project plan;
- provide the link for applying product strategy to product development;
- provide measurable checkpoints to monitor progress;
- establish milestones that emphasize a sense of urgency.

In fact, current practices indicate that the highest attrition of programmes in the funnel takes place at concept screening, with the second largest number of cancellations taking place in the next, business planning, phase. Consequently, programmes are eliminated much earlier in the NPD process than in the past, resulting in less time and money being spent on a particular idea[32]. Modern day corporate portfolios of NPD projects are therefore wasting less money on unsuccessful products[33].

Weaknesses in the innovation management methods

Regardless of the gains to be achieved through an effective NPD framework, there still appears to be much room for improvement. Recent analysis of various NPD frameworks and the programmes being executed within them indicated weaknesses which give cause for concern, and in some cases result in the NPD programmes having a negative impact on the success of the organization[34]:

- around 24 per cent of companies who have implemented an NPD framework have reported worse 'Time to Market' performance;
- 63 per cent of company executives have stated that they are 'somewhat' or 'very' disappointed in their firms' new product efforts;
- additionally, it has been identified that 46 per cent of resources invested in new product programmes are wasted on technical and commercial failures.

Consequently, it is not surprising that this less than startling rate of success has resulted in many studies aimed at identifying associated problems and inefficiencies. In support of this, some studies have shown new product success not to have improved over the last 30 years[35].

According to work performed by Cooper and Kleinschmidt[36], potential problems may arise with the implementation of a new product development process. More bureaucracy and tighter controls can thwart creativity, and slower decision making is a deadly plague for the introduction of any formal process. Indeed, many of the problems identified appear to be caused by implementation-related issues rather than any fundamental failing of the NPD framework.

New developments in managing the innovation process

The discussion thus far has presented a structured innovation process system that currently represents the state-of-the-art process. However, new developments are taking place that are taking the innovation process on towards a more advanced stage. One of the most interesting developments is the iterative model of Hughes and Chafin[37]. Hughes and Chafin propose a value creation model, which they call the Value Proposition Process (VPP). Such developmental models show great potential to become the new generation approaches to innovation management.

The Hughes and Chafin model of new product development

One means of making this transformation is the Value Proposition Process (VPP). The objectives of this development approach are continuous learning, identifying the certainty of knowledge used for decision making, building consensus and focusing on adding value.

Value Proposition Process

The VPP was designed to improve the efficiency and effectiveness of multifunctional project teams through continuous learning, identifying the certainty of knowledge, building consensus, and focusing on adding value to customers and end-users. To fully leverage this process, the organization in which the team operates must have a culture that supports improvement and innovation, is flexible and encourages change.

The objective of the VPP is to determine if the organization can convert an idea or an opportunity into a proposition that adds value to the end-users, the company and the value chain. In short, the team must answer a basic question: can we do it right? The VPP consists of a framework of continuous planning cycle, called the Value Proposition Cycle (VPC), and an integrated screening methodology, called the Value Proposition Readiness Assessment (VPRA).

Overview of the Value Proposition Cycle

The VPC comprises four iterative loops, addressing the following activities: capturing the market value of the proposition (does the customer care?); developing the business value (do we care?); delivering a winning solution (can we beat the competition?); and applying project and process planning (can we do it?).

Only a few companies have focused on modelling the relationships between value measures. For example, how is customer satisfaction related to economic value added? How is employee motivation linked to added shareholder value? These questions need to be part of a company's plan for understanding how it adds value. Critical questions to be answered at each loop are as follows:

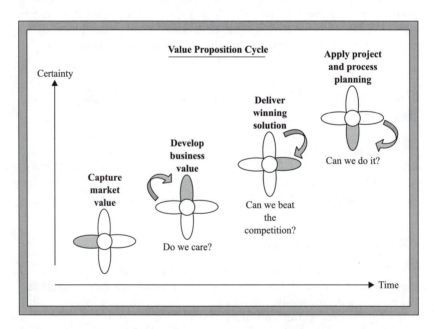

Figure 7.11 Value Proposition Cycle. *Source*: Hughes, G. D. and Chafin, D. C. (1996). Turning new product development into a continuous learning process. *Journal of Product Innovation Management*, 13, 89–104.

- Capture market value – does the customer care?
- Develop business value – do we care?
- Deliver winning solutions – can we beat the competition?
- Apply project/process planning – can we do it?

The VPC also provides a logical framework for the VPRA methodology. This methodology is based on a series of screens along each loop in the VPC, as shown in Figure 7.12. These screens summarize the success factors for the company. The number of success factors will vary according to the product newness, the amount of risk and the number of product ideas to be screened. New and risky products with a high cost of failure will require more items in the screen. A large line extension can use a reduced set. For a large number of product ideas, a reduced set of items is appropriate for the first screening and then a larger list for the final screening.

The VPP, as a multifunctional teaming methodology to screen ideas, is part of a more encompassing life cycle process. The VPP described

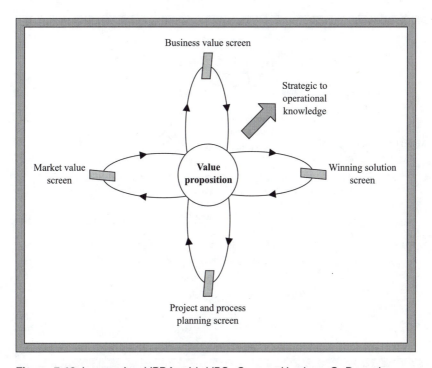

Figure 7.12 Integrating VPRA with VPC. *Source*: Hughes, G. D. and Chafin, D. C. (1996). Turning new product development into a continuous learning process. *Journal of Product Innovation Management*, 13, 89–104.

focuses on answering the question: can we do it right? However, there is an even more basic question that should be answered first: is it the right thing to do? After the VPP, there is another question: can we do it right the first time? And once the product or service begins to be commercialized, there is an ongoing evaluation question: did we do it right? This question must be answered from the point of view of the four stakeholders: the customer, the employee, the suppliers and the stockholders. A four-loop iterative process can be used to answer each of these questions, forming the portfolio life cycle.

Value Sensing Cycle

The portfolio life cycle process can begin at any point in the life cycle if a product already exists. A really new product would begin at the idea generation stage, known as the Value Sensing Cycle (VSC), which appears in the left in Figure 7.13. This cycle continuously scans the market, the business environment, competition and technology to iden-

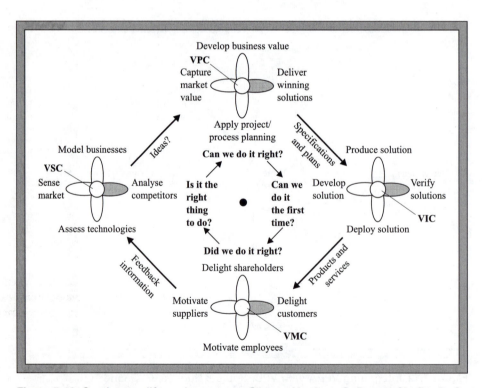

Figure 7.13 Continuous life cycle process. *Source*: Hughes, G. D. and Chafin, D. C. (1996). Turning new product development into a continuous learning process. *Journal of Product Innovation Management*, 13, 89–104.

tify new ideas or opportunities. These ideas are screened and reduced to a manageable few, which are then passed along to the VPC.

Value Introducing Cycle

Once the team and the organization have used the VPC and agreed that they can do it right, the proposition is translated into the final specifications and plans, and fed into the Value Introduction Cycle (VIC). This cycle consists of the fully characterized and highly disciplined process to develop, produce, verify and deploy the solution initially to all target market segments and, over time, any additional market segments. The output of this cycle is products and services, and the required support infrastructure that provides the input for the Value Management Cycle (VMC).

Value Management Cycle

The VMC, at the bottom of Figure 7.13, continuously screens market and business performance to answer the question: did we do it right? The monitoring is from the point of view of our customers, our employees, our suppliers and our stockholders. Critical questions must be answered at each of the four loops in the VMC. Do our customers perceive that they are paying a fair price for the benefit received? Do the project team members feel motivated by what they accomplished? Do we have strong supplier partnerships that will assure our receiving a favoured customer treatment from them? Are we profitable and adding shareholder value? Metrics from each of these four loops are an important part of the CEO's dashboard. Critical feedback from the VMC is linked and fed into the VSC to complete the life cycle.

Macro-models of innovation in organizations

So far, we have looked essentially at micro-level structuring of innovation. Moving to a look at innovation from a higher level of abstraction it is possible to discern the key features of importance. Tang[38] captures this overview in suggesting that there are four basic problems. These are:

- a human problem of managing attention to the need to innovate;
- a process problem in managing new ideas into good currency;
- a structural problem of managing part–whole relationships;
- a strategic problem of institutional leadership.

From this, six constructs of innovation are identified:

- information and communication;
- behaviour and integration;
- knowledge and skills;
- project raising and doing;
- guidance and support;
- external environment.

Table 7.1 shows the linkage of these constructs to the key concepts. From the six constructs, the associated key concepts and their interactions, a picture of innovation emerges. This is captured in the integrative model of innovation in organizations shown in Figure 7.14.

Accordingly, an organization is encompassed by its external environment. The organization interacts with its external environment through exchanges of information, ideas, goods and services, which include the organization's innovation outputs. At the centre of innovation is the core process of project raising and doing. The results of project raising and doing are new products, processes and services. There are two enablers

Table 7.1 *Constructs and Concepts for the Model of Innovation in Organizations*

Construct: information and communication
  Concepts: flow of information and technology, use of information technology, information as source of knowledge and stimulus for innovation.

Construct: behaviour and integration
  Concepts: behaviour traits, creative behaviours, motivation to innovate, team roles, cross-functional integration.

Construct: knowledge and skills
  Concepts: creativity, intelligence, insights, bisociation, domain-related knowledge and skills, tacit and explicit knowledge, knowledge creation, learning and training.

Construct: project raising and doing
  Concepts: opportunity and problem finding, problem solving, product and process development stages, uncertainty reduction.

Construct: guidance and support
  Concepts: organization's mission, task, structure, strategy, resources, operation systems. Shared values, leadership style.

Construct: external environment
  Concepts: economic rules and innovation, national innovation system, industry structure, culture.

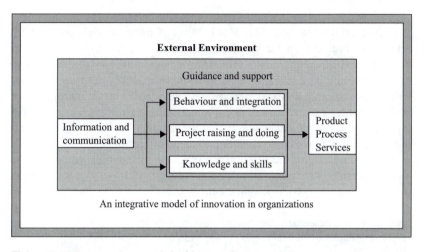

Figure 7.14 Integrative model of innovation.

for this core process. The first is knowledge and skills, and the second is behaviour and integration of individuals, teams and functions. The enablers and the core process influence each other. Positive outcome and progress in the project foster teamwork, whereas a long period of negative results will have the opposite effect. Knowledge is created through doing a project and knowledge so created will reinforce future projects. Information from the external environment, as well as from within the organization, provides inputs and stimulates project raising and doing through the staff of the organization. Availability of information, knowledge and skills, together with creative behaviour and the integration of people in the organization, determine the ability and inclination of staff to raise projects and find innovative solutions. How innovative an organization is depends on the guidance and support, which are defined in terms of the mission, tasks, strategy, systems and resources of the organization. Ultimately, top management underpins the entire innovation process by providing the proper guidance and support in response to the external environment.

Thus far, we have examined thoughts on how innovation management processes have evolved into their current state of being. This is instructive in that it highlights a trajectory of continuous improvement in the approaches and also because it emphasizes the need to build upon the current legacy of systems in place. The effectiveness of the approaches/ frameworks is very much contingent upon the specific context a company faces. This means that generic and unquestioned adaptations of frameworks and associated tools are likely to result in failure. Success requires careful understanding of the specific constraints and opportunities, both internal and external to the organization, and a selection and adaptation of an innovation framework that best capitalizes on this context.

In highlighting Hughes and Chafin's model, we present a possible trajectory of development. The Hughes and Chafin model presents an attempt to improve on the currently popular stage/gate system, which is atypical of the 5G innovation systems. The model highlights the need to capture iterative and learning features more thoroughly than earlier innovation processes. It is also driven by a stronger focus on delivering value, and using this as a yardstick of decision making. In contrast, Tang's model highlights the generic challenges facing management of innovation. Taken individually, the models represent moderate improvement on current understanding of the innovation process. Taken together, however, the models are highly representative of the evolutionary trajectory for the next generation of innovation management processes.

Problems in innovation

The major problems to surface in managing innovation are outlined as follows.

Inadequate resources

Shortage of resources (time, money, people) occurs because often:

- Too much attention is given to current activities, leading to insufficient efforts for long-term and radical activities. The present versus future conflict is a central source of contradiction on resources.

- Resources are too thinly spread out. There is a tendency to consider too broad a range of development directions with limited resources. It is better to focus on fewer directions for better results.

- Excessive projects. This occurs when there are too many programmes in the innovation product development portfolio. Consequently, people work on too many projects, leading to a tendency to pull expert individuals off one project to fix another one. This can cause serious disruptions in project progress.

Not knowing the customer

Customer orientation is particularly important in successful innovation. It is surprising that many employees, not only scientists and engineers but even marketers, do not understand their customers. The problem is not just a lack of market research making the organization unsure of customer needs, but largely a result of the company's inability to effectively transmit the 'voice of the customer' internally. This requires the company to devise ways of correctly exposing employees to customers' needs.

Unsupportive top management

Lack of commitment from top management strongly dampens innovation. Leadership that leans toward excessive retrospection and possesses attitudes that reinforce 'we have always done it this way' deadens radical innovation. Management by signalling and reinforcing the norms of behaviour either encourages or stifles innovation. Innovation begins and ends at the top.

One way to try to combat negative tendencies and turn them into positive ones is to introduce initiatives for creativity. Encouraging open communication and providing creativity training are good techniques for doing just this. However, at times it may be necessary to mandate sharing activities across functional disciplines, for instance through events such as get-together lunches, etc.

Poor decision policies

Poor decision making hinders innovation. This can arise from several sources:

- *Lack of explicit criteria*, which makes justification difficult.
- *Too many good ideas*, which makes setting priorities difficult.
- *Biases of senior management*, especially if toward a single dominant functional area such as marketing or engineering, can actually be very troublesome for well-rounded decisions to be reached.
- *Delayed decision making* usually builds frustration. Good companies make quick decisions and provide rapid feedback. Decisions that take longer than 2 months often deflate the energy to get things done. The net result – frustration in the recipients.

Lack of co-operative behaviour in the project management process

Problems in project management cover areas such as competitive behaviours within the innovation portfolio. These lead to individual teams in the portfolio fiercely battling for resources. One or two individual teams may end up winning out, but the organization as a whole loses.

Additionally, poorly developed and poorly understood organizational goals produce focus on narrow individual team gains. This leads to a lack of synergistic actions and behaviours.

Poor management planning and direction

Vagueness resulting from poor planning leads to frequent changes in priorities. This compounds the problems that already may exist from the chopping and changing of personnel from one project to the next. Consequently, scarce resources are wasted by running in many and often wrong directions.

Internal marketing's role in managing the company for innovation

The role of IM in innovation is multi-faceted, and in this section we will focus discussion on the following areas that directly or indirectly affect a company's success or failure in innovation:

- organizational culture
- structures, process and context
- employee communications
- people
- core competency
- integration.

Internal marketing plays a role in these because it can reinforce and emphasize aspects that help innovation to take root.

Organizational culture and leadership

Organizational culture embodies a set of deep-seated beliefs and basic assumptions that are shared by members of an organization. Culture works mainly at the unconscious level. It is the lens through which employees and the organization view themselves and their environment. Organizational culture is a representation of the artefacts, actions and norms of the organization. It captures the 'way of the organization': how its people dress; how they greet one another; how they interact; how they make decisions; what is important to them; what is not and so on.

Organizational culture encompasses symbols, cues and actions, both physical and intangible. Thus, it is possible for astute leadership to emphasize some values and de-emphasize others. This opens up the possibility of moulding cultures that are more conducive to innovation. Whilst the possibility exists, it is nevertheless difficult.

Through its focus on 'employees', IM helps the process of identifying current behaviours and probes why they are occurring. Once specific employee behaviour patterns have been established, it is then possible to create specific IM programmes to induce behaviours for enhanced innovation.

Internal marketing indicates to leadership what kind of messages and cues they need to amplify and communicate to get innovation embedded throughout the organization. Internal marketing is a tool that can be used to build in-depth understanding of the workplace environment. Through this understanding, it is possible to identify different employee segment needs. Internal marketing provides managers with insight and tools to customize internal strategies to enhance and improve programme implementation. Internal segmentation is made on the basis of employee behaviours and needs. Clearly, encouragement and direction take on greater meaning if they are focused and more appropriate, rather than one pill for all symptoms. Internal marketing identifies the type of things leadership personally need to promote. For example, if a CEO attends all major meetings, personally gives out awards and tells stories about major sales successes, but does not visit the shop-floor at all, then it suggests a top-down emphasis that places low value on its workers, despite the masquerade of personal involvement. Internal marketing can engage in 360-degree assessments of leadership involvement and objectively assess the weaknesses or contradictions that leadership/managerial actions and behaviours are causing. In this way, IM helps identify gaps in the leadership's armoury. Internal marketing does this by its internal research antennae, which allow it to listen to the pulse of the internal organization.

Internal marketing identifies and compiles stories that exist within the organization of innovation successes and role model individuals. After compiling the critical stories that stress the desired attributes of behaviour for innovation, IM can then package the stories in an appropriate format so that they can be retold throughout the organization. In so doing, IM penetrates the unconscious mind and moves it toward sought-after innovative behaviours. For example, companies like 3M and Hewlett-Packard abound with stories of innovators and innovations. Such stories become part of the organizational folklore, and inventive individuals become heroes and legends. The stories typically make a clear point about a company's culture and are often told to almost every newcomer to the company. This socialization helps to pass on the culture and acts as a powerful guide to actions. Another important feature of culture is that it transcends functional boundaries and its impact. It may look rather nebulous but it is organization-wide and endures over long periods of time.

To the extent that IM can strengthen or change cultural elements that favour innovation, then it can move the company toward innovation.

Structures, processes and context

Internal marketing can be used to examine hierarchies, processes, sub-processes and interfaces, and to assess whether innovation activities are hindered or given priority. For example, it is difficult for a company to successfully pursue ideas to successful commercial outcome if its culture requires multiple levels of approval for all expenditures, and favours strict observance of all rules and procedures. Innovative companies like Hewlett-Packard allow workers up to 15–25 per cent of their work time to pursue innovative projects on their own. This one practice speaks volumes about Hewlett-Packard's cultural attitude to innovation. It signals the importance that the company places, which is stronger than any programmes of 'forced' action.

Internal marketing is an approach and a force for empowerment, which attempts to unleash the inventive energy of each and every employee. The culture of a company, coupled with structure, act as primary facilitative agents in this task. Clearly, structures, processes and culture have a far-reaching impact on innovation success. For example, employees may have many excellent innovative ideas, but if the firm's structures and processes discourage or prohibit such ideas from reaching those with the power to evaluate and implement them, then ideas rarely bear fruit.

Internal marketing examines what needs to be done, and by whom. Internal marketing can be used to identify the type of role that innovation agents need to play to execute innovation strategies. These roles can vary from plant (who creates the infectious enthusiasm for a new idea) or sponsor (encouraging ideas from below and nurturing their development) to commander (giving orders and expecting obedience). Each is appropriate under different organizational circumstances and situations. Which role is appropriate for whom is dependent upon the individual's orientation towards the desired goal at that specific moment in time. This links strategic implementation to the specific skills and capabilities of the individual. By implication, this necessitates first knowing the skills and capabilities of each employee before they can be usefully deployed. Some individuals are naturally good at sponsorship, because of their ability to network at many different levels within the organizational hierarchy. Others may be more gifted in development and idea generation. Internal marketing helps in the assessment of these skills for specific innovation projects. This assessment is made more visible because IM looks at a deployment of individual competence from an opportunity cost point of view, which is taken from the organizational viewpoint as well as from the employee's perspective. Moreover, IM is important because it links specific individuals to the strategic context by assessing the strategic sense of specific competence deployment. For instance, while it is usually advocated that the role of sponsor is more appropriate than that of commander in fostering a culture of innovation, this may not necessarily be so. Situations may arise at times of acute crisis when the leader has to push forcefully a particular course of action to ensure survival or break a bottleneck that is unwilling to yield to participative management and sponsorship. Internal marketing assesses the internal context and then assesses the appropriateness of strategic actions and the likely side-effects that may arise. Internal marketing also prepares appropriate internal PR to lessen and ameliorate negative consequences of a specific course of action.

Internal marketing builds an understanding of the organization environment, organizational hierarchy, organization politics and structures. Through this understanding, IM plays an important role in the nurturing of the right environment for innovation. Internal marketing helps reflect on concrete practical experiences. People's behaviour (both managers and employees) has to be evaluated in terms of agreements, guidelines and envisaged objectives, and expectations by others.

Internal marketing helps companies to approach innovation as an 'open' system, whereby innovation participants are given control over initiatives and employees are entrusted to organize themselves efficiently[39]. In environments of trust, employees are more prepared to do what is necessary, even where it entails breaking existing conventions, rules and routines. The simple maxim used by the US store Nordstrom, 'use your good judgement in all situations'[40], is simple yet a very powerful reminder of the impact that trust can have in energizing the organization toward motivated action.

Employee communication, personalization and space for improvisation

Communication is an indispensable activity in the functioning of all processes, but it is critical in highly cross-functional ones such as innovation. Based on communication, problematic situations can be analysed and interpreted, and solutions can be sought and developed. It is, of course, imperative that the relevant stakeholders are involved in the communication process.

As companies have evolved, so have the lives of employees. In the past, tangible internal products (such as pay and benefits) were the main motivational drivers for improved productivity. Increasingly, though, the benefits (meanings) that internal products convey have come to be very significant[41]. Just as external marketers came to appreciate the maxim 'positioning is not something you do to a product, it is what you do to the minds of your consumers'[42], internal marketers have to understand that positioning is not something you do to the internal product, it is what you do to the minds of the employees. Once the hearts of employees are won, invariably the minds will follow[43]. Vital in this process is the connection firms make with their employees. The connection or relationship creates an emotional state in which employees respond through feelings, rather than through cold facts. Ensuring an appropriate fit between form and feelings is critical.

Internal marketing, by creating messages and appealing to the emotions, can provide firms with a rich source of advantage. Moreover, since employee behaviour is socially constructed, idiosyncratic and largely holistic, it calls for a richer analysis of the employee experience. This requires an immersion in the 'consumption' experience of the employees. Companies that just measure aggregate trends and statistics achieve little in the way of insight on how to really motivate their employees. Aggregate employee satisfaction figures are typically lagging measures; often they are out of date pictures of yesteryear's sentiment. At worse, the aggregations hide the realities of employee dissention and demotivation. It is important to note that IM itself needs to resort to ethnographic probes of the organizational milieu, otherwise it will end up constructing superficial messages based on superficial insight, resulting in little real impact. This suggests the need for differentiated messages for different employee segments. Internal marketing mandates more than strait-jacket appeals for efficiency. Internal marketing forces companies to be more empathic in the design of their communications to employees. If companies do not appreciate the existence of different employee segments and their different needs, they will continue to produce messages that hold little meaning for the targeted segments. Broad and diffuse messages create distance between the employee and the organization, and in worst scenarios confusion in action. In other words, IM personalizes!

Internal marketing can be used to communicate broad goals, but also articulate specific plans and actions for development.

Exhibit 7.1. McVitie's: involving employees to get a strategy and values buy-in

McVitie's marketing director Will Carter believes it is important to get all staff involved and ensure that all staff are on board, even those with little customer contact. This means carefully designing an internal marketing programme for all

(continued)

staff, not just those who are customer facing. Ignoring non-contact employees creates divisions and conflict. This demands an exhaustive and at times exhausting programme of communications by senior management. Carter has thought of a number of ways to create involvement and across-the-board organizational buy-in.

One approach was to take staff from the shop floor to see the company's products in retail settings. The brief of these visits was simple: look at the company's brands and come back and discuss what they saw, what opportunities and threats they perceived for *their* business. According to Carter '[things like this] are hugely rewarding in getting people to look at our brands and our marketplace outside their normal place of work.'

These initiatives were driven by an increasing recognition that in a company like McVitie's there was a strong need to generate a common understanding of what are the goals and what is the strategy throughout the business. That means communicating consistently throughout the business across functions and down into the organization. It is important to remember not to compartmentalize the messages. This demands a pretty extensive and intricate strategy communication programme within the organization.

After developing strategy, the most critical step is to communicate it through the organization. Carter's approach was one that involved setting up a programme of relatively small meetings with groups of managers, shop-floor manufacturing staff and sales staff. The goal was to ensure that the business was aligned in terms of the brand priorities and values that were important to the company, and the cultural and performance values and measures that the company was aiming to adopt. In this way, it became possible for the company to harness the energy and work of each employee, such that it made strategy come to life.

In this process, McVitie's complemented the use of traditional internal communications media with a lot of time in face-to-face meetings and briefings with all its employees.

Source: Mazur, L. (1999). Unleashing employees' true value: employees can be your company's most valuable marketing asset. *Marketing*, April, 22–4.

Traditional approaches to innovation proceed through careful reviews of the environment, data gathering and execution of an innovation project plan. However, such conventional planning models have reached their limits in dealing with high levels of turbulence in the business environment. This necessitates 'improvisation'[44] within the structured innovation process. Improvisation introduces the notion that the composition of and execution of plans occur simultaneously[45]. Given that NPD markets are increasingly experiencing environmental turbulence, it is expected that the criticality of communication and space for improvisation will grow significantly into the future. While structured planning has its merits, it tends to bear down upon the organization a machine-like rationality. Acting like this serves only to drive underground the realities and complexities of organizational practice, such as those embedded within the power and politics processes, and the fact that actions and planning are interactive acts, and need to be so in highly dynamic environments. Efficient improvisation calls for high levels of trust, teamwork and integration between business functions. Internal marketing plays a role, allowing improvisation to take place within the innovation process. Improvisation enables firms to be responsive in fast changing markets. By communicating the overall direction and behavioural norms, IM allows relaxation of rules and procedures, which can be an important stimulus to promote radical innovation and experimentation. Formal procedures are suggested to stifle innovation and creativity, and often are inappropriate as vehicles to bring about radical growth. Tightly structured approaches to product development are more appropriate primarily when the companies are solely aiming to compete in those environments that represent incremental growth opportunities[46].

Internal marketing allows team members to engender a sense of shared destiny for new products, the development of mutual trust and respect for alternative points of view. It is a medium to convey details of technical performance levels of products, and information about the product development process and its related systems. It does this by building high levels of teamwork and mutual trust among team members. In effect, the introduction of IM provides an 'enabling' environment for innovation.

People: the creative engine of innovation

A vital ingredient, which adds value to innovation projects, is that of motivated employees. Increasingly, following Maslow's hierarchy, as individuals' basic needs are met, there is a corresponding 'need' to strive towards higher and more self-actualizing aspects of the work experience[47]. Too often, work within modern corporations parches the human spirit[48]. Canfield and Miller suggest that there was a time when it was possible to equate being 'hard at work' with 'heart at work'. The farmer loved his land and animals, and the seamstress took great pride in her handiwork[49]. Unfortunately, in the modern corporation, more and more work has been placed on the shoulders of fewer workers in drives for efficiency. Historically, such events were driven by scientific management, but in recent years, similar repercussions have occurred through the effects of a shortsighted application of BPR and organizational de-layering. These moves have made the organizational environments barren and sterile places of work. Applied in their extremes, these philosophies have robotized the workplace and stripped employees of their dignity as thinking beings.

To get innovation and creativity, companies must re-engage the hearts and minds of employees. Without this, a great deal of creative potential in organizations will continue to lie untapped. One reason for the failure to cultivate motivation is the failing of companies to sufficiently link into the needs of their employees. If they want a workforce that is both creative and committed, they must think about and set about nurturing the types of relationships that make business work through an under-standing of employee needs. Thus far, if companies have focused on building relationships with employees at all, then they have done so at a superficial level, often deploying crude rational inducements. Needs of employees are both rational and emotional.

Internal marketing scrutinizes the rational and emotional content to build pictures of the reality of the corporate environment. Only in this way is it able to create 'packages' to fully meet the needs of employees. Internal marketing is a philosophy based on the understanding that it is through the application of subjective emotions and empathic awareness that employees are able to make judgements that end up in the realiza-tion of the long-term corporate interests. Recently, the term 'emotional intelligence' has been coined to address the many issues in this area[50]. Emotional intelligence refers to the process of knowing and under-standing feelings, and being able to marshal those feelings to the best effect for the individual and organization, coupled with the ability to empathize with others, leading to successful relationships[51]. Given its link with motivation of employees, the need for screening measures in this area is considerable. Internal marketing is an important tool for this. Internal marketing tries to understand employees by adopting a stance that scrutinizes skills and competencies from a vantage that goes beyond hard quantitative paper-based qualifications. Internal marketing forces a rounded understanding of the organizational readiness for a particular new initiative by examining the full set of needs of the organization (demand of organization upon the employees) in direct relation to the full set of needs and aspirations of the employee (demands of the employee upon the organization). It is when there is balance in both these demands that conditions become conducive to motivated implementation of innovation and therefore long-term prosperity.

Accepting the view that innovation is endemic within individuals, man-agers are immediately faced with the dilemma regarding recruitment and channelling talent in a way that is consistent with the organization's goals. Internal marketing plays an active role in selecting and nurturing the range of individuals necessary for innovation success. Truly creative individuals are not always easy to manage. According to Jain and Triandis[52], the kind of people who are most likely to succeed in an innovative organization are those who are analytical, curious, independent, intellectual, introverted, and who enjoy scientific and mathematical activities. Such people tend to be complex, flexible, self-sufficient, task oriented and tolerant of ambiguity, and have high needs for autonomy and change and a low need for deference.

Internal marketing is a useful tool because it pays attention to those aspects of human behaviour that could increase the creative potential of organizations, namely employee motivation. Until now, companies have resigned themselves to accepting that employees will only utilize a tiny fraction of their brainpower during work. In too many instances, employees disengage, so to speak, their brains before entering work premises.

Training and education: for roll-out and deployment

Once a product is ready for launch, there is a need to scale up all operations. This increases the number of people and teams dramatically. To achieve consistency in delivery, the company must invest heavily in both internal and external training programmes for its employees. The training is to build competencies in programmes, processes and controls for development of a new product. If turnover among employees is high, then the competence challenge becomes even more pronounced. Success in roll-out requires management to build and sustain partnerships with a larger number of employees. In attempting to do this, the company needs to cater for the different internal market segment needs. One way of doing this is to examine the training needs along two dimensions, Needs (company needs) versus Gains (personal gains), which can be mapped as a matrix to augment traditional employee classification. An extension of this is to try and understand the shape of employees' current and future value chain and a firm's positioning against that value chain.

Core competencies

As we have noted, IM is uniquely placed to maintain or modify a company's culture, because it cuts across functional boundaries. The same is true of managing a company's core competence. Because IM is not part of any one functional domain, it is best positioned to manage the firm's core competence.

Internal marketing can be used to stress the set of related strengths that makes up its distinctive competence. Distinctive competence is any competitive advantage that one company has over others in its industry and which cannot be easily copied. It can be constituted within a core function, such as manufacturing, or a support function such as IT. A firm's core competencies represent a cohesive sets of skills and techniques used to design, develop, distribute and support a firm's products or services. Competencies can be grouped into four general types: market-based insights, product-based, manufacturing process-based and support-based capabilities. These competencies vary among industry sectors, as well as among firms within the same industry.

If innovation is to be part of a company's core competence, then it must possess a high degree of co-ordination and integration. It is also important to remember that innovation is not a one-for-all activity. It comprises many shades and variations. Different types of innovation strategy draw upon different skill sets. For example, to be an inventive winner of first mover advantages requires certain kinds of co-ordination, while attempts to innovate by being a fast follower calls for somewhat different co-ordinative efforts. Thus, innovation competence is based on different forms and skills of co-ordination and integration.

Effective new product development usually requires external competencies among suppliers and partners to supplement internal competencies. Rarely can any one company possess all the resources and skills to build an entire product itself. Successful firms nurture strong internal competencies for product development, but also they rely on partners and suppliers for other necessary competencies. The role of IM, therefore, extends into the full innovation chain. Partner companies in the development chain must be closely aligned to the innovation aims of the company and motivated to work towards this common goal. Just as a firm must market internally to its employees, so it must market internally to its innovation chain partners. Trust and mutual understanding are of utmost importance in these partnerships. Actions of IM are to ensure that this is so.

To create outcomes from competencies, a corporation must target its competencies in specific directions. The problem is that most companies hardly understand their real core competencies. Many pay lip service to the concept, but few are really able to pinpoint their core competencies, let alone deploy them. Even worse, fewer still know the source of their competence basin. Nurturing them is even more difficult. Internal marketing's role is to create an assessment of core competencies, and plans for their nurturance and deployment. Internal marketing does this by building deep insight into the form and function of the organization. Also, since not all competencies are in-house, there is a need to strategize how best to acquire them from outside. This requires a long-term core competence plan of, firstly, how the company will source competencies and, secondly, how it will use its competencies. The plans must be of the now and of the future. Internal marketing, by linking current competencies to planned strategies, assesses the gap in competencies to realize the plans. This creates a strategic dialogue which forces strategic competence planning, not just strategy planning. Unfortunately, most organizations stop once they have made strategy plans. They hardly ever successfully make the transition from strategy plans to strategic competencies planning, which is at the heart of making actions occur and strategic plans to become realities.

This approach may be summarized as a set of basic questions that need to be asked:

- What is the competency requirement for the planned innovation strategy?
- What is the current status of resources?
- What is the gap between competencies required for the planned strategy and the current status?
- How can this gap be closed? That is, what resources – people, technology and capital – are required to develop necessary skills and competencies for product development success?
- How can the competencies be transformed into a distinctive competence?
- How can the competencies be leveraged to create value proposition for end-consumers?
- How will the company refresh and rejuvenate critical competencies?

Integration

Innovation is dependent on the input of *all* relevant viewpoints and arguments. If innovation is based on partial inputs, then there is likely to be a sticking point within the implementation cascade. Integration of all inputs is of great importance.

Innovation is not a monolithic entity. It consists of individual subsystems and system interfaces, which themselves can be the focus of improvement and innovation. The subsystems are based on specific capabilities and component processes, both within and external to the firm. Only through the integration of these subsystems can the final outcome be successfully produced. The effectiveness of integration can substantially impact the cost incurred to the total organizational system. If all efforts are integrated, the net result is a continuous stream of value-rich products over extended periods of time. Effective integration in innovation generates many generations of market-driven products, which are the foundation for a firm's long-term competitive position. Integration is arguably the most difficult yet most important challenge facing innovating firms.

Every individual within a company has the important task (and also the responsibility) in the creation of innovation. Management has to provide the conditions for openness to all stakeholders and viewpoints. These conditions take shape in many different ways: in leadership style, structuring of the organization, communication, strategy and culture for innovation.

Exhibit 7.2. B&Q: values for quality and consistency

B&Q has managed to instil a distinct B&Q personality by directing its efforts to make its employees its brand ambassadors. According to B&Q's communications controller Lorian Coutts, this has been in place since the company was founded some 30 years ago. Current management's task is to ensure that this continues. 'They have seen in the past what works and know a good thing when they see it. That includes its well-publicized "over-50s" hiring policy, and using staff in all its advertising.'

B&Q's over-50 policy came about from a belief that its customers would feel more comfortable if they could talk to someone who has hung a door, not just to some spotty youth with little experience of DIY.

Each morning B&Q runs 'energize' sessions, which are designed to encourage staff to work together and voice their opinions on how to run the store. At the heart of the way B&Q runs its business is its 'purpose and values statement', which comprises a set of five values. This values set eschews the corporate speak of many mission statements, opting instead for simplicity. The values that B&Q wants its employees to adopt and work toward were formed through the product of staff liaison, and are:

- a down-to-earth approach;
- respect for people;
- being customer driven;
- being positive; and
- striving to do better.

(*continued*)

As Coutts explains: 'One of the difficulties of having a business with 286 sites and over 22 000 people is trying to have a brand consistency. We are consciously trying to get our people to behave in a certain way to each other as well as to customers.' B&Q's approach of achieving this has been one of consistently reinforcing and symbolizing these values as behaviours in day-to-day practice.

Source: Mazur, L. (1999). Unleashing employees' true value: employees can be your company's most valuable marketing asset. *Marketing*, April, 22–4.

Internal marketing makes us realize that people are central in the equation of organizational success. Because IM links the employee to strategy, it takes implementation to the very core of its enabling agency: the employee. This direct link helps to cut through the layers that often act as multipliers of confusion, conflict, frustration and eventually inaction. Internal marketing links specific strategy programmes to developing competencies, which are in turn linked to each individual's intelligence, creativity, responsibility and experience. By so doing, IM not only manages the individual, but also the collective that makes up the organization. Internal marketing thus influences the formation of a 'corporate identity' and 'collective mind'. These influences set in place foundations for an integrated innovative creative organization. This means more than just putting together individual qualities and capabilities, however important each individual and personal contribution may be. Internal marketing works by bringing the individual into the collective. It is in this combination that individual creativity is transposed to organizational innovation and learning. Internal marketing's view of organizations can be said to be personalistic, in that it stresses the primary importance of the individual within and outside the organization, as a source of sense-making for the organization, yet it is operationalized through a strategic lens. In this way, IM aligns the individual into a collective unit, performing in concert to the orchestra of strategic coherence and alignment.

Internal marketing understanding is shaped by descriptive anthropology where individuals and their environment get shape and meaning in a continuous mutual interaction. Internal marketing examines the irrevocable relationship of employees to themselves, to other people, to the organization and the world they live in. More than this, IM is characterized by the capability to reflect on organizational functioning, its environment and societal context. Customers and employees are key agents in this value-adding process. Internal marketing helps the understanding of this. Internal marketing does not just reflect on the past, but also anticipates what is yet to come and influences the future.

Summary

Today, the process of innovation is as important to firms as ever. The development and commercialization of successful new products is probably the single most important task of organizations. Developing new products though is not only a very complex task, it is also very risky. With average success rates for new products of around 60 per cent, ensuring that appropriate procedures are in place to guide new products through the organization is a crucial task. However, there are signs that early NPD modelling approaches are becoming dated. Changes in the business environment with respect to time compression in development, coupled with the need to get closer to customers, is leading managers to seek fluidity within structure.

Ensuring the creative potential of organizations is maximized is now crucial. Yet there is a huge discrepancy between the actual creativity levels of individuals within organizations relative to their full potential. There is a natural human tendency to be motivated through creative actions. Providing an environment whereby innovation and creatitivity become an emergent property of the organization will become increasingly important as business pressures continue to intensify in the years ahead. Managing innovation and creativity is difficult. It involves organizing and managing the organization proactively, and requires the balancing of short- and long-term considerations, external as well as internal requirements and constraints, and quality of product design (performance of NPD output) against the innovation process (e.g. speed, cost). Meeting performance demands on the polar dimensions in many respects leads to contradictory requirements. Internal marketing reconciles the contradictions by planning for the holistic by examining and managing the employee in the macrocosm (organizational) of individual (micro) action.

As Jain and Triandis[53] state: 'The most important element in innovation is ... people. They are the vessels that hold the skills and possess the capacity for action that translate results into useful products.'

Internal marketing is a concept to create circumstances and conditions (resources) to be successful in today's (and tomorrow's!) highly competitive environments.

References

1. Cooper, R. G. and Kleinschmidt, E. J. (1991). *Formal Processes for Managing New Products: The Industry Experience*. Hamilton, Ontario: Faculty of Business, McMaster University.

2. Cooper, R. G., Edgett, S. J. and Kleinschmidt, E. J. (1998). *Portfolio Management for New Products*. Reading, MA: Addison-Wesley.

3. Trygg, L. (1993). Concurrent engineering practices in selected Swedish companies: a movement or an activity of the few. *Journal of Product Innovation Management*, **10**, 403–15. Pawar, K. S., Menon, V. and Reidel, J. C. K. H. (1994). Time to market. *Integrated Manufacturing Systems*, **5** (1), 14–22.

4. Anthony, Shapiro and M. McGrath (1992). *Product Development: Success Through Product & Cycle-time Excellence (PACE)*. London: Butterworth-Heinemann.

5. Pawar, K. S., Menon, V. and Reidel, J. C. K. H. (1994). Op. cit.

6. Wheelwright, S. C. and Clark, K. B. (1992). *Revolutionary Product Development*. New York: The Free Press.

7. Griffin, A. (1997). PDMA research & new product development practices: updating trends & benchmarking best practices. *Journal of Product Innovation Management*, **14** (November), 429–58.

8. Barczak, G. and Wilemon, D. (1989). Leadership differences in new product development teams. *Journal of Product Innovation Management*, **6** (4), December, 259–67. Barczak, G. and Wilemon, D. (1991). Communications patterns of new product development team leaders. *IEEE Transactions on Engineering Management*, **EM 38** (2), November, 101–9. Cooper, R. G. (1990). Stage-gate systems: a new tool for managing new products. *Business Horizons*, **33** (1), Spring, 44–56. Calantone, R. J., Vickery, S. K. and Droge, C. (1995). Business performance and strategic new product development activities: an empirical investigation. *Journal of Product Innovation Management*, **12** (June), 1–10.

9. Cooper, R. G. (1988). *Winning at New Products*. Gage Educational.

10. Griffin, A. (1997). Op. cit.

11. Cooper, R. G. and Kleinschmidt, E. J. (1988). Resource allocation in the new product process. *Industrial Marketing Management*, **17** (August), 249–62.

12. Urban, G. L. and Hauser, J. R. (1993). *Design & Marketing of New Products*. Englewood Cliffs, NJ: Prentice-Hall.

13. Haffenden, P. A. (1990). Reducing time-to-market. *Professional Engineering*, December, 44–51.

14. Pawar, K. S., Menon, V. and Reidel, J. C. K. H. (1994). Op. cit.

15. Trygg, L. (1993). Op. cit.

16. Zahra, S. and Ellor, D. (1993). Accelerating new product development & successful market introduction. *SAM Advanced Management Journal*, Winter, 9–15. Zirger, B. J. & Hartley, J. L. (1994). A conceptual model of product development cycle time. *Journal of Engineering Technology Management*, **11**, 229–51.

17. Murmann, P. A. (1994). Expected development time reductions in the German mechanical engineering industry. *Journal of Product Innovation Management*, **11**, 236–52.

18. Gehani, R. R. (1994). Concurrent product development for fast-track corporations. *Long Range Planning*, **27** (2), 40–47.

19. Murmann, P. A. (1994). Op. cit.

20. Power, C. (1993). FLOPS – too many new products fail, here's why – and how to do better. *Business Week*, 16 August, pp. 34–9. Gehani, R. R. (1994). Op. cit.

21. Rothwell, R. (1994). Towards the fifth-generation innovation process. *International Marketing Review*, **11** (1), 7–31.
22. Rothwell, R. and Zegveld, W. (1985). *Reindustrialization and Technology*. Harlow: Longman. Towner, S. J. (1994). Four ways to accelerate new product development. *Long Range Planning*, **27** (2), 57–65. Quotation from p. 50.
23. Rothwell, R. (1992). Successful industrial innovation: critical factors for the 1990s. *R&D Management*, **22** (3), 221–38.
24. Anthony, Shapiro and McGrath (1992). Op. cit.
25. Ibid.
26. Reported in Cooper, R. G. and Kleinschmidt, E. J. (1991). Op. cit.
27. Larson, E. and Gobeli, D. H. (1989). Significance of project management structure on development success. *IEEE Transactions on Engineering Management*, **36** (2), May, 119–25.
28. Trygg, L. (1993). Op. cit.
29. Cooper, R. G. and Kleinschmidt, E. J. (1988). Op. cit. Cooper, R. G. (1990). Op. cit. Frey, D. (1991). Learning the ropes: my life as a product champion. *Harvard Business Review*, September/October, 46–56.
30. Anthony, M. T. and McKay, J. (1992). FROM EXPERIENCE: balancing the product development process: achieving Product and Cycle-time Excellence in high technology industries. *Journal of Product Innovation Management*, **9**, 140–7.
31. Pawar, K. S., Menon, V. and Reidel, J. C. K. H. (1994). Op. cit.
32. Page, A. L. (1993). Assessing new product development practices and performance: establishing crucial norms. *Journal of Product Innovation Management*, **10**, 273–90.
33. Griffin, A. (1997). Op. cit.
34. Power, C. (1993). Op. cit. Lee, M. and Na, D. (1994). Determinants of technical success in product development where innovative radicalness is considered. *Journal of Product Innovation Management*, **11**, 62–8. Trygg, L. (1993). Op. cit.
35. Booz, Allen & Hamilton (1968). *Management of New Products*. Chicago: Booz, Allen & Hamilton. Booz, Allen & Hamilton (1988). *New Products Management for the 1980s*. New York: Booz, Allen & Hamilton. Page, A. L. (1993). Op. cit.
36. Cooper, R. G. and Kleinschmidt, E. J. (1991). Op. cit.
37. Hughes, G. D. and Chafin, D. C. (1996). Turning new product development into a continuous learning process. *Journal of Product Innovation Management*, **13**, 89–104.
38. Tang, H. K. (1998). An integrative model of innovation in organisations. *Technovation*, **18** (5), 297–309.
39. Regine, B. and Lewin, R. (1999). *The Soul at Work: Unleashing the Power of Complexity Science for Business*. New York: Simon & Schuster.
40. Freemantle, D. (1999). *What Customers Like About You, Adding Emotional Value*, p. 40. London: Nicholas Brealey.
41. Cude, B. J. (1980). An objective method of determining the relevancy of product characteristic. *Proceedings of the American Council of Consumer Interests*, pp. 111–16. McCracken, G. (1990). Culture and consumer behaviour: an anthropological perspective. *Journal of the Market Research Society*, **32** (1), 3–11.

42. Ries, A. and Trout, J. (1981). *Positioning: The Battle for your Mind.* New York: McGraw-Hill.
43. Feig, B. (1997). *Marketing Straight to the Heart.* Printed in the US. New York: AMACOM.
44. Moorman, C. and Miner, A. S. (1998). The convergence of planning and execution: improvisation in new product development. *Journal of Marketing*, **6** (July), 1–20.
45. Hutt, M. D., Reingen, P. H. and Ronchetta, J. R. (1988). Tracing emergent processes in marketing strategy formation. *Journal of Marketing*, **52** (January), 19. Mintzberg, H. (1994). *The Rise and Fall of Strategic Planning.* New York: The Free Press.
46. Anderson, R. and Tappin, S. (1999). The vision that will keep you growing. Report by the PA Consulting Group, Buckingham Palace Road, London.
47. Covey, S. R. (1990). *The 7 Habits of Highly Effective People.* New York: Franklin Covey.
48. Canfield, J. and Miller, J. (1998). *Heart at Work: Stories and Strategies for Building Self-esteem and Re-awakening the Soul at Work.* Crawfordsville, IN: McGraw-Hill.
49. Ibid., p. xi.
50. Goleman, D. (1996). *Emotional Intelligence: Why It Can Matter More Than IQ.* London: Bloomsbury. Goleman, D. (1999). *Working with Emotional Intelligence.* London: Bloomsbury.
51. Goleman, D. (1996). Op. cit.
52. Jain, R. K. and Triandis, H. C. (1990). *Management of R&D Organisations. Managing the Unmanageable.* New York: John Wiley.
53. Ibid., p. 21.

chapter eight

Knowledge management, learning and internal marketing

Introduction

More than a decade ago, Peter F. Drucker foretold the coming of the age of the knowledge worker. Workers, in this age, were the critical capital. Whereas machines stay in the factory floor, knowledge goes with the person. The knowledge era began in the 1970s with the advent of IT. It took shape with the birth of personal computers. This technological revolution has given rise to more changes in management practice than any other previous period. With each passing generation, computers have become more powerful, making information storage, processing and transfer widely available. The knowledge economy has made information, and the knowledge of how to use it, more powerful than ever. At the same time, unfortunately, it has reduced the 'shelf-life' of each piece of new knowledge. Knowledge is the source of competitive advantage, because it is a vessel of human experience and insight capable of potential action.

With the development of the global economy, knowledge management and learning (KM&L) has risen to higher prominence. In this new era, the approach to employees has changed from one treating them as machine-like appendages to intellectual capital possessing strategically valuable and renewable experience.

While clearly knowledge is an asset, it is often not treated as such and is hardly ever consolidated into corporate accounts. Because of such neglect, intellectual capital often walks out of the company and suddenly reappears in the offices of competition. The market value of some corporations can be multiplied several fold. The difference between these and other organizations is in their employees. Individual skills, know-how, relationships and contacts add value and generate wealth. The way organizations tap into their intangible assets can increase the value of these assets to the organization. Employees may possess certain knowledge, but organizations do not benefit from that knowledge unless they put in place an adequate structure and processes to capture, support and enhance it.

In a survey in *Fortune* magazine[1], executives were found to be searching for a new business paradigm. In the 1980s, over 50 per cent of the Fortune 500 underwent some form of restructuring exercise. Executives, however, were not convinced that these new 'decentralized, lean and mean' structures were likely to meet the challenges ahead. They believed that they would not be:

- *Fast enough* to match foreign competitors' product development or identify an opportunity in the marketplace.

- *Keen enough* to deliver higher levels of customer service or achieve leaps in productivity.

- *Smart enough or sensitive enough* to manage a polyglot workforce or satisfy the needs of its best employees.

While these companies were busy disfranchising their employees (people with the knowledge) with poorly thought out changes (downsizing, rightsizing and re-engineering), technology was increasing the power of knowledge and information. The emerging knowledge economy was about ideas first, services second and products third. Companies that were busy with de-layering failed to appreciate what the employee actually brings 'to the table' in today's workplace. For instance, when older employees are dispensed rather than retrained, it is quite possible that the company is losing persons who hold the experience and share the values that a company desires. Teaching a new young replacement the same can be a costly task. Consequently, the cost of getting 'lean' often shows up in poor financials. Why? Because many companies have found they need to re-hire the same employees as expensive external consultants. One of the causes for this myopia is the 500-year-old Venetian 'double entry' accounting system, which is unable to assign a value to knowledge that employees possess. Treating people as an undifferentiated resource can levy a heavy penalty. The problem is that companies have yet to come to terms with intellectual capital (IC).

Knowledge management and learning

Knowledge management and learning offer ways to harness the potential of employees. Knowledge and learning are intertwined concepts. New knowledge is the outcome of learning, and new knowledge when it is applied feeds into the building of a higher level of insight and learning.

Organizational learning is a process in which an organization's members actively use data to guide behaviour in such a way as to promote the ongoing adaptation of the organization[2]. It is a process by which managers become aware of the qualities, patterns and consequences of their own experiences, and develop mental models to understand these experiences[3]. Knowledge, on the other hand, is closely linked to organizational memory, which allows the organization to call up past events, remember what was done – what worked and what did not work – and avoid the 'reinvent the wheel' syndrome.

Peter Senge highlighted the link between learning and knowledge in stating: 'Learning in organizations means the continuous testing of experience, and the transformation of that experience into knowledge – accessible to the whole organization, and relevant to its core purpose'[4]. Not only does experience need to be continuously tested (with an aim, not just to test), but also the relevant parts of that experience must be shared with appropriate people in the company. Companies renew themselves through processes of organizational learning[5]. Implanting new knowledge involves innovative behaviour, and learning is the means through which change occurs. Knowledge management (KM) is intertwined with learning. Learning is an essential aspect in examining organizational change processes. Companies are routine-based, history-dependent systems that respond to experience. In other words, they are experiential learning systems[6]. The company's past affects its future capability of change. Learning brings about changes in current routines and institutes new capabilities[7].

Change and learning reinforce each other. Change tends to invalidate known answers and so demands continuous learning. New knowledge is attained through learning. Learning generates change, which in turn can again lead to learning, etc. The knowledge–learning cycle can lead to continuous improvement if utilized properly. Learning is more than getting everyone to understand systems and their architectures[8]. It is also about discerning and managing interrelations. To really embed knowledge and learning in the workplace involves not just developing new capabilities, but also making fundamental shifts in the mindsets of the individual and collective units.

The learning organization is built upon four pillars[9]:

1 Philosophy (in which vision, values and purpose are important).

2 Attitudes and beliefs (in which there is genuine caring and commonness of aims, and the willingness to change and learn).

3 Skills and capabilities (in which systems thinking is developed, along with a shared commitment).

4 Tools (systems tools) that can be used to learn throughout the organization.

Developing knowledge and learning foundations requires companies to share beliefs, attitudes and vision. In a study of successful learning organizations, it was found that the first principle is the need for a vision, upon which organizational members can base their future learning requirements[10]. Secondly, this vision must be shared throughout the organization. Peter Senge[11] notes that one 'cannot have a learning organization without shared vision'. Without a strong pull toward a common goal, the forces in support of the status quo can be overwhelming. Shared perspectives provide focus and energy for sharing knowledge and learning. 'It's not what the vision is, it's what the vision does' that is important[12].

Barriers to learning

Barriers to learning or disabilities are an ingrained part of all organizations. Common barriers that can debilitate the transition into a learning organization are[13]:

- 'I am my position' (the manager or employee who places loyalty to the job before loyalty to the firm – 'functional myopia').
- 'The enemy is out there' (when the true enemy is almost invariably 'inside' the organization).
- Illusion of taking charge (when proactivity is really 'reactiveness' in disguise).
- Fixation on events rather than processes.
- Delusion of learning from experience (is commonplace because we rarely directly suffer the consequences of many of our decisions; there is usually a separation between decision and consequence, allowing us to live the delusion that learning has taken place).
- The myth of the management 'team'.

Five statements that serve as guideposts as to what a learning organization is and is not are[14]:

1 It is not just a collection of individuals who are learning.
2 It demonstrates organizational capacity for change.
3 It accelerates individual learning capacity, but also redefines organizational structure, culture, job design and assumptions about the way things are.
4 It involves widespread participation of employees – and often customers – in decision making and information sharing.

5 It promotes systemic thinking and building of organizational memory.

It is a fact that all organizations learn, but only learning organizations *consciously* learn.

Knowledge management directs and enhances organizational decisions as to how, where and when to create and account for new knowledge. Knowledge management prevents the loss of critical knowledge due to retirement, rightsizing and employee mobility to other firms. When proactively supported by senior management, knowledge management encourages the employee to create, share and benefit from knowledge. The business problem that knowledge management attempts to solve is that often knowledge acquired through experience isn't reused because it isn't shared in a formal way. The ultimate goal of knowledge management is to give the organization a capacity to be more effective every passing day by the gathering of institutional memory, very much like human beings who possess a capacity to become more effective and mature every day with the accumulation of thoughts and memories[15].

The implementation of knowledge management is an organizational change process that involves learning and often requires an extensive cultural change. In this process, managers are responsible for shaping organizational culture by advancing knowledge management awareness and values, for the development and deployment of strategy for knowledge, for the development and communication of knowledge management policy, for setting knowledge management goals, and putting in place knowledge management systems and processes.

Different types of KM

Over time, many different varieties of knowledge management have appeared on the scene. Binney[16] puts forward a KM spectrum that usefully covers an extensive range of KM approaches and applications (Figure 8.1).

Transactional KM

In transactional KM, the use of knowledge is embedded in the application of technology. Knowledge is presented to the user of a system in the course of completing a transaction or a unit or work, e.g. entering an order or handling a customer query or problem. An example of transactional KM is case-based reasoning. 'Case-based reasoning provides a method for representing past situations (cases) and retrieving similar cases when a new problem is input. Given a description of a problem,

	Transactional	Analytical	Asset Management	Process	Developmental	Innovation and Creativity
KM Applications	• Case-based reasoning • Help desk applications • Customer service applications • Order entry applications • Service agent support applications	• Data warehousing • Data mining • Business intelligence • MIS • Decision support systems • Customer relationship management (CRM) • *Competitive intelligence*	• Intellectual property • Document management • Knowledge valuation • Knowledge repositories • *Content management*	• TQM • Benchmarking • BPR • Lessons learned • ISO 9xxx, six sigma, etc.	• Skills development • Staff competencies • Learning • Teaching • Training	• Communities • Collaboration • Discussion forums • Networking • Virtual teams • R&D • *Multi-disciplinary teams*
Enabling Technologies	• Expert systems • Cognitive technologies • Semantic networks • Rule-based expert systems • Probability networks • Decision trees • Geospatial information systems	• Intelligent agents • Web crawlers • Relational and object DBMS • Neural computing • Push technologies • Data analysis and reporting tools	• Document management tools • Search engines • Knowledge maps • Library systems	• Workflow management • Process modelling tools	• Computer-based training • Online training	• Groupware • Chat rooms • Video conferencing • Search engines • Bulletin board • Push technologies • Simulation technologies

Portals, Internet, Intranets, Extranets

Figure 8.1 Spectrum of knowledge management. *Source:* Binney, D. (2000). The knowledge management spectrum – understanding the KM landscape. *Journal of Knowledge Management,* 5 (1), 21–32.

the system searches for similar known cases. The system asks the user questions (proactively) about the problem to narrow the search for similar problems'[17]. Other examples of transactional KM include help desk, customer service, order entry and field support applications.

Analytical KM

Analytical KM provides interpretations of, or creates, new knowledge from vast amounts or disparate sources of material. In analytical KM applications, large amounts of data or information are used to derive trends and patterns – uncovering that which is hidden due to the vastness of the source material. It turns data into information, which, if acted on, can become knowledge.

Traditional analytical KM applications such as management information systems and data warehousing analyse the data or information that are generated internally in companies (often by transactional systems). Traditional analytical KM applications focus on customer-related information to assist activities such as product development functions. These are now being complemented by a range of competitive or business intelligence applications that incorporate external sources of knowledge or information. Such competitive intelligence applications are being used to analyse and understand what is happening in their marketplace and assess competitive activity.

Asset management KM

Asset management KM focuses on processes associated with the management of knowledge assets. This involves either:

- The management of explicit knowledge assets which have been codified in some way; or
- The management of intellectual property (IP) and the processes surrounding the identification, exploitation and protection of IP.

Once captured, the assets are made available to people. This element of the spectrum is directly analogous to a library, with the knowledge assets being catalogued in various ways and made available for unstructured access and use.

Knowledge assets are often created as a by-product of 'doing business' and are kept for future use. What differentiates this element from analytical systems is that the assets are often more complex and less numerous. They may also require some level of intervention in order to codify them.

For example, capturing project or product development history, experiences or work products often requires some intervention.

Process-based KM

The process-based KM element covers the codification and improvement of processes. Process knowledge assets are often improved through internal 'lesson' sessions and internal and external best practice benchmarking.

Developmental KM

Developmental KM applications focus on increasing the competencies or capabilities of an organization's knowledge workers. This is also referred to as investing in human capital[18]. The applications cover the transfer of explicit knowledge via training or the planned development of tacit knowledge through developmental interventions such as experiential assignments or membership in a community of interest.

Innovation/creation KM

Innovation/creation-based KM applications focus on providing an environment in which knowledge workers, often from different disciplines, can come together in teams to collaborate in the creation of new knowledge. The innovation/creation of new knowledge is the one receiving the greatest attention currently. The focus in this element is on providing an environment in which knowledge workers of various disciplines can come together to create new knowledge.

An alternative method of classification is in terms of knowledge strategies. Hansen et al.[19] suggest that businesses followed two mutually exclusive knowledge management models, called *codification* and *personalization*.

1 *Codification strategy* – the approach by which knowledge is carefully extracted from people, codified into documents and stored as knowledge objects or products in databases, from which it can be accessed and used easily by many staff within a given organization. People gain insight from documents.

2 *Personalization strategy* – this is an approach that focuses on knowledge sharing via person-to-person contact. People gain insight from other people.

For the codification approach, significant IT support is required. For the personalization model, IT is much less important than social interaction. Fundamentally, KM has much wider implications than data management and information management. Many commentators observe that KM is not new. What is new is the phenomenal growth of technologies that make it easier to implement KM systems. Technology is simply a catalyst in the KM movement. As technologies continue to evolve rapidly, especially in the areas of collaboration and search engines, they will enable more sophisticated KM. Notwithstanding its importance; technology is not the biggest challenge in implementing effective KM. Indeed, there is some evidence that there is no direct correlation between IT investments and KM, or business performance[20]. The bigger challenge is of organizational cultural issues, such as departmentalism, that often divide allegiances and block the transfer of knowledge from individual minds into the organization at large. Another barrier is the poverty of far-sightedness of senior management, who often fail to support knowledge and learning behaviours.

Internal marketing and knowledge management and learning

The metamorphosis of an organization into a knowledge-led organization can be aided by internal marketing. Internal marketing enhances the correct performance of knowledge management.

Internal marketing allows the organization to enhance customer service and customer care. It does this by building internal competencies and understanding of who the customers are and what they want. Knowledge and learning is driven by an appreciation to improve customer outcomes through continually building and upgrading organizational insight. Knowledge and learning are the capacity to pass that learning on from one individual to the next, from one department to the next, and from one generational time period onto the next. It is easy to see that internal marketing can be used as a tool to help knowledge management and learning.

Ballantyne[21] links knowledge management and internal marketing by first putting forward two methods of internal marketing:

1   *Transactional marketing* (aiming to satisfy customers' needs profitably)

   (a) To capture new knowledge.

   (b) To codify knowledge.

2 *Relationship marketing* (aiming to create mutual value with customers or other stakeholders)

(a) To generate new knowledge (through cross-functional project groups, creative approaches, innovation centres, quality improvement teams, etc.).

(b) To circulate knowledge (through team-based learning programmes, skills development workshops, feedback loops, etc.).

In each case, the marketing methods are internally directed. These can be depicted as a matrix of internal marketing activity (see Figure 8.2).

In terms of knowledge management, the role of internal marketing is knowledge renewal and occurs in two main ways:

1 Knowledge generation – the creation or discovery of new knowledge for use within the organization, with external market intelligence as input.

2 Knowledge circulation – the diffusion of knowledge to all that can benefit, through the chain of internal customers to external customers.

In terms of learning, Ballantyne proposes four distinct modes. These modes are:

1 *Energizing – learning how to work together on useful marketplace goals that are broader than the bounds of any individual job des-*

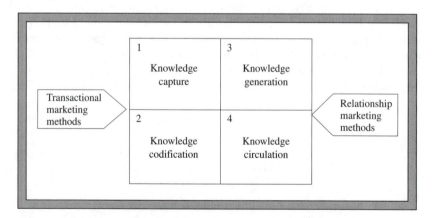

Figure 8.2 Internal marketing and knowledge management. *Source*: Ballantyne, D. (2000). Internal relationship marketing: a strategy for knowledge renewal. *International Journal of Bank Marketing*, 18 (1), 274–86.

cription. What people feel explains a great deal of the what and how and by what means they want to achieve. To energize employees, it is necessary to be able to touch their deeper values and motivations in some way or another. Energizing is the energy of renewal that comes directly from doing an act[22].

2 *Code breaking – learning how to apply personal resources of 'know-how' in working together to solve customer problems, create new opportunities and change internal procedures.* The primary source of knowledge is the individuals themselves. Learning to trust is fundamental. Companies 'learn' through their employees. Employee insights are tested by action, in which it becomes possible to observe what works and what doesn't work. To find out whether the insight has wider application, it becomes necessary to test the personal know-how in group settings. Such wider demonstrations also serve to provide confidence to challenge entrenched internal policies and procedures.

3 *Authorizing – learning to make choices between options on a cost-benefit basis and gaining approvals from the appropriate line authority.* To change any particular process or policy it is necessary to get support through a well-documented argument. An understanding of the broader context is helpful in this. This also requires advocacy and listening skills, as well as support of senior management who possess the power to influence.

4 *Diffusing – learning how to circulate and share new knowledge across managerial domains in new ways.* The diffusion of 'new' knowledge is more than one-way communication. It requires dialogue. 'Can we trust them?' is the question staff often ask themselves. Trustworthy actions from management are the secret of gaining staff buy-in.

Feedback from each activity helps to adjust the direction of the cycle as a whole and the activities it comprises. This action and feedback pattern acts as a reinforcing circle. Each learning mode is complementary to the whole. Working in this way, the whole becomes more than the sum of the parts.

Generating new organizational knowledge is closely intertwined with dialogue. The process of organizational learning is not the same as having a knowledge repository. Even more importantly, learning does not occur just through the capture and processing of information from the market and adapting to it. It requires actively reshaping the assumptions on which existing knowledge is built. This reconstruction of meaning is central to knowledge renewal.

Mapping the four learning modes onto Nonaka and Takeuchi's[23] four-phase theory of knowledge creation, Ballantyne highlights the concept of knowledge renewal (see Figure 8.3).

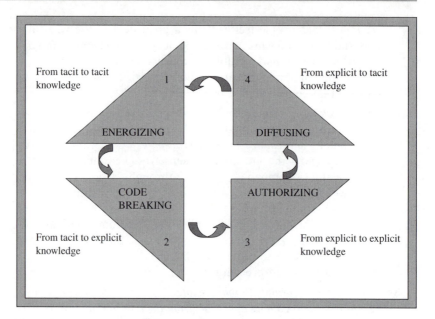

Figure 8.3 Internal marketing as knowledge renewal. *Source*: Ballantyne, D. (2000). Internal relationship marketing: a strategy for knowledge renewal. *International Journal of Bank Marketing*, 18 (1), 274–86.

1 *Energizing – developing common knowledge (socialization: knowledge interactions from tacit to tacit)*. What is at issue at this phase in knowledge renewal is the willingness of employees to pass on to each other their hard won know-how. The processes involved in capturing new knowledge can be quite subliminal. We may be able to do certain things without really understanding what we are doing and how we are doing them. This makes the task of transfer more difficult. This phase is 'energized' by the sharing of tacit knowledge, a tacit to tacit process, thus amplifying common knowledge under conditions where trust is present.

2 *Code breaking – discovering new knowledge (externalization: knowledge interactions from tacit to explicit)*. This phase is about moving tacit knowledge to explicit through creative dialogue. Creating staff overlaps between departments helps to create a climate for knowledge discovery. This underpins frequent and higher quality interaction between departments. In 'overlapping' work situations, managers and other employees are challenged to re-examine what they take for granted. This leads to 'code breaking'. By using their common knowledge, workers in teams can convert insights generated in dialogue into possible new solutions to customer problems. Teams expand the scope of alternative options and thereby widen the source of new knowledge creation. In a supportive environment, mutual obligation soon develops, which feeds back into the process. This phase is characterized by inter-action in the discovery of new knowledge.

3 *Authorizing – obtaining cost-benefit knowledge (combination: knowledge interactions from explicit to explicit).* The transfer of knowledge in this phase is from explicit to explicit. Two-way dia-logue between departments based on trust contributes to readiness to make decisions. Readiness feeds back into further dialogue. Obtaining cost-benefit knowledge is an analytical task familiar to every organization and yet it is a difficult one to make. There are always competing agendas in large organizations and often insuf-ficient knowledge of the impact on current or proposed policies. This phase is characterized by bringing together explicit knowl-edge on costs and benefits.

4 *Diffusing – integrating knowledge (internalization: knowledge inter-actions from explicit to tacit).* The final knowledge transfer is from explicit to tacit. Managing knowledge is not just a matter of pro-cessing information. There is a need to circulate, test, integrate and codify new knowledge into new designs, policies, processes and training programmes.

According to Ballantyne, underlying this knowledge renewal process is a cycle that moves from commitment to trust, trust to obligation, obliga-tion to trust, and from trust back to (re) commitment.

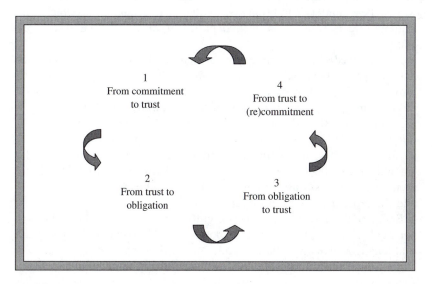

Figure 8.4 The cycle of trust and commitment.

Personal commitment is of two types:

1 Commitment to achieve something or to behave in a certain way involves a personal view of the likely beneficial outcomes of internal marketing.

2 Commitment inspired by obligation to others. This involves consideration of reciprocal benefits in order to get things done.

Ballantyne suggests trust is a precondition for obligation but not for personal commitment. Trust means that reliance was placed on another person (or happening) in relation to an expectation. There was some risk involved, or even faith (as in 'blind' trust), and certainly some confidence in others as a consequence of past experience. The strength of internal marketing is its intent, coupled with trusting employees and being trustworthy. The much neglected fact is that organizational knowledge is created through interaction and dialogue. The traditional marketing mindset based on the competitive premise blinkers companies to the fact that collaboration is central to much of, if not most, knowledge creation. It is therefore at the heart of creating competitive advantage. Collaboration means the involvement of multiple participants. Marketing departments may play a leading role but the cycle of activity demands collaboration between many different units. For instance, 'energizing' and 'diffusing' involve new learning behaviours and thus may require high input from HRM, and 'code breaking' and 'authorizing' require more support from operational departments. Rather than dominance and dictat, internal marketing works best under conditions of equal partnership, in which the leading role is rotated as each department or actor takes the more active role.

For knowledge and learning management not to become a passing fad, it must really take hold in the minds of practising managers. It has to move out of the realm of an 'interesting idea' to become a 'usable idea'. This means getting managers to recognize that knowledge and learning is something they should and could be doing. The role of internal marketing in this is to help give knowledge and learning personal relevance, i.e. engage managers' motivations. Internal marketing helps to turn the 'should and could do' to 'want to and will do'. If this can be done, then KM becomes a usable idea: notably one whose value is recognized and therefore motivated into realization.

Bailey and Clarke[24] are very insightful in developing the notion of personal relevance, which we transpose to the IM context. They suggest that managers can appreciate the relevance of KM by relating the knowledge to be managed into four distinct domains of managerial focus (see Figure 8.5).

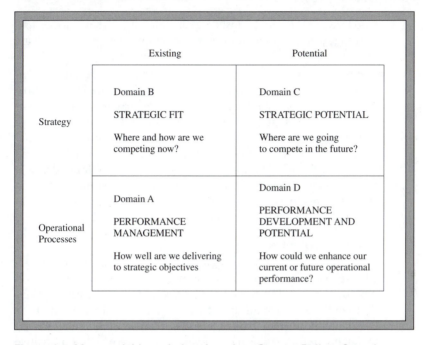

	Existing	Potential
Strategy	Domain B STRATEGIC FIT Where and how are we competing now?	Domain C STRATEGIC POTENTIAL Where are we going to compete in the future?
Operational Processes	Domain A PERFORMANCE MANAGEMENT How well are we delivering to strategic objectives	Domain D PERFORMANCE DEVELOPMENT AND POTENTIAL How could we enhance our current or future operational performance?

Figure 8.5 Managerial knowledge domains. *Source*: Bailey, C. and Clarke, M. (2001). Managing knowledge for personal and organizational benefit. *Journal of Knowledge Management*, 5 (1), 58–67.

1 *Domain A:* The Performance Management Arena – prompts decisions and actions to influence performance.

2 *Domain B:* The Strategic Fit Arena – prompts decisions and actions about customer management, product portfolio, marketing, competence requirements, etc.

3 *Domain C:* The Strategic Potential Arena – prompts decisions about investment and development of organization, people, markets, technology and competencies.

4 *Domain D:* The Performance Development and Potential Arena – prompts decisions and actions to develop products, processes and competencies.

Bailey and Clarke point out that knowledge management is about the generation, communication and exploitation of ideas. Managers can understand the actionability of knowledge management by locating normal managerial activities in terms of generating, communicating and exploiting ideas in one of the four managerial knowledge domains.

Personal relevance is important because:

1   Knowledge starts and finishes with individuals. Knowledge and learning cannot take hold without employees since it occurs through them.

Employees are central agents who surface, share and exploit tacit knowledge. Managing knowledge relies on individual effort and co-operation. Without a high trust environment, individuals place themselves at considerable risk in performing knowledge activities. So unless individuals are able to see the personal relevance (*'what's in it for me?'*), then the knowledge and learning initiative will suffer. Internal marketing is a key tool for addressing this challenge. By looking at the employees as customers, it explicitly attempts to examine the cost-benefit for the employee in making the knowledge transaction (sharing, surfacing, etc.).

2   Sharing is not a natural activity.

Examples of this are highlighted in the many failures of knowledge repositories, despite large amounts of investments in technology for sharing. The reason is that companies make assumptions that employees have an innate desire to share information. They could not be further from the truth. Sharing has to be induced through careful management. Even if an employee has a positive attitude toward sharing, the grind of daily pressures works against the time-consuming effort of updating information and sharing knowledge. Consequently, the motivation to share is low.

Put simply, knowledge management and learning will not work if people are unable to see the personal value of KM activities. Without personal motivation, it is unlikely that KM will become integrated sufficiently to create bottom line results.

3   Perceived personal relevance is a precondition for the motivation to think and act differently.

Questions of how to incentivize, reward and recognize knowledge management and learning are preceded by important questions about how the adoption of a KM frame of reference actually benefits the individual. In other words – why should any manager or employee adopt knowledge and learning perspective?

Clearly, knowledge and learning requires managers to think differently about organizational work and KM activities require managers to change how they invest their effort and time.

Personal relevance is critical when people are considering doing something they do not have to do, especially if it incurs considerable personal expense and is not easily recompensed. To gain and sustain commitment to valuing KM, personal relevance needs to tap into something more fundamental than immediate extrinsic gain. For example, why should a senior executive risk investing organizational resource and personal reputation to create favourable conditions for knowledge management? Changing the culture may fail and therefore damage his reputation or the positive effects occur so far into the future so as not to be of any benefit to him. Similarly, why should a line manager invest his already pressured time in knowledge-sharing activities outside of his or her immediate area of operational concern? Something more than extrinsic reward is required to motivate and engage in KM activities. Managers need to see how KM can enhance their personal effectiveness in achieving what they want to do, in a way that would not otherwise be possible relying on their current way of thinking.

By paying specific attention to the issue of real personal relevance, in getting involved in a specific set of activities, it becomes possible to:

1 Bring clarity to where and with whom individuals need to focus their effort in order to gain maximum organizational and individual benefit.

2 Highlight to employees and managers alike what ideas to use to enhance their personal influence in their organizations.

Both these issues are critical for organizations and individuals. Relevance is achieved if people in every role can see how knowledge management and learning enhances their effectiveness.

Employees can increase their personal effectiveness if they are able to focus their expert knowledge in a way that naturally contributes to organizational success. In turn, this enhances the visibility of their personal contribution and enables personal influence to grow. Internal marketing is a highly useful activity in this. If internal marketing can help to bring the right ideas, at the right time to the right people, then it enables effective knowledge management. More than this, if internal marketing can help people see the relevance of why they should engage in knowledge activities it becomes a true enabler of knowledge management. Internal marketing's adoption of a cost-benefits transactional approach for employees tackles the very heart of the notion of personal relevance: what is the gain to the employee for engaging in a specific organizationally directed action and what is the cost of doing so. Internal marketing explicitly attempts to address these two questions.

Understanding role differences

Bailey and Clarke also note that the distribution of organizational responsibilities through managerial roles has a significant impact on the management of organizational knowledge. In most organizations, the responsibility for the domains in Figure 8.5 rests with particular managerial roles. Due to the effects of organizational hierarchy, managerial roles are differentially positioned to generate, communicate and exploit information. They provide access to different realms of ideas, different groups of people and different opportunities for utilizing ideas. For example:

- *Senior executives* – are positioned to take an external focus and possess an internal overview. They have shareholder insight and the organizational power and visibility to influence the communication and exploitation of ideas. Because of this, they are able to generate ideas about future direction (domain C), communicate this to senior colleagues for implementation and ensure that this information is exploited for organizational gain.

- *Functional managers* – are well placed organizationally to understand strategic direction as well as operational performance. They are able to generate information about gaps in current strategic capabilities (domain B) and work with managers to improve performance in these key areas.

- *Front-line managers* – are well placed organizationally to understand strategically relevant performance requirements as well as operational issues. They know about current performance levels (domain A) and work to improve alignment and productivity.

- *Technical specialists* – are well placed to understand technical problems and possibilities, such as know-how to enhance products, services or competencies (domain D) and work with managers to exploit these ideas.

Explicitly recognizing that each manager has unique access to generate, communicate or exploit is an important condition of effectiveness. However, faced with multiple tasks, competing agendas, pressures of time, change and ambiguity, it is all too easy for managers to become disconnected from how they can really add value. Under these conditions, managers easily lose sight of their unique focus. They begin to under-utilize or, worse still, undermine others' contributions. As Bailey and Clarke state: 'Senior executives can find themselves in domain B, "Shooting from the hip" – generating short-term reactive strategic shifts, without apparent relation to future strategy or current capability. Functional managers can find themselves "hands on", "lost in operational detail" in domain A, "seizing the reins" – taking control. Meanwhile, front-line managers, "head down" in domain A, just get on with the job – turning the handle – and technical specialists resort to producing quick fixes expensively or "divorced from reality", "indulging in ivory tower thinking" in domain D. And as for domain C – strategic potential – it appears that there's no one there!'

If a company is to become a high performer, then it must focus managers on their unique role and learn how to leverage it for organizational benefit. This comes from the ability to direct the right ideas to or from the right people in the right way from one knowledge domain to another. This is the hallmark of effective, influential and organizationally valuable individuals. Appropriate change comes about when the right knowledge is made available, shared and used to organizational advantage. In other words, to be effective, managers need to keep a focus on their own role but be active in other knowledge domains by communicating relevant information within and across domains.

Effectiveness is about the successful flow of ideas. It hinges on where individuals get ideas from, to whom they communicate them to, and how successful they are in getting them exploited when they are not in a position themselves to get ideas directly or to exploit them. This is the fundamental issue of managerial influence – how to get someone to act on an idea they would not otherwise do.

To illustrate this notion of greater personal effectiveness, each of the roles is elaborated next.

Front-line managers

Performance management (domain A) is the essential focus for front-line managers. Front-line managers' focus of knowledge is about the operations that enable the delivery of strategic goals. Their prime activity is to establish, monitor and manage the operational processes using that knowledge. However, to add value they need to look beyond this domain. They need to seek and communicate ideas gained through their work activity to others who can exploit them in other domains. It is this activity which leverages tacit knowledge and potentially creates value, and enables effective change. Success in this provides the individual with personal credibility, influence and visibility.

What this highlights is that for front-line managers to be organizationally effective and enhance their personal status they need to:

■ Understand and work with the bigger organizational picture.

■ Have a view about wider business issues, to enable them to better position their ideas about performance, competence and technical issues in context.

■ Know who in their organization has a managerial interest in the different domains.

■ Understand what is actionable by people in these other roles.

■ Think and act outside the box so as to influence others who can take action around issues of significant organizational currency.

The personal motivation for front-line managers to adopt a KM perspective lies in understanding exactly how, by generating, communicating and exploiting information from within domain A, they can increase their visibility and credibility. The use of internal marketing can help in all of these areas.

Senior functional or operational managers

Senior and operational managers' role is to co-ordinate and implement strategy through the expertise and activities of their own specialist disciplines. They have access to information about functional requirements, performance expectations, resource, and technical capability and potential. Their activities focus on using that information to ensure continuing strategic fit (domain B). To add value, these managers need to combine their knowledge with that of other managers in domain B. In this way, they facilitate co-ordinated business effort. These managers need to use their knowledge to align operations with strategy and be informed of any newly emerging trends or organizational competencies. They also need to know about *how* and *where* to invest in development activities (technical, product, people) to create the greatest organizational benefit.

Managers in these roles need to work with peers across the organization on the issues in domain B to:

■ Generate and share ideas about how well the organization is performing against current strategic aspirations.

■ Understand new strategy requirements against the company's internal competency profile.

■ Exploit ideas through agreed changes to maintain strategic fit.

Managers in these senior roles are often trapped in functional mindsets. They narrowly optimize operational performance, forgetting how the pieces of functional expertise come together to create overall performance. This leads to optimizing parts but sub-optimizing the whole. Unfortunately, it is common for managers in these roles to find themselves dragged down into the minute details of their own operational responsibility. Often, they end up focusing on areas of past success and strength rather than rejuvenating and building for the future. The net result: they put all their energies in a narrow area of knowledge leverage, ignoring other alternatives which in the long run may hold higher potential and impact. In this way, they seriously under-leverage the potential of knowledge.

To be more influential, these managers need to be able to think and act more from a general management viewpoint, not just their own specialist perspective. They need to:

- Know which managerial knowledge is critical to future strategic direction and operational performance.

- Appreciate what others uniquely bring to the table.

- Be clear about what and how they really add value to their organization, so that their contribution to the strategic fit arena can be properly put in context.

- Be critical about how their own specialism makes a difference to others.

The motivation for managers in these roles to adopt a knowledge and learning perspective is to be able to understand and use the real added value of their specialism, overcome frustrations in getting co-operation from their peers and be able to extend their sphere of influence in getting things done.

Senior executives

Top management ask and address the question of 'Where are we going to compete in the future?' (domain C). They are positioned to develop and exploit strategic ideas and to set conditions for the flow of knowledge around the business to ensure that managerial decisions are taken effectively to address continual change requirements. To add value, they need to leverage external knowledge that others are not party to, make informed judgements about trends in the uncertain future so that they can create clarity of direction. They then need to communicate well and widely that which is fundamental and critical to organizational success.

All too easily, senior executives become stuck in current strategic, or even operational, issues in domain B and lose sight of the need to generate the questions about domain C issues. Senior executives have to step up from managing to leading. They must use their organizational visibility to convey what is strategically important. They must focus their activities to create knowledge cultures that value creating, sharing and leveraging knowledge. Their value-adding activity is to develop a clear vision of strategic potential. This requires a deep grasp of the external business and industry environment to spot opportunities. Visions in themselves are insufficient. Senior executives must devote time to communicate them in ways that are relevant to those around the organization who are best placed to implement them.

Senior executives' motivation to adopt a KM perspective lies in being able to:

- Understand where to focus their time to maximize organizational impact.

- Know where and how to promote better utilization of other managerial resources.

- Know what to focus on in communicating to people throughout the organization so as to influence culture and performance.

Technical specialists

The task of enhancing operational performance (domain D) is the primary focus of 'technical' specialists (e.g. R&D experts, IT specialists). Typically, these roles bring specialist knowledge to bear upon the processes, products and challenges of the company.

The major knowledge management challenge for this group is how they can really leverage their specialist know-how for organizational advantage and not become ivory tower thinkers disconnected from the real world of business. The emphasis for this group is to be able to communicate and exploit ideas with the rest of the business, particularly with front-line managers in domain A and senior executives in domain C. There is the need to translate specialist knowledge in managerially relevant terms. This means getting beyond technical jargon and overcoming the tendency to communicate technicalities at the expense of explaining how something works in a language others can comprehend.

Overall, internal marketing's role is to help the process of establishing personal relevance. Internal marketing can do this by:

1 *Establishing status* (of current engagement).

2 *Establishing focus and energy*. Where are people spending their energy and time?

3 *Establishing effectiveness*. How well are people performing in these knowledge tasks/domain areas?

4 *Establishing conduciveness*. How good is the company in creating the conditions for employees to create and share knowledge in and across domains?

5 *Establishing improvement areas*. What are the improvement areas and how can improvements be made?

6 *Establishing actions*. What can be done to improve their influence and benefits?

7 *Establishing accountability*. Who needs to do what and when?

8 *Establishing communication*. How effective is the company at helping the individual to generate, communicate and exploit ideas for organizational benefit? What could increase this effectiveness?

9 *Establishing individual cost-benefits.* In what ways are people benefiting in carrying out knowledge activities?

10 *Establishing relevance.* Are knowledge activities relevant to them? Do they enhance their influence, position, etc.?

11 *Establishing leverage.* What knowledge should the company be seeking to leverage? With whom? What are the benefits of this to those involved?

12 *Establishing organizational cost-benefit.* In what way and to what extent does the organization benefit from these activities?

Internal marketing can be used to conduct an internal audit to define the personal relevance, current status and actionability of engaging in knowledge activities. Internal marketing can also be used to tackle a host of other interpersonal and organizational factors, especially the issues of power and politics. Managers, when they begin to generate, communicate and exploit knowledge in their own and across domains, inevitably begin to challenge the status quo. This sets in motion changes that start to alter power balances. Often, such shifts lead to power and political strife. Not only does internal marketing play a role in communicating change and channelling relevant information, the way the communication is managed influences the social and political context. Internal marketing, if used properly, can also be used to understand and manage the socio-political context.

Internal marketing communications for knowledge management and learning

Communication is a critical factor to the successful implementation of any change in an organization. This is even more critical for a knowledge and learning organization. What is often missing in workplace communications is the listening aspect. Listening is critical in understanding what the other person heard and perceived. This is especially critical when a message (e.g. strategy) is passed through many layers of the organization. Each layer filters the information through its own bias before passing it on to the next. Appelbaum and Gallagher[25] propose a model of how the communication loop needs to be closed for an organization to progress in the intended direction (see Figure 8.6).

As we noted earlier, knowledge management and learning organization is very much about dialogue. The flow of ideas throughout the organization plays an important role in knowledge creation. Communication is not just verbal. A company communicates not just through explicit messages, but also by its measurement system, its reward system and through

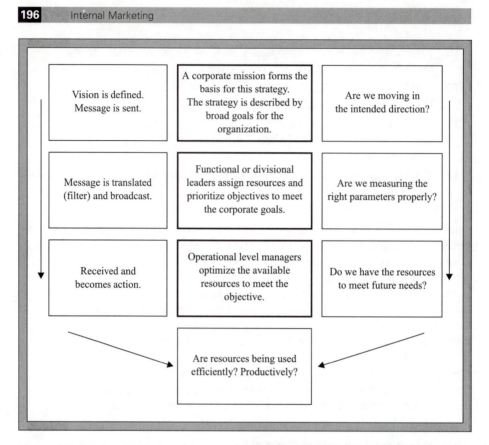

Figure 8.6 Closing the communications loop. *Source*: Appelbaum, S. H. and Gallagher, J. (2000). The competitive advantage of learning. *Journal of Workplace Learning*, 12 (2), 40–56.

its structure. This includes actions such as training and development and any other artefact that is created. Particularly powerful is the communication that occurs through the articulation of objectives. The power of objectives is often underestimated. Once decisions concerning objectives are cascaded into the company, they can have a profound impact. Once defined by a list of objectives and a set of measurements and rewards, an organization will perceive that everything not on the list is unimportant.

Measurement and communication

Vision and strategies of a company dictate what needs to be measured. Measurement must be linked to goals and cannot be mutually exclusive.

Once a company has devised its plans, the next step is to communicate it to its employees. Measuring non-financial indicators is an important step in communicating (what is important), training (what to look at, what to train for) and organizational development (how performance in one area impacts upon the group). Selecting the appropriate measurement metrics is critical. Kaplan and Norton[26] suggest the use of a balance of performance drivers and outcome measures to determine if an organization is making progress toward its goals. The balanced scorecard, by incorporating a broad set of measures, adopts a holistic view of an organization. As Kaplan and Norton note: 'flying an airplane with the altimeter is fine, until you run out of fuel'. This contrast holds well for companies whose sole preoccupation is the monthly bottom line. If measurement is narrow then it drives a very narrow set of behaviours. The risk in this approach is one of gaining in a single area but sub-optimizing the totality, especially so if the company ignores critical variables[27]. Vision and strategies of a company dictate what needs to get measured and the measurement must be linked to goals, and the two cannot be mutually exclusive. To measure an employee it is necessary, likewise, to take a holistic view. One way of doing this is to construct an employee balanced scorecard (see Figure 8.7). An employee scorecard should be constructed not simply to reflect efficiency and productivity (as is typically reflected in rewards and pay), but also include less tangible factors, such as how does the job enhance a person's skills and competence, how does it bring joy and motivation, and how does it enhance the self-esteem of the individual. Taking an encompassing view of the employee and his job allows for a more balanced assessment of what to do and how to move an individual toward customer consciousness.

A knowledge and learning organization must have an appropriate measurement system. Without measurement systems and tools, it is difficult to move from theory to reality because there is no reliable feedback to build improvements upon. Measurements assess the current, in order to determine which actions must be taken to manage the progression towards a learning organization[28]. Metrics must be:

1 Meaningful.
2 Manageable.
3 Measurable.

Each of the three Ms indicates why it is so difficult to find examples of learning organizations.

Knowledge management is concerned with which knowledge should be available where, when and in what form within an organization. Internal marketing is concerned with assembling, synthesizing and packaging knowledge to enable effective transfer and action. Internal marketing is therefore a fundamental enabler of KM. Internal marketing attempts to

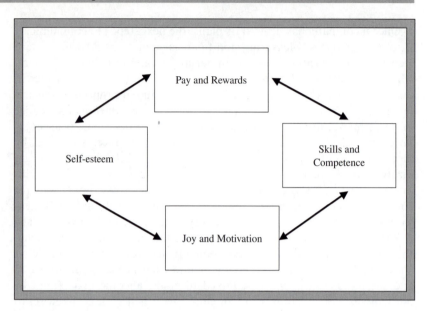

Figure 8.7 Employee balanced scorecard.

improve the processes and systems used to transfer and manage knowl-edge, and does it as an ongoing, continuous critical function. Internal marketing in this respect works like a proposal to its employees, to engender specific types of actions and behaviours. Proposals are, first and foremost, '*products*' that include a host of information and educa-tion. Through a choreographed process of generation, transfer and con-gealment, the internal marketing proposal is designed to sell both the benefits derived from implementing desired actions from the employee, and also training and tools to accomplish all required activities. In addi-tion, the proposal must convey not just tangibles but speak to the intan-gible values of the individual.

One of the most important aspects of internal marketing is commu-nication with employees. Internal communication lets employees know what is going on so that they can do their jobs effectively and efficiently. This is the basis for serving external customers and internal customers well. Internal cues and communications signal to employees which activ-ities are acceptable and which are not. Pronouncements issued from senior management in company reports are not very good at dispersing and internalizing strategic knowledge throughout the company. Getting people to share their knowledge requires new processes but, more impor-tantly, it requires setting a new covenant between employer and employ-ees. Workers have to be reassured that they will still be valued after they give up their know-how. In short, it involves treating the employees as partners in the firms.

Leadership and internal marketing communication

Top management play a visible role. Senior managers act as knowledge and learning champions. Their actions are very important cues in supporting implementation. What they do and how they facilitate programmes lends support to the idea of knowledge management. Their actions can help to overcome resistance, help the sharing of ideas and enhance involvement in activities that promote learning. They can trigger a positive learning cycle, which embeds new concepts and ideas via a process of materialization and internalization. Subsequently, action is created.

Figure 8.8 illustrates the example of the promotion of learning through materialization, internalization, support and commitment, and practical activity. In the case of a positive cycle, ideas are actively transformed into action in the implantation of knowledge management thinking. Learning functions as a mechanism by which new ideas and thinking are implanted. Applied to the process of organizational implementation, learning occurs through the stages of materializing ideas, internalizing ideas and concepts, gaining support to the idea, preparing a plan of action and, finally, activity. This cycle of four stages represents an ideal framework for a cyclical learning process. Through participation in continuous organization-wide training, people learn the idea of knowledge management and resistance is gradually overcome. In the course of the process, people also learn new working methods. Mental integration of organization members increases involvement and supports implementation.

Figure 8.9 shows a negative cycle of implementation. This leads the organization to avoid effective learning. When managerial perceptions

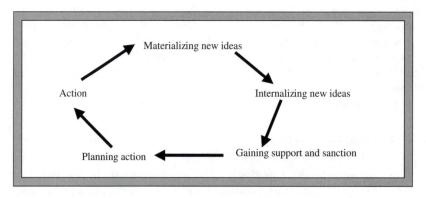

Figure 8.8 The positive implementation cycle.

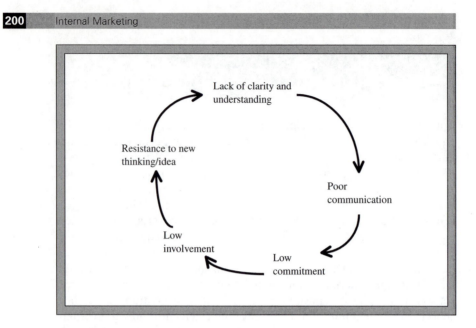

Figure 8.9 The negative implementation cycle.

are unclear, employee commitment is adversely affected. Vagueness and low commitment have an unfavourable effect on the progress of the KM programme. Ideas are not shared and sufficient support to the knowledge and learning effort is not gained. As a consequence, the effort falters and ends up failing to prosper across the organization.

Nucor's Chairman's Kenneth Iverson notes in reference to the company's learning efforts: 'We've tried a lot of technologies, and our success is probably 30 per cent the result of new technology – and 70 per cent due to our people'[29]. Clearly, employees are the primary factor driving the success of his firm. This is an important aspect of the knowledge economy: as companies invest in technology they overlook the fact that the payback is dictated by people using equipment and systems, not the machines themselves. Indeed, as Sheridan[30] goes on to suggest, there are two fundamental ingredients: I think you need a good strategy, but you also need to do the dailies well. Building an effective global company is 10 per cent strategy and 90 per cent implementation of the daily requirements.

The implications of this for organizational learning are:

1 Companies making decisions based only on financials will not fully utilize all of the assets that they have at their disposal.
2 Investment in technology, although important, is not the final answer. Developing a company that captures the ideas and knowledge of the people that engineer the system brings a greater return.

Knowledge management implementation is an incremental process. It needs to start by the development of a common language for knowledge management. This occurs through materialization of ideas. Adopting and internalizing knowledge management thinking is a major challenge of learning. If this is not tackled adequately, unclear perceptions will develop and lead to a weak common foundation. This results in insufficient support for the knowledge initiative, which weakens commitment to it. Low commitment generates resistance to the adoption. This is a challenge for top management, in particular. In order to avoid transient knowledge management efforts, top management must internalize and communicate the values and vision to create a common language and increase commitment. This is one of management's most significant tasks in creating a knowledge management culture. Promotion of concepts, values and principles cannot be overstated.

Language is a very important aspect of communication. And 'languaging' is the art of word choice[31]. To ensure that knowledge is understood and shared effectively and efficiently, companies must develop and implement an enterprise-wide vocabulary. Great care is needed in defining or redefining the *images* employees hold and the *language* the organization uses. Language exerts a profound influence on perceptions of ourselves, our companies, products and indeed our entire world view. Consequently, language impacts the way we manage and the way we behave.

In this role, it is important to remember to use metaphors and *transformed iconography* (or 'word pictures'), because they expand the domain of possible and realizable interactions and approaches. They are rich transporters of information. 'Metaphors allow the transfer of bands of information where other means only transfer smaller bits'[32]. New metaphors and words create not just new linguistic domains, but enable capture and promotion of new concepts, thoughts, discourse and behaviours. Used properly, these can help guide business actions. They offer senior managers a multidimensional mode of understanding and transfer mechanisms.

The implications of communication for organizational learning are:

- Communication, sending and receiving, ties pieces of the learning jigsaw together.
- Managers need to realize that they are communicating in everything that they say and do, and they communicate most clearly when the two align.
- There are filters everywhere; just because your message was clear in your mind does not mean that it is clear for everyone to whom it may have been intended.

Undoubtedly, the most common internal marketing application is in the crafting of internal communication strategies. When this is done in parallel with external marketing communications, advertised promises stand a better chance of being fulfilled to the required level of performance, because staff are better prepared to perform them.

A story that has become part of IBM folklore describes how a young engineer who was responsible for a very risky project that cost $10 million went to Thomas Watson, president of IBM, after it was found that the project could not be implemented. 'I guess you want my resignation,' said the engineer to Watson. Watson replied: 'You can't be serious. We just spent 10 million dollars educating you.' Watson's behaviour influenced the IBM members' willingness to take risks, especially in the area of new ideas and development.

Leaders influence organizational values relevant to the functioning of the organization. Even more, just as leaders influence values, they also influence the forms of thinking, the level of motivation and the behaviours relevant to organizational learning. They exert this influence through several channels. Jan Carlzon[33], CEO of Scandinavian Airlines (SAS), coined the phrase 'moments of truth' to refer to those critical episodes of behaviour that transmit clear messages about 'what is important here', 'how to behave', 'who is important', ' who is a role model in the company' and so forth. These actions become behavioural co-ordinates for others in the organization. Popper and Lipshitz[34] highlight three channels of leadership influence:

1 *Time devoted by the manager*. There is a saying that 'the urgent tends to take precedence over the important'. The daily tasks, the need to meet short-term schedules, often take precedence over dealing with important long-term issues. Allocating 'manager time' is thus a clear signal to the staff as to what is more important and what is not. The fact that managers who are extremely busy with urgent tasks invest 'manager time' (which is a very expensive resource) in some actions and not in others influences employees' order of priorities. The fact of allocating precious 'manager time' to an issue conveys an unmistakable message concerning the importance of that value.

2 *Managers' attention*. Managers' attention has an effect similar to the investment of 'manager time'. Managers who consistently pay attention to certain subjects send a clear message about its importance. For instance, a manager of a company wishing to convey the message that client satisfaction was more important than profits didn't let a day pass without asking every local manager what the clients said about them and their service. This consistent interest conveyed a message that eventually became internalized.

3 *Reward and recognition*. Channels of reward and recognition are the most common means of influence in organizations. They establish criteria regarding the desired behaviours. These channels

include various bonuses, letters of appreciation, promotion, attractive assignments, allocation of resources, and punishment.

Managers who value and reward learning activities reward people who contribute to organizational learning. They use aspects of learning as part of the process of evaluating employees, and make learning activity a criterion for promotion. By doing so, they reinforce the behaviours required for knowledge creation and learning. On the other hand, punishment for mistakes and impatience reduces the likelihood of sharing and transfer. Even worse, they can totally stop the behaviours of sharing, dialogue and communication that are so essential for learning and knowledge management.

The channels of influence described above affect people's actual willingness to put organizational learning on the organizational agenda. However, even if learning becomes part of the agenda, that in itself is not enough. To manage knowledge and learning the company must root it deeply in the culture of the organization.

The main problem in creating and maintaining learning organizations lies in the tendency of people to safeguard their 'positive image' (this is why most people tend to report successes and try to avoid reporting failures and mistakes, even though there might be important lessons to be learnt from failures)[35]. One major challenge in building learning organizations is to reduce the impact of 'defensive routines'. Since 'defensive routines' are the natural tendencies of people, there is a need to create psychological conditions that change these tendencies and encourage people to be more accountable, more willing to be transparent, more facts (or issue) oriented: in short, less defensive. In this sense, leadership's actions are highly influential because they have high impact in creating an *atmosphere* that affects learning processes in organizations. The aspects of leadership that generate values conducive to learning are[36]:

- Transparency (i.e. relating to facts without defensive routines).
- Issue orientation (focusing on performance).
- Accountability (freedom from the tendency to avoid personal responsibility).

Indeed, 'eliminate fear from the organization' was one of the principles formulated by Deming for introducing TQM to organizations. This principle came from an understanding that 'improvement teams' become mere ritual if those involved in them do not feel the psychological safety that allows them to bring up facts and discuss them openly even if the facts were unpleasant. Psychological safety is a state in which people feel safe to candidly discuss their mistakes: what they think and how they feel[37]. Behaving in new ways and doing things differently can involve some degree of unlearning. This can be emotionally difficult, and often raises anxiety due to feelings of incompetence[38]. People act transparently and investigate their own mistakes with integrity when they are psychologically safe rather than under threat. Leaders facilitate organizational learning if they are able to inspire trust: trust in their leadership and trust in the processes and system, and specifically, trust in the 'rules of the game' maintained in the organization.

The importance of trust to organizational learning has been demonstrated in some studies[39]. Establishing 'conditions of trust' is no less than establishing 'psychological conditions for effective organizational learning'. Gambetta[40] suggests that building of trust requires:

- Consistency.
- Keeping promises.
- Discretion.
- Morality.
- Fairness.
- Openness.
- Accessibility.

Corporate leaders who are able to inspire trust possess four key characteristics[41]:

1 *Idealized influence*. Words reinforced by behaviours form a collective and social orientation. Leaders influence by role modelling their behaviour to match their words.

   Example: CEO Ralph Larsen of Johnson & Johnson explained his readiness to lose $240 million in earnings in the Tylenol case because 'if we keep trying to do what is right, at the end of the day we believe the market will reward us'. Senior executives of the company consistently devote considerable time and energy to maintain in practice the 50-year-old credo created by Robert Wood Johnson, son of the founder. The credo emphasizes honesty, integrity and respect for people.

2 *Inspirational motivation*. Leaders motivate and inspire by creating impelling visions of the organization's future in which the organization is seen to prosper. These leaders praise acts done for the common good, express optimism about the future of the organization, show enthusiasm for shared success and radiate confidence that the aims will be achieved. They exhibit clarity and commitment in thought and action.

3 *Intellectual stimulation*. Leaders can provide intellectual stimulation by exhibiting a willingness to constantly examine the status quo and not to see the existing situation as an immutable fact. Leaders who can stimulate their employees intellectually help their people to look at old problems in new ways, encouraging them to 'think differently'. They legitimize creativity and innovation.

4 *Individualized consideration*. Leaders who are high in personalized attention are able to inspire and motivate their employees. They achieve this by treating each employee as an individual with needs, abilities and aspirations different from those of others. They help strengthen their workers' capabilities and overcome their weaknesses through training and guidance. They don't punish mistakes but show a willingness to see mistakes as opportunities for learning. When mistakes are made, they are more concerned about asking what happened than finding out who is to blame. Success is not taken for granted but studied as part of the developmental approach.

These leadership behaviours contribute enormously to the formation of values and atmosphere that is conducive to knowledge management and learning. Such leaders are transformational leaders because they inspire high levels of trust. They are able to elicit a more idealistic and ethical level of thinking. They generate more collaboration and sharing, more openness and honesty, more credibility, more willingness to take responsibility, and higher quality performance.

Exhibit 8.1. Virgin: values and leadership as symbols for employee behaviour and action

As companies struggle to find something that gives them a competitive edge, it is no longer sufficient to energize employees through publication of bland corporate newsletters or hold annual outings. Companies have to try to use insights and strategies that they have deployed for acquiring and holding on to external customers on their employees as well. This has led many to turn their attention to internal

(continued)

marketing, which while it might possess the appeal and glamour of above-the-line advertising, is increasingly being perceived as a highly effective means of delivering to customer expectations.

It is a fact that in many corporations employees feel undervalued, uninvolved and lack confidence in their organizations' leaders and vision. This sums up the challenge for internal marketing programmes. In these circumstances, as Anne Gilbert, director at the Marketing & Communications Agency (MCA), highlights: 'Asking people to be brand ambassadors is almost like getting them to be internal customers. It means thinking like a marketer. Instead of having fizzy drinks or crisps as the product, the product is the organization, and its goals and its people are the target market. So, just as with external marketing, you have to know what makes them tick, and what motivates them. Why would they buy the goals and objectives?'

Alison Copus, general manager of marketing at Virgin Atlantic Airways, notes that this involves a lot more than coming up with mere mission and vision statements: 'What counts are your values, and planting those values into employees' hearts and minds: I think values are more powerful than rules or mission statements because of two things. First, whether they are employees or customers, they give you something with which to identify. And that identification is a very, very strong bond...Second, if you have one shared set of values – shared between your customers and employees – you have a sporting chance of saying what you mean and meaning what you say at every point of contact.'

Copus considers the little things to often be the most important. For instance, the last thing she would wish to lose from her marketing budget is the annual party, to which all employees and their partners and children are invited.

Virgin has a big advantage when it comes to instilling common shared identity and brand values: Richard Branson, who epitomizes and embodies these values. Branson's personal actions and behaviour in relating to employees is crucial in setting the tone of Virgin's employee-focused culture. In Virgin's case, successfully getting its employees to buy into the values of Virgin and its leader is at the heart of its success and truly defines the way it operates.

Source: Mazur, L. (1999). Unleashing employees' true value: employees can be your company's most valuable marketing asset. *Marketing*, April, 22–4.

Leaders promote knowledge and learning in three key ways:

1 Putting learning *on the agenda* as a central issue. This they do through their ability to influence key channels (namely 'manager's time', 'manager's attention', and the organization's reward and recognition aspects).

2 Building the *structural* foundations needed to turn individual learning into organizational learning (processes and systems for enhanced sharing).

3 Creating cultural and psychological conditions that facilitate learning (i.e. establishing 'conditions of trust').

A simple template for initiating a knowledge management and learning programme is given below as a set of steps.

■ **Step 1**. Organizing for KM must start off with education and training for top and upper level managers. This prepares the ground for the sharing of knowledge thinking and getting the entire organization involved.

■ **Step 2**. Mapping the company's intellectual capital and competencies against strategic demands made by the external environment.

■ **Step 3**. The next step in practice is to formulate a knowledge and learning policy, and put it forward in an understandable and sufficiently concrete form to guide daily operations. Top managements' deep commitment is required when the policy is put into practice. This is the way to get lower level (middle) managers and the organization members involved in a continuous move toward a positive learning cycle.

■ **Step 4**. Communicate a clear vision for the firm.

■ **Step 5**. Develop a business language, or lexicon, with shared meanings and nuances to foster generalized understanding of strategic goals.

■ **Step 6**. Put in place structures and systems to facilitate multi-directional flow of knowledge throughout the organization to meet employee requirements.

■ **Step 7**. Put in place assessment frameworks to ensure behaviours are aligned to desired actions.

■ **Step 8**. Act on feedback to align the company to strategic goals.

Summary

In conclusion, succeeding in the new world requires a sophisticated understanding of the rules of competition and a deep appreciation of the competencies of the company itself. Managers who think strategy is easy, and implementation more difficult, do not put enough effort into strategy. Certainly, sophisticated understanding doesn't come from 3-day strategy retreats. On the other hand, you can't implement any strategy if you haven't developed a plan, communication tools or a feedback system.

On their own, calls to mobilize energies of the organization do little to ensure the survival of companies in the modern era. The new world is filled with flux and demands flexible open structures and understanding. Management hierarchies that characterized the twentieth century have become very dated in the face of new challenges. New approaches based on partnership that incorporate values such as co-operation, caring, creativity, empathy and connectedness are needed for the knowledge era. Building and sustaining competitive advantage requires leveraging the collective knowledge base of a company and fostering a 'learning organization'. This demands more than simply investing capital into existing infrastructures and systems of management. In such environments, translating meaningful opportunities into market successes means that employees cannot be treated as mindless cogs in a machine or line items on a financial spreadsheet. Knowledge management is more than just sending employees to a training school; it is about the ability to harness and use the knowledge for competitive advantage. It is also about the ability of an organization to learn from itself, its mistakes, its inefficiency and its employees. Managers must identify gaps between what they have and what they need to have if they are going to create the organizational structure to implement the strategy.

Internal marketing is an unusually slippery concept, easy to visualize and yet exasperatingly difficult. Internal marketing is a concept that is socially constructed and context-specific in nature. It cannot be understood without relating the concept to the company, organization or person who gives meaning to it. Furthermore, internal marketing is holistic. This is, in fact, an argument for internal marketing adoption, since it plays a role in all functions and operations in an organization. It is a 'total' managerial approach for co-ordination and integration. Managers practising internal marketing will play an important role in combining and integrating different perspectives. Using internal marketing management can create a commonly shared and clearly understood language for the entire organization and put it in systems, processes and structures to get the sharing actions enacted. To do this, however, managers must themselves first build a deep understanding of internal marketing, if they are to use it as a means to enhance organizational knowledge and learning.

Knowledge and learning do not constitute a simple 'me too' experience. They require much work. A company has to consider what it wants to be and *what resources* it has (strategy). It needs to share the strategy with employees (*communicate*). It must define progress and success (*measurements*), then look for gaps between their current reality and future reality (*feedback*). Finally, it must strive to narrow the human resource gaps (*hire, train and develop*). This process is one of continuous internal marketing.

Good ideas and good intentions that are poorly designed and improperly implemented soon become extremely costly experiences. Introducing new initiatives such as knowledge management easily wreaks havoc if expectations, resources and commitment are not aligned. The knowledge management journey is not a simple one: it challenges many fundamental beliefs and operating principles. It takes sustained effort and time because it involves changing employee behaviours, perceptions and beliefs, and not just rearranging the organizational furniture.

References

1. Field, N. E. and Yang, H. (1990). The organisation that learns. *Fortune*, 12 March, p. 133.
2. Edmondson, A. and Moingeon, B. (1998). From organisational learning to the learning organisation. *Management Learning*, **29** (1), 5–20.
3. McGill, M. E. and Slocum, J. W. Jr (1993). Unlearning the organisation. *Organisational Dynamics*, **22** (2), 67–79.
4. Senge, P. M., Roberts, C., Ross, R. B., Smith, B. J. and Kleinter, A. (1994). *The Fifth Discipline Fieldbook: Strategies and Tools for Building a Learning Organisation*, p. 24. New York: Doubleday.
5. McGill, M. E. and Slocum, J. W. Jr (1993). Op. cit.
6. Dixon, N. M. (1994). *The Organisational Learning Cycle: How We Can Learn Collectively*. London: McGraw-Hill.
7. Mezias, S. J. and Glynn, M. A. (1993). The three faces of corporate renewal: institution, revolution, and evolution. *Strategic Management Journal*, **14**, 77–101.
8. Senge, P. M. (1990). *The Fifth Discipline: The Art and Practice of the Learning Organisation*, p. 73. New York: Doubleday.
9. Senge, P. M. et al. (1994). Op. cit.
10. Bennett, J. K. and O'Brien, M. J. (1994). The 12 building blocks of the learning organisation. *Training*, **31** (June), 41–8.
11. Senge, P. M. (1990). Op. cit., p. 209.
12. Senge, P. M. (1990). Op. cit., p. 154.
13. Ibid.
14. Watkins, K. E. and Marsick, V. J. (1993). *Sculpting the Learning Organisation: Lessons in the Art and Science of Systematic Change*, p. xii. San Francisco: Jossey-Bass.

15. Angus, J., Patel, J. and Harty, J. (1998). Knowledge management: great concept ... but what is it? *Information Week*, No. 673.
16. Binney, D. (2000). The knowledge management spectrum – understanding the KM landscape. *Journal of Knowledge Management*, **5** (1), 21–32.
17. Davenport, T. H. and Klahr, P. (1998). Managing customer support knowledge. *California Management Review*, **40** (3), 195–208.
18. Edvinsson, L. and Malone, M. S. (1997). *Intellectual Capital: Realizing your Company's True Value by Finding its Hidden Brainpower*, 1st edn. New York: Harper Business.
19. Hansen, M. T., Nohira, N. and Tierney, T. (1999). What's your strategy for managing knowledge? *Harvard Business Review*, March/April, 106–16.
20. Malhotra, Y. (1998). Knowledge management for the new world of business. < http://www.brint.com/km/whatis.htm >
21. Ballantyne, D. (2000). Internal relationship marketing: a strategy for knowledge renewal. *International Journal of Bank Marketing*, **18** (1), 274–86.
22. Katz, D. and Kahn, R. L. (1966). *The Social Psychology of Organisations*, pp. 14–29. New York: Wiley.
23. Nonaka, I. and Takeuchi, H. (1995). *The Knowledge Creating Company: How Japanese Companies Create the Dynamics of Innovation*. New York: Oxford University Press.
24. Bailey, C. and Clarke, M. (2001). Managing knowledge for personal and organisational benefit. *Journal of Knowledge Management*, **5** (1), 58–67.
25. Appelbaum, S. H. and Gallagher, J. (2000). The competitive advantage of learning. *Journal of Workplace Learning*, **12** (2), 40–56.
26. Kaplan, R. S. and Norton, D. P. (1996). *The Balanced Scorecard: Translating Strategy into Action*. New York: The Free Press.
27. Sheridan, J. R. (1997). The best vs the rest: a glimpse at the strategies, strengths, and management styles behind the numbers. *Industry Week*, August, 70.
28. Appelbaum, S. H. and Reichart, W. (1998). How to measure an organisation's learning ability: a learning orientation – part 1. *Journal of Workplace Learning*, **9** (7), 225–39.
29. Sheridan, J. R. (1997). Op. cit.
30. Ibid.
31. Roos, J. and Oliver, D. (1999). *Striking a Balance: Complexity and Knowledge Landscapes*. Maidenhead: McGraw-Hill.
32. Lissack, M. R. (1996). Complexity metaphors and the management of a knowledge based enterprise: an exploration of discovery. < http://www.lissack.com/writings/proposal.htm >
33. Carlzon, J. (1989). *Moments of Truth*. New York: Harper & Row.
34. Popper, M. and Lipshitz, R. (2000). Installing mechanisms and instilling values: the role of leaders in organisational learning. *The Learning Organisation*, **7** (3), 1–12.
35. Argyris, C. and Schon, D. (1996). *Organisational Learning: Theory Methods and Practice*. Reading, MA: Addison-Wesley.
36. Popper, M. and Lipshitz, R. (2000). Op. cit.
37. Popper, M. and Lipshitz, R. (1998). Organizational learning mechanisms: a structural and cultural approach to organisational learning. *Journal of Applied Behavioural Science*, **34** (2), 161–79.

38. Schein, E. (1993). How can organisations learn faster? The challenge of entering the green room. *Sloan Management Review*, **34** (2), 85–92.
39. Heavans, S. and Child, J. (1999). Mediating individual and organisational learning: the role of teams and trust. Paper presented at the 3rd Conference on Organisational Learning, Lancaster, 6–8 June.
40. Gambetta, D. (ed.) (1988). Can we trust trust? In *Making and Breaking Cooperative Relations*, pp. 213–38. New York: Basil Blackwell.
41. Bass, B. M. and Avolio, B. J. (1996). *Manual for the Multifactor Leadership Questionnaire*. Palo Alto, CA: Mind Garden.

Section III

Internal Marketing Case Studies

Atlantic Richfield Company: using internal marketing to implement change

The Atlantic Richfield organization (ARCO) consists of a number of semi-autonomous operating companies, with a corporate overseeing unit. The operating companies are variously engaged in oil and gas development, petroleum products and services, coal, copper, chemicals, transportation, international oil and gas development, and new ventures. The major companies are scattered around the USA, with major operating arms having headquarters in Los Angeles, Dallas, Philadelphia and Denver. The management philosophy historically was, and continues to be, one of decentralization and local autonomy.

While many other companies were still considering whether to introduce teleconferencing, debating whether it was an effective tool or a technological fad, ARCO took the lead. As early as 1979, ARCO had began to consider this option.

Two years in after its introduction by ARCO's electronics and telecommunication (E&T) department, ARCO operates a seven-site full-motion video-conferencing system linking facilities in Alaska and the continental US, which has received praise from many satisfied users. Over 90 per cent of the users evaluated ARCOvision (the name given to the company's video conference) as successful and a useful tool for enhancing business communications.

The video conferencing success story is underpinned by successful internal marketing. The journey began with internal market research to investigate the appropriateness of the product for the company.

The challenge

Like any pioneers, ARCO faced a major challenge when it first thought of overhauling ARCOnet (Atlantic Richfield's voice/data network) into a video-conferencing service. Although they were spurred by an enthusiastic CEO who felt video conferencing could supersede the Boeing 747 as a vehicle for long-distance communications, the electronics and tele-communications (E&T) department faced uncertainty on a number of fronts.

- In 1979, no vendor could provide a satellite-based system that served both the continental US and Alaska, which was a basic requirement for the ARCO system.

- Teleconferencing had a decidedly mixed record of accomplishment. Success stories for video conferencing were so few that its very viability was in question. Systems installed on an experimental basis often went begging for use.

- The telecommunication planners did not know whether they faced a receptive or a resistant audience for this new technology. They had no clear notion of who the prospective users were and how they might use video teleconferencing. Essentially, they did not have a good handle on the Atlantic Richfield marketplace.

At the time, ARCO constituted nine semi-autonomous operating companies with major operating company headquarters in Los Angeles, Dallas, Philadelphia and Denver, and with larger operational arms located in Anchorage, Prudhoe Bay (Alaska's North Slope), Houston (Channelview), Louisville, Independence (Kansas) and Waterbury (Connecticut). Even though the operating companies shared the parental umbrella of ARCO Richfield, there were many differences among them, especially in terms of their receptivity to new ideas. A communication service initiated by corporate planners had the potential to be seen either as a good idea or as an unwanted infringement on the operating company autonomy.

Determined to succeed in E&T, planners turned to the Telecommunications Research Group (TRG) – part of the Annenberg School of Communications, University of Southern California – for advice. TRG, who were familiar with the technology and the difficulties of introducing new ideas in corporate settings, set about helping the ARCO team ask and answer the questions necessary to successfully design and implement an innovative communication service. TRG's advice was that the design team consider the Atlantic Richfield organization as a marketplace, and video conferencing as a new product that the team wished to introduce.

TRG proposed a two-pronged research programme:

- gather detailed information about the Atlantic Richfield marketplace;

- initiate interest via 'marketing' of video conferencing.

The logic behind this was that prospective users were largely unaware of the technology and of Atlantic Richfield's plans to implement it. Thus, there was a need to inform or create 'positive' awareness in the market-place, and the design teams needed information about the operating companies, the potential users and uses, and the system requirements.

Internal market research

With the two aims in mind, TRG began internal market research at ARCO by conducting 135 interviews with management to introduce the concept of video conferencing and get an early gauge on potential users' reactions and requirements.

The internal market investigation provided many valuable insights. It highlighted:

■ *Receptivity to the concept.* ARCO's management appeared recep-tive to the idea of 'electronic meetings'. They saw many potential possibilities, yet were cautious about embracing the idea without better knowledge of how it would influence the way they worked.

The internal market research also highlighted that although ARCO had thus far justified video conferencing using a travel displacement rationale, most people stressed positive rather than negative aspects of travel. While employees did not appear to be averse to eliminating some of their travel (long trips for short meetings, trips to locations with particularly difficult access – Alaska in the winter, for example), in general, travel substitution seemed an 'unwise' marketing theme.

Overall, it seemed ARCO personnel were much more intrigued with video conferencing's potential to improve or enhance com-munications with remote locations. What excited them about video conferencing was the potential to do things that currently were impossible or impractical to accomplish. Conversely, only those at the highest organizational levels seemed to get excited about a reduced travel budget.

■ *User needs.* The internal market research also picked up on user requirements for the system. They wanted a system that approxi-mated as closely as possible to face-to-face communications. It also had to be reliable, very easy to use, unobtrusive and flexible. This meant designing a system that would be 'simple and transparent'. Busy executives wanted to be able to walk into the room and meet. Users also wanted a room that felt like a typical ARCO conference room, not a television studio. Security was another precondition for success, because much of the work within ARCO (such as oil-lease bidding) involved highly sensitive materials.

The internal market research helped:

- *Planners set design parameters*, i.e. easy to use, reliable, flexible, secure, comfortable, like other Atlantic Richfield conference rooms, etc. These preferences ran counter to many earlier video conference designs, which provided users with total control over cameras and other system components but were not particularly easy to use.

- *Alert the team to change the marketing theme.* The initial marketing stressed ARCO's plans to introduce video conferencing as travel and cost savings. This led to user concerns about costs: Was this a wise investment? How much would it cost to use the system once it was installed?

  It became clear that planners had to take great care to emphasize the positive and eliminate the negative. Creating positive predispositions toward video conferencing during the design phase was an important first step toward building a ready market for the service. The ensuing publicity and talks with potential users downplayed system costs and emphasized using video conferencing to replace undesirable or nuisance travel.

While system planners directed their attention to the technical matters such as how to provide full-motion, colour and life-size images, TRG set about building a more detailed profile of potential users and their needs. This was done through a random-sample survey of 980 management employees from the different ARCO operating companies. The survey sample design was designed to be representative for all ARCO operations, i.e. location, job types and management levels.

Good internal market research can, by itself, spark interest and involvement in eventual consumers. The in-depth research survey of employees did just that. The 12-page questionnaire got an overwhelming response (87 per cent), with some employees even calling in to ask why they had not received the questionnaires. Many responding employees elaborated in detail how they would use it, what kinds of graphic support they would need and what other locations should be considered, while others provided insights and suggestions about internal marketing, training and how to support usage over the long term.

The survey results revealed not just support and interest in the concept of video teleconferencing, but also differences in perception between different levels and job types over the how and whys.

For example, engineers indicated the highest use of the system because of their heavy travel schedules. Employee relations personnel wanted more face-to-face contact with those in remote locations. They wanted an easy-to-use system that could capture high levels of detail (facial expressions, for example).

Motivational triggers also varied for the different management levels:

- lower-level managers were motivated by the desire for better communications with remote locations;
- higher-level executives were motivated by having an easy-to-use alternative to travel.

Job type and level profiles developed from the survey results permitted ARCO room co-ordinators to tailor their introductory demonstrations to the needs and interests of the different user groups.

The survey also highlighted network modifications. Based on current travel and communication patterns, and employee projections of use, it became evident that system planners needed to add Channelview (Houston) and drop the New York City node, where there was little support for the concept.

A further survey of 300 was conducted over the telephone to get a better picture of the kinds of meetings that potential users were willing to video conference. The emerging profile indicated that meetings averaged about eight participants, with over three-quarters of all meetings involving 12 people or less. Company meetings were typically supported with a variety of visual aids, including viewgraphs, slides, chalkboard, geophysical maps, written documents and computer printouts. The meeting profile directly influenced design of the room and facilities, including how many seats to place in the room and the range of graphic aids. These needs were used to build conference room facilities.

Internal market research on the potential consumers (ARCO management and professional personnel) and the product (ARCOvision) was the first step of the programme. It contributed significantly to the auspicious start. Internal market research was used by the design team to help it create the 'right' tool for the ARCO 'marketplace'. Internal market research collected invaluable information about potential users and their work, the corporate culture and the technology. Clearly, knowing the 'market' pays off, more than 40 per cent of the firm's managerial and professional employees tried ARCOvision in its first year, with only a few indicating that they would not be using it again. Since the system was launched, in Autumn 1983, usage climbed steadily. It was evident that the planners had understood the internal users and designed a 'product' that proved highly useful right from the very beginning.

Supporting components of ARCO's internal marketing

The company utilized a range of activities to reinforce its internal marketing.

Media interest

The 'selling of ARCOvision' began with a mass media send-off. Members of the press were invited to tours in each conferencing site and intercity press conferences were held, such as Los Angeles reporters interviewing Philadelphia officials via ARCOvision. This led to a great deal of both national and local coverage. Articles were also written in ARCO's internal newspaper, announcing the launch of the system and providing details on how to arrange demonstrations.

Video communications

Two videotapes were produced to help market the network internally and support its usage. The first tape described ARCO's communication history and entrance into the world of video communications, and gave a brief overview of the system. This partly humorous tape was used as part of lunchtime ('brown-bag') seminars to ARCO employees. The second was a 5-minute tape explaining how to use ARCOvision. The 'how-to' tape, available in the ARCOvision waiting rooms, was usually played before each meeting in the early months of the system's operations.

Poster campaigns for constant communication

Poster campaigns emphasizing the advantages of video conferencing over travel, the easy-to-use nature of the system, and video conferencing's value as a decision-making tool were also developed and distributed periodically to all ARCOvision locations. Users were also given ARCOvision pins to mark their first video conference. This proved to be a very popular practice and it was to continue for many years.

Promotional efforts

Internal marketing was continuous throughout the first year of operations and involved a range of promotional activities. These included:

- a contest at holiday time with a video conference for family and friends as the prize;
- a slogan contest for ARCOvision coffee mugs.

To keep reminding users of the facility and get them to use it, mugs with the winning slogan, such as 'Keep Productivity in Focus', on the front and 'I use ARCOvision' on the back were awarded for five uses of the service.

To keep the momentum going and also troubleshoot any problems, a conference co-ordinator staffed each ARCOvision room. The co-ordinator was made responsible for conference scheduling, solving routine problems, and developing and maintaining internal marketing momentum. These individuals were carefully selected for their ability to interact successfully with other personnel. They were instrumental in making users comfortable with video conferencing and encouraging repeat usage. They served as system advocates in each of their respective locations, seeking out new users and following up with reminders to 'old' customers of the service. The co-ordinators' demonstration sessions were an extremely useful opportunity for marketing the tool. They demystified the system and encouraged usage through 'success stories' passed on to them. Many users credited the co-ordinators with getting video conferencing off to a good start. Early feedback forms were overflowing with comments about the helpfulness and importance of the conference co-ordinator.

Outcomes

The system's real market test was during the first few months of operations. It was important to make a positive impression on the system's initial users, because both good and bad news travel fast. ARCOvision, because of good internal marketing, did make a good impression on its first customers, who were pleased with what they experienced and were able to provide valuable feedback on how to make the new service even better.

Indeed, when problems were detected system implementers were quick to act on sources of dissatisfaction. Chairs were changed, graphics capabilities improved, graphics guidelines provided and screens altered to improve image quality along the edge of the picture. Users saw their suggestions reap results. Approval ratings climbed along with usage.

Usage did not happen automatically. Internal marketing training and follow-up support were important factors in getting employees to internalize the availability and utility of a new communications option.

ARCO's CEO was right. Video teleconferencing could compete effectively with the Boeing 747. However, making it successfully happen was more about good internal marketing than it was about technology.

Source: Svenning, L. and Ruchinskas, J. (1986). Internal 'market research' program is yielding successful videoconferencing foe ARCOvision. *Communications News*, **23** (2), February, 48–52.

Case Study 2

Aydlotte & Cartwright Inc.: reward and recognize your employees

Aydlotte & Cartwright Inc., USA, is an agency providing advertising, marketing and public relations services to the healthcare industry, founded by William Aydlotte, who handles the creative side, and Jeane Cartwright, who manages the business and customer service side. From personal investments of $8000 from both partners, it quickly developed into a multi-million dollar business specializing in services for the healthcare industry.

On the first day of each month, every employee at Aydlotte & Cartwright receives a $10 allowance for the soft-drink machine. Despite the obvious cost, the company finds that the return on investment in terms of employee satisfaction is worth every dollar, according to Bill Aydlotte. The same is true for the firm's 'birthday present' to each employee – a day off with pay during the month of his or her birthday.

The allowance and day off are part of Aydlotte & Cartwright's internal marketing programme, conceived by the firm's partners, Bill Aydlotte and Jeane Cartwright. The concept of internal marketing was originally developed to help their clients. Aydlotte recounts facing a roomful of angry physicians who had fired the previous advertising agency. It did not take long for Aydlotte to work out that the physicians were angry because they had not been heard by the hospital or the former agency. So, he asked for their thoughts and ideas, and he listened. After the session, he came away with the account, which remains with Aydlotte & Cartwright.

The experience led Aydlotte & Cartwright to focus on the importance of internal marketing. 'It sounds simplistic' he says, 'but internal marketing is basically listening to the employees and staff in a hospital or company, telling them what is happening and what we are going to do.' Often, employees do not know what is going on in their organization. They feel excluded and as a result are not committed to or do not support their company's programmes. If, however, employees feel included in the company's decisions, they begin to take pride in their work and their employer.

While developing internal marketing programmes for their clients, Cartwright and Aydlotte began to look at their own fast-growing company. The two partners soon arrived at the conclusion that they, too, could benefit from such a programme. 'We ask a lot from our employees, and they give it' Cartwright explains. 'Our experiences with our clients demonstrated that it would mean a lot if we show our appreciation for those efforts.'

Internal marketing was particularly pertinent since the firm was growing rapidly, and the partners wanted to find ways to remain close to employees, as well as help old and new members know each other better and build strong relationships. The key to good internal marketing, Cartwright suggests, is to show employees they are appreciated and heard. From this comes improvement in morale and productivity. Another point to remember is to implement these kinds of programmes before employees become disgruntled or less productive, and before they want to leave the company.

'We have found that employee support can make our advertising work for the client more successful' Aydlotte notes.

Apart from the soft-drink allowance and birthdays off, the firm has put in place the Big Idea Award. This is given to any employee whose idea has improved or could improve business operations, contribute to humanity, or 'make agency life a little easier'. The winner gets a statue, two entertainment tickets and recognition in the agency newsletter. Since setting up the award, the company has been inundated with ideas, and competition for the award is intense. The award is taken seriously, but it contains an element of fun that also helps to spark creativity.

An in-house newsletter is also part of the programme. It communicates news within the agency, such as awards granted to employees and the firm, new business, employee birthdays, items from the agency's suggestion box and even bits of gossip.

Cartwright notes that employers do not have to offer complicated incentive programmes to make a difference. Aydlotte & Cartwright's internal marketing programme is simple and easy to implement. Maybe that is the reason why it has been so successful.

As Aydlotte remarks, at the end of the day 'Internal marketing is really just a fancy term for showing employees we care, we appreciate your efforts, and we want to hear what you have to say.'

Source: Schonbak, J. (1991). Internal marketing worth every cent. *Business, Atlanta*, **20** (10), October, 16–17.

Barclays Card Services (BCS): getting employees to live the brand

An important issue facing companies when dealing with their employees and persuading them to follow defined actions, especially when making difficult decisions such as redundancies, is to maintain integrity of the internal marketing communications.

Sonja Roberts, head of Barclays Card Services (BCS) Communications and Marketing Change at Barclaycard, is a firm believer in the honest approach. Barclaycard has, since the early 1990s, been driving change in its operations through its Living the Brand programme. During the late 1990s, the bank went through a major business change programme, which forced it to marry job losses with brand values.

Under these conditions, according to Roberts, 'Transparency is key. It takes a lot of commitment from the top. It's no good my going around saying those at the top are committed. The way it worked for us was to get senior people on the road supporting events so that what we have now is woven all through the business strategy.'

Barclaycard started the Living Brand initiative in 1995, as a vehicle to actively spread brand focus throughout the business. The Living the Brand programme put every single person through a series of workshops and activities. The logic behind these sessions was to build brand awareness, understanding, commitment and action.

The aim was to get employees thinking about the brand generally and then think about Barclaycard and where the company wanted to take it. After that, the bank developed and ran numerous more workshops, with each one carefully targeted at different audiences across the business. Within a period of a few years, the entire business was covered about two to three times, with workshops tailored according to the segment group: senior managers, back office, front line and so on.

In addition to enlisting and making 'visible' senior management commitment to keep the initiative alive when things were not going smoothly, Barclay's found that it was important to track and measure success. While to some extent there had to be a certain amount of blind faith, since it is very difficult to pinpoint the precise impact of internal marketing, BCS developed a brand tracking system to try to gauge what affects the brand and what does not. This information was considered vital enough for board members to scrutinize it every month.

One of the worst mistakes companies make is to mouth the right words but take little action. Unfortunately, there is a lot of that around, with many corporations simply making glib statements about how open, accessible, listening and caring they are toward their employees. What is worse than not being open, honest and not caring about your employees' views is saying you are and not reflecting it in action. In such instances, it is far better to just keep quiet. Success in this sector is very firmly rooted in the skills, capabilities and motivation of employees. In Roberts' words: 'I have seen, over the course of my career, the issue of how you deal with your staff becoming more and more critical. There are other important assets, of course: we know that our data, for example, is a very important asset. But at the end of the day, it is our people that make the difference, whether they are the people manipulating the data or talking to customers. You can't be in this business unless you have effective customer service. The real differentiation comes from customer contact. And we have more than 10 million customer service calls a year – that's 10 million potential opportunities for building relationships.'

Source: Mazur, L. (1999). Unleashing employees' true value: employees can be your company's most valuable marketing asset. *Marketing*, April, 22–4.

Case Study 4

Barnardo's: enhancing corporate identity through internal marketing

A national communications exercise by Barnardo's found that its employees knew as little about the charity's operations as did the public. The exercise was prompted by Barnardo's decision to re-brand itself through national TV and radio advertising. This led to the 18-month exercise, which discovered that a large number of its employees held outdated views of the charity's work. The outcome was the development of several training and communications programmes to rectify the perceptions and change attitudes.

Internal marketing exercise

Questionnaires, workshops and interviews with a cross-section of managers, staff and many of the 200 000 volunteers revealed surprising results about the nature of Barnardo's 'brand image'. For example, many of its staff believed that the charity had been running orphanages for more than 20 years, yet this was not the case at all.

Barnado's set up an internal marketing department from its HR and advertising teams. The first test for the charity's newly formed internal marketing department was to interpret employees' feelings about the organization. Banner McBride, a new agency specializing in 'behavioural change', claimed that Barnardo's approach to employee relations is becoming increasingly popular with commercial companies who are keen to manage their own change programmes.

Banner McBride's managing director, Michael Pounsford, highlighted: 'This exercise has been an essential way of getting every member of staff involved in the brand's success. Barnardo's was very keen to avoid its volunteers seeing TV and radio advertisements and being concerned that money wasn't being spent on children.'

However, Pounsford also notes that many HR departments in large organizations may be missing a trick by not working closely enough with marketing professionals to communicate their values and objectives, especially in times of change. 'Marketing is seen to put an emphasis on lasers, lights and dry ice at the expense of more thoughtful HR thinking. But the two together can help to manage change very effectively.' John Grounds, head of communications at Barnardo's, admitted that his department needed to be more aware of 'mutual support' and consultation. 'I don't think we are as far down that line as we would like to be, but we are talking to the same audience, so we need to develop a close relationship.'

The fact is that many HR and marketing departments have, historically, been guilty of being overly secretive, often to the detriment of their organizations.

Source: Welch, J. (1988). Barnardo's points the way to HR and marketing link-up. *People Management*, **4** (1), 13–14.

Boatmen Trust Company: creating success through internal network relationships

Trust and estate business was once a major part of the banking industry. Over the years, brokers, investment advisers and lawyers, all wanting part of the lucrative market, have eroded this business. One of the reasons for the decline has been in the poor handling of sales. In the past, banks generated new business by relying heavily on personal contacts. However, with increasing competition business cannot be handled that way any more. Trend statistics within financial services over the last few decades highlight this:

■ the number of firms managing money for individuals has increased more than six-fold

■ employment and the number of firms managing money and registered with the Securities and Exchange Commission have more than tripled

■ mutual funds have grown more than 10-fold

■ banks, insurance companies and trust companies account for less than 30 per cent market share of investment accounts, down from 70 per cent in 1969

■ nearly every major brokerage house is now in the trust business.

Internal marketing

According to William F. Ottinger, senior vice president marketing at Boatmen's Trust Company, St Louis, USA, success in the trusts markets isn't a mystery, but the sum of many small things done well. To compete in this market requires delivering very high quality, and trust service levels thrive externally when they are successfully promoted internally. 'It sounds simple enough' says Ottinger. 'But actually accomplishing it is another story. At Boatmen's we're always looking internally at ways we can make the trust company and the bank work together. Otherwise, you forget where the customer is in the process.'

Internal selling

The essential first step in any trust marketing effort is selling internally. Senior management needs to buy into and give priority to the importance of non-interest income to all areas of the bank in order to make the internal marketing programme work. This helps remove many internal barriers.

Senior management need to agree on the need to stimulate trust business within a banking organization, and make an unswerving commitment to remove any territorial disputes.

Prospecting internally means getting retail and corporate bankers to be encouraged to refer, without reservation, customers to the trust department. The Boatmen's Trust Company generally seeks prospects with $200 000 plus in liquid assets. Of the bank's 2.5 million customers, 5 per cent fall into this category, creating a pool of opportunity for the trust company in its own backyard.

To prospect effectively within the bank, a substantial percentage of funds earmarked for external marketing needs to be shifted to the internal marketing programme. In the first 1 or 2 years, it is not unusual to spend more marketing money internally than externally, especially if the sales programme is being revamped to take advantage of the bank's customer base.

Internal education

After winning support from senior management, the next step is internal education of trust capabilities by the 'marketing' of trust capabilities and trust service priorities to other areas of the corporation, including the bank and investment subsidiaries. The best trust prospects are already customers of the bank, but reaching them can prove to be very difficult, especially if an organization embraces a territorial mindset or is product-driven rather than client-driven.

According to Ottinger: 'Trust offices must constantly educate their peers in other areas of the company about the customer desired by trust... By education, I don't mean a lengthy manual about a trustee's duties product features and benefits. Provide profiles of customer service needs and problems. Then educate other areas about how some of these situations may be solved by a trust service relationship.'

In this internal education part of the internal marketing initiative, banks need to promote the distinct advantages they have over non-bank competitors. For instance, only banks can offer a wide array of trust arrangements. While brokerage houses and other financial institutions may offer similar products, only full-service trust departments have the resources and expertise (specialists) to advise clients in complex areas of trusts and investments. Moreover, because their fees are not based on sales, their advice tends to be much more objective.

One way to develop trust business is by first selling current fee business – investments that clients pay to have managed and getting adjunct sales later. This strategy is quite contrary to the traditional way the industry has operated: banks were so intent on selling their estate services that the non-bank competition weaned the more liquid customers to mutual funds, cash management accounts, annuities and traditional brokerage accounts. As a result, current fee accounts became not only more difficult to locate, but more difficult to sell.

Strong internal communications have helped Boatmen's executives to educate and boost the trust business.

'You can spin your wheels conducting numerous seminars and producing newsletters which may prove fruitless in generating leads...It's important for trust bankers to take the initiative in educating others – not just the retail side of the bank, but commercial lenders, investment officers and others, as well.'

Apparently, the strategy is working. The trust company's total assets are $51 billion and assets under management total $30 billion. According to Ottinger, Boatmen Trust receives more than 100 referrals a month from bankers.

Internal network and relationships

Selling current fee services is, by itself, insufficient to kick-start the trust business. It takes an active internal referral network. In fact, when searching for the bank's best customers, all areas of the bank must be included. Too often, the trust salesperson calls on the same branch bankers repeatedly, ignoring other referral sources. Instead, salespeople must talk with corporate bankers, the brokerage department, and private banking, correspondent bankers and any area of the bank in contact with affluent customers.

While the concept of internal 'networking' sounds great, how does the trust officer get the attention of other busy, goal-driven bank officers? A network is no good if it is not going to be tapped. Moreover, while it may be possible to accomplish a great deal working from a referral system, the key to success is to provide incentives for other areas to provide referrals. This means that incentives and referrals must be a two-way street.

'Internal territoriality is one of the most destructive forces to providing a high level of service – when you start putting fences around customers, then the whole sales, marketing and service process breaks down,' Ottinger stresses. 'Therefore, it's important that the referral process works both ways.'

Since the best trust prospects are already customers of the bank, adding them as trust department customers can be a challenge. This means that some parameters need to be set up before prospecting within the bank. The trust department's positioning on bank deposits must be perfectly clear. For example, the trust department cannot afford to appear as if it is trying to poach deposits into its domain. The trust sales force must emphasize that it is targeting non-deposit assets, including assets held in S&Ls, in brokerage accounts, at competitive banks and in mutual funds. If, at some point, it is necessary for a customer to shift deposits to a trust account, the banker must be notified first to clarify the reason and how the customer benefits. The advice is simple: if you can avoid giving surprises to your banking colleagues then collaboration increases and conflicts are minimized. Boatmen approach this challenge by concentrating on the following key areas:

- ■ *Avoid territoriality*. Cultivates personal relationships that cut across organizational lines to encourage retail and corporate bankers to refer high net worth prospects to the trust company.

- ■ *Profile trust prospects*. Educates employees by focusing on the needs of the customer. For example, rather than providing trust manuals or long-winded presentations summarizing a trustee's duties or the responsibility of an executor, Boatmen provide profiles of a typical customer problem, how it could be solved by a trust service and how a banker benefits financially from a referral.

- ■ *Maintain contact with internal sources*. Boatmen have found that there is no substitute for keeping the 'Trust Story' in front of bankers. Periodic seminars, quarterly mailings, lengthy technical product descriptions and casual contact often do not produce a volume of leads. Trust bankers must constantly educate peers about the types of customers desired by the Trust, not features and benefits of trust and investment services.

- ■ *Create a strong incentive compensation programme*. In a well-designed programme, the selling efforts of the sales staff, administrators and portfolio managers, plus the bankers and their profit centres, need to be interlocked, ultimately rewarding everyone involved. At Boatmen, the compensation programme is based on the first year's fees. The banker who refers the account receives 20 per cent of the first year's fees and his department receives 40 per cent. This is in addition to bonuses paid to the trust sales staff and/or the trust administrators and trust investment managers.

- *Repeatedly sell the incentive programme to employees.* Repetition is a key part of the referral bonus programme. It is critical to continually 'advertise' the referral programme to bankers and reinforce the dollar amounts paid to specific bankers.

- *Internal referrals are a two-way street.* Remind other employees that the trust department is a good source of referrals. It is risky to always seek a handout without returning the favour. Boatmen developed a programme to refer qualified, new trust customers to its private banking function. Because trust customers have a large amount of money to invest, they are often good private banking candidates. Additionally, Boatmen track the amount of direct deposits from the trust company back into the bank as a result of trust relationships.

Recruiting the right people

Boatmen also place a high emphasis on getting the right people. Marketing trust services effectively means the right person must be in the salesman's seat. For Boatmen, sales ability is a key sought-after trait, with technical knowledge second.

Boatmen hold clear thoughts on the type of people they want. They want a staff of closers, not counsellors. When hiring trust sales staff, Boatmen's advice is:

- Hire only high-activity, high-energy-level individuals. There is no substitute for the willingness to work. Persistence is the greatest sales attribute in the world.

- Hire proven closers with a financial background. Ex-brokers can be good prospects; many have received excellent sales training, but are looking to work in an industry offering good compensation.

- Hire salespeople who are primarily motivated by money. Such people want to sell quality and want to be substantially rewarded when they are very successful. Give them the chance to earn six-figure compensation.

- Provide salespeople with a lucrative incentive programme that rewards success. Monitor the progress and performance of these salespeople closely.

- Allow 12–18 months for a new salesperson to prove him or herself. Each salesperson should be able to produce a minimum of twice his salary in current fees. If there are doubts after this period, the wrong person has probably been hired and an immediate change should be made.

- Avoid protecting sales positions because of seniority or office politics. Each position should be quantitatively judged based on current fee results.

- Set sales goals based on the individual, territory, sales experience and management expectations.

- Train salespeople, either in-house or using a qualified outside training programme, to sell trust services. In addition, expect the sales manager to assume much of the responsibility for training sales people.

- Provide sales staff, administrators and investment managers with as much information as possible on trust services, investment performance and pricing. In addition, circulate information about the competition, including an analysis of fees related to mutual funds, brokerage accounts, wrap accounts and annuities.

- Encourage salespeople to innovate and differentiate themselves from the competition. Without innovation and differentiation, trust departments are in danger of becoming just another option in the financial services arena. They need to leverage their strengths in order to gain new business and increase profitability.

External marketing to supplement internal marketing effort

All the trust department's time clearly cannot be focused internally. Internal effort must be complemented with external effort to cultivate external referrals. Many banks use public seminars to sell trust department services. However, while public seminars are an acceptable marketing tool to use every few years, alternative ways such as educating attorneys and CPA firms about investment performance, competitive fees and quality staff of your trust department may yield better results. Most of the professional community is aware of trust department capabilities as executor and trustee. However, answering questions about investment return, the costs of trust services and the turnover ratio among staff may increase referrals from these groups.

Sources: Ottinger, W. F. (1991). Making the case for Trust. *Bank Management*, **67** (11), November, 37–40. Anonymous (1992). Internal incentives boost trust referrals. *Bank Marketing*, **24** (4), April, 42–4.

CSX: appreciating the cost–benefit trade-off for employee change

Over the last two decades or so, the railways industry roadmap has witnessed considerable change. Successful railway managers have been changing what Peter Drucker calls 'the business theory'. Driving this change is not technology, because it remains essentially the same – diesels still pull cars on four-wheel trucks, using air brakes and knuckle couplers. What has changed is attitude. Those companies that could change did, and evolved into companies that we see on the map today. Those who did not perished. One of the success stories in managing this transition is the American railtrack company, CSX.

The big question is how does a railway company like CSX change its business theory? CSX's success can be attributed partly with coming up with a new paradigm and partly with being able to firmly implant it within the company. In the management of this transition, internal marketing was a crucial step in the process of change. Otherwise, railway staff who felt threatened by a change in the status quo would have resisted change tooth and nail. The only way to market change internally was to make it non-threatening and to show employees how it meets their needs for increased productivity, more job satisfaction, or even perhaps more tangible rewards.

Internal marketing to identify internal needs

Internal marketing can often help identify employee needs that otherwise one would never consider. For example, in the mid 1980s, Seaboard planned to improve accuracy and timeliness in a number of clerical areas. To assess the viability of this, they decided to do some internal market research. To management's surprise, the results of the internal marketing exercise uncovered that clerical groups had an entirely different agenda. They were raising a number of workplace-related hygiene concerns that were hampering their ability to do their jobs. Factors such as:

- noise levels in the work area;
- secondary smoke;
- strict group break times;
- limited washroom facilities;
- inflexible working hours.

Once management addressed these issues, employees felt empowered to make the real changes in the work process. Soon thereafter, employees overhauled their billing process to reduce errors and increase timeliness. Morale went up, mistakes went down, and so did the cost of failure.

Eventually, Seaboard merged with Chessie to form CSX. Many of the people who ran Seaboard (or Chessie) remained in position because they were good at managing the transition, in which internal marketing played a notable role.

Employees are at the centre of paradigm shifts

In the new world of the 1990s, competitive intensity cut out the luxury of making mistakes and redoing work. Change was rapid and there was a need to constantly adjust and adapt because the validity of the current business theory was questioned daily. Assumptions regarding the outside (customers, connections, cabotage supply) and assumptions about the inside (skills, train size and scheduling, track maintenance) are what drive the business theory. But these internal assumptions must be ever-changing, at the very least in line with changing external assumptions. The danger is that they are cast in stone and ossify the company in the process. That is what had happened to once great companies like IBM and GM, resulting in their severe experience of difficulties.

Keeping the company vibrant and flexible means constantly rethinking internal and external assumptions. Managers can no longer say 'we know', they must move to a position in which they say 'let's ask'. And there are no better people to begin asking than your own employees. No matter what some commentators may say, in most cases employees are the most dedicated and the most knowledgeable about what they do and about what their companies do – or should be doing – because they face the coalface every day of the week.

Changing hearts and minds, not just directions

At the beginning of the 1990s, railroads traditionally operated a batch process, yet customers wanted customization. The pull was in two opposing directions: the ultimate batch is a unit train while the ultimate customization is a private fleet of trucks. The railroad trade-off becomes: how far can I customize my batch without hurting economies of scale? The shipper's trade-off is: how far can I batch my custom movements without hurting flexibility? Making these trade-offs work depends on the ability of workers in each organization to make changes in their assumptions about the work.

Some time earlier, the Milwaukee and New York Central tried short, fast, frequent freight trains over short distances. They were not very successful: the reason was that they were running a custom process with a batch mentality. The people who had dreamed up the idea had failed to consider their internal market and failed to do any internal marketing. Now, on the other hand, it is common to see short custom trains, mostly on short lines. The technology is not different but the attitude is.

Sharing thinking and involving means getting things done

To be effective at managing change through internal marketing, you must begin by marketing a willingness to embrace change – at all levels of management. Change is nowhere nearly so threatening when it's understood, and when it's a something you've been involved in thinking up and developing. The fact is that employees, and that applies to all sectors, intuitively embrace changes in the way they work when they can see *tangible benefits for their customers* (shippers in the case of railway freight), *for themselves* (rewards – extrinsic as well as intrinsic) *and for the company* (in the efficiency of their operations). The truth is, insofar as management let them, employees will and do initiate change to achieve organizational ends.

Source: Blanchard, R. H. (1993). Change – or die. *Railway Age*, **194** (3), March, 64–5.

Eastman Chemical Company: implementing TQM through internal market focus

Eastman Chemical Company, a chemical giant, has over 450 product markets and employs over 17 000 people. Its operations cover the globe. Eastman has been a leader and pioneer in its field, and has won many accolades, such as the Malcolm Baldridge Quality Award. Eastman was, until 1 January 1994, a wholly owned subsidiary of the Eastman Kodak Company.

Eastman's success, however, has not always been guaranteed, but has required a lot of effort and hard work. Back in the 1970s, the company was floundering. According to Robert C. Joines, a former vice president of quality, the wake-up call arrived one day when a key customer of Eastman (which was then a division of Kodak) bluntly put to them 'Your product is not as good as your competitor's'. This came as a shock to the company because it had always considered itself to be customer focused, and indeed had invented and patented the product in question. It was clear that if the company did not quickly put its house in order that it would rapidly lose market share and the threat of going out of business appeared a serious one. Eastman responded by taking the issue of customer feedback much more seriously, and by the early 1980s customer feedback was a central part of the operational planning process.

To develop customer responsiveness further, in 1983, the company formulated a quality policy that was to set the tone and direction of future initiatives. In 1984, the company started training in the tools of quality, namely SPC and the accompanying traditional tools of quality such as process flowcharting. Shop-floor workers were asked to chart their progress and post it for all to see. Unfortunately, for some employees these charts became 'rat charts', because the company had not been able to drive fear out of the workplace. One employee's comment typifies the underlying sentiment: 'You are asking all of us using SPC to post all our mistakes. How *will* these things be used?' These sentiments brought out to senior staff the cultural contradictions that existed within the company: a conflict between the hierarchical, structured and disciplinary corporate culture with the open, honest, trusting environment demanded to run an effective SPC and other quality initiatives.

Cognizance of the cultural tensions led, in 1985, to the development of the Eastman Way.

The Eastman Way

Eastman people are the key to success. We have recognized throughout our history the importance of treating each other fairly and with respect. We will enhance these beliefs by building the following values and principles:

Honesty and integrity. We are honest with ourselves and others. Our integrity is exhibited through relationships with co-workers, customers, suppliers and neighbours. Our goal is truth in all our relationships.

Fairness. We treat each other as we expect to be treated.

Trust. We respect and rely on each other. Fair treatment, honesty in our relationships, and confidence in each other create trust.

Teamwork. We are empowered to manage our areas of responsibility. We work together to achieve common goals for business success. Full participation, co-operation and open communication lead to superior results.

Diversity. We value different points of view. Men and women from different races, cultures and backgrounds enrich the generation and usefulness of these different points of view. We create an environment that enables all employees to reach their full potential in the pursuit of company objectives.

Employee well-being. We have a safe, healthy and desirable workplace. Stability of employment is given high priority. Growth of employee skills is essential. Recognition for contributions and full utilization of employee's capabilities promote job satisfaction.

Citizenship. We are valued by our community for contributions as individuals and as a company. We protect public

(*continued*)

> health and safety and the environment by being good stewards of our products and our processes.
>
> **Winning attitude**. Our can-do attitude and desire for excellence drive continual improvement, making us winners in everything we do.
>
> *Source*: extract from *To be the Best*, Eastman Chemical Company publication, ECC-67, January 1994.

While the plans, for the Eastman Way, to nurture an open trusting environment were being thought up, some employees were asking: 'We have always been honest. Why do we need to emphasize trust now?' Others noted that SPC was about looking at data not trust. These types of questions indicated to the company that it needed to examine and understand internal employee perceptions and attitudes before it could move forward. So, employees were surveyed and from this internal marketing research effort the company found that there was poor communication throughout. Specifically, it found that:

1 Management must communicate what it is doing and why it is doing it.
2 Employees are the key to accomplishing anything the company wishes to do.

Based on these insights, The Eastman Way was developed, which subsequently became a strong foundation for the quality initiatives that were to follow.

Initiatives leading to winning the Quality Award

Year 1985

In 1985, a quality initiative, which started in manufacturing and then expanded organization wide, began to look at internal customers, external customers and suppliers. Its aim was to get the company to become more customer focused.

Year 1986

In 1986, senior management implemented their own quality process. In this, they had to identify their customers, understand their needs and develop measures to make sure that these needs were being met. This culminated in the implementation of a computerized internal customer satisfaction survey. The success of this programme was largely attributed to the fact that management was walking the talk, so to speak.

Year 1987

The quality focus was expanded from individuals to interlocking teams. Each team consisted of several members and a supervisor. The supervisors constituted another team with other supervisors and so on upwards. By 1995, about 99 per cent of employees were working as part of teams, using quality tools to drive continuous improvement.

By 1987, Eastman also began to focus on employee empowerment. In its effort Eastman quickly discovered that it couldn't empower people who:

- don't care;
- don't have authority;
- don't have appropriate skills.

With regard to skills and authority, the company began to ask questions about each unit's purpose and focus. Why did the unit exist? What was it doing? How did it support the overall organization? Only once these fundamental questions were answered was it possible for management to start addressing how to provide skills, authority and responsibility. As far as the issue of caring was concerned, Eastman decided to undertake a specific survey to find out what were the issues at stake. Eastman discovered that the key problem was the appraisal system, which was then changed in 1990.

Year 1988

The company applied for the Malcolm Baldridge Award, and learnt a lot from the site assessment.

Year 1990

Eastman registered to the ISO 9000 and built competencies for JIT systems deployment.

The company assessed all of its divisions against the Malcolm Baldridge Award criteria. Based on this and its earlier survey findings, it started to overhaul its appraisal system. Before the change, the appraisal system force ranked individuals on a bell-shaped normal curve. This system, as the quality guru Deming had noted, automatically identifies half the employees as below average. The consequence is that a great number of high quality people are classed as poor performers. After a 6-month review of the system, the company concluded that one improves nothing by *only* appraising. This led to the realization that improvements come about by working on the system and not by scoring people. This led Eastman to shift its focus from grading employees to developing them.

Year 1991

The company developed its strategic intent: to be the world's preferred chemical supplier. At the same time, the company was reorganized from a hierarchy to a hub-spoke structure.

Year 1992

Eastman initiated a supplier recognition programme, to reward and involve suppliers in its quality efforts.

Year 1993

Eastman won the highly prestigious Malcolm Baldridge Award.

Later that same year, Eastman expanded its commitment by announcing its 'responsible care pledge' for the environment, health, safety and community.

Eastman's internal market focus

After the findings of its employee survey in 1986, the company knew that it had to reorient itself to create skills, empower and motivate if it was to succeed in the external marketplace. By providing JIT and other training, as well as delegating authority downwards, Eastman was able to address the first two objectives. The task of motivating, however, was much trickier. Eastman knew this, in reality, demanded a two-fronted action:

1 Remove the impediments to motivation.

2 Provide employees incentives to keep them focused on corporate goals and objectives.

Put simply, this meant that management had to be able to answer the perennial employee question: 'What's in it for me?'

After this realization, the company undertook to remove several motivational stumbling blocks:

- *Fear of losing one's job*. The company pledged that it would never lay off anyone as a consequence of quality improvements. This was to create a common mindset, in which the belief is grounded that as processes improve and productivity improves people would be able to accomplish more. This was an important motivator for improvement.

- *Performance appraisal system*. The performance appraisal system was abolished. As Joines noted, only those at the very top of the appraisal system objected to its removal. 'The traditional system of telling people "We have determined that you are not in the top third of performers, go and do better" just didn't motivate. What's wrong with telling employees they are all in the top third, thereby making themselves feel better about themselves? When you do they will go out and win battles for you.'

- *Employee suggestion scheme*. The old scheme rewarded individuals with money for their suggestions. It was found that this process conflicted with team spirit, so the company abandoned it.

Motivating employees is not an easy task. It requires a change in the company and management's mindset. Eastman noted that there are three things in this:

1 Management must identify and focus on a unifying theme.
2 The theme needs to be communicated throughout the organization.
3 Teams are needed to implement management action plans.

Russell Justice, a technical associate and a champion of quality through motivation, suggests that *how* management responds to these challenges is just as important as the tasks themselves. For example, there are three scenarios to empowering employees:

- *Scenario 1*. Management tells employees they are empowered, gives them the task and walks away. Outcome – decline in enthusiasm for the task.

- *Scenario 2*. Management tells employees they are empowered and gives them a task, subsequently discovers that there are problems and punishes employees for their failure. Outcome – sharp decline in motivation and performance.

■ *Scenario 3.* Management tells employees they are empowered, gives them a task, monitors the results and applauds them for their efforts. Outcome – commitment, enthusiasm and performance.

Praise is an accelerator for performance. It is part of the positive cycle of human behaviour reinforcement. Justice notes: 'Behaviour is not a function of procedure. Behaviour is a function of consequences.' The question for a company then is: 'How can the company create the right consequences of behaviour to further its corporate goals?' Eastman tackled this question by:

■ offering positive reinforcement to the best behaviours;
■ making everyone feel like a champion;
■ rigorously measuring the results of business processes;
■ encouraging employees to learn from their experiences.

These practices were organized into a seven-step process to unify the company around common goals. Eastman calls this process 'Leadership for Accelerated Continuous Improvement'.

Leadership for Accelerated Continuous Improvement

The seven steps of this process are:

1 *Focus and pinpoint.*
Focus is about getting everybody to share the same goals. Pinpoint is about specifying in measurable terms. This helps to get employees see how their objectives fit in with the overall corporate objective. To attempt this, management should use simple tools that everyone can understand and use. For example, interrelationship diagrams.

2 *Communicate.*
The objective is to let employees know what is important and why it is important. As Eastman's chairman noted: ' If you want people to join you on this journey, if you want them to be enthusiastic and take responsibility for what needs to be done, there has to be lots of communication.'
    Eastman undertakes organization-wide communication by publicizing its vision and mission. Corporate communications must help employees understand:

    (a) What is being improved?

(b) Why is it important for the customer, to the company, to me?

(c) What has the management team committed to do to help?

(d) What, specifically, is the company asking me to do?

Eastman has found that one good way of seeing if the communication has been effective is to get employees to restate what they are going to do.

3 *Translate and link.*

The team must next translate company-wide objectives into their own language and environment. For example, whilst management may talk about the objective in financial returns, or market shares, teams need to transpose these into relevant items such as cycle time compression, higher reliability and so on.

4 *Create management action plan.*

Management must create a plan with specific action, which includes measures and metrics to reach the objective. Each team member is asked to know what tasks needs to be done, why they are important and what the team is going to do to get them done. In drawing up these plans, managers need to examine policy, possible system changes, barriers to success, training requirements, resources needed and any other problems that need to be addressed to reach the goal.

The methodology is to try to get managers to be proactive and progressive in making their plans. By using problem-solving techniques, they can make mistakes on paper rather than during implementation.

5 *Improve processes.*

At this stage, employees work together to solve problems. Eastman, has drawn up a very successful six-step team process to create and maintain improvements:

(a) identify the problem;

(b) use the tools to solve the problem;

(c) plan the solution implementation;

(d) execute and measure the results;

(e) document what was done;

(f) strategize how to maintain the level of improvement.

6 *Measure and provide feedback.*

Eastman insists on simple, clear, visual feedback to employees. Eastman's mottos amplify this: 'feedback is the breakfast of champions'; 'if you don't measure performance, you can't improve it'.

Eastman has created rules for feedback, and the key of these include:

(a) feedback should be visual (posted), frequent, simple and specific;
(b) the baseline performance should be used for comparison;
(c) the past, current period and goals should be posted;
(d) the best ever score should be posted;
(e) a chart should be immediately understandable;
(f) a good scorecard allows comments and annotations.

7 *Reinforce behaviours and celebrate results.*
Celebrating positive results can provide a big boost to morale and energy. However, Eastman noticeably goes beyond this stage, to one of learning from success, since a party in itself is not enough. At celebrations, team members are encouraged to revisit how they achieved their success.

Eastman is also very wary to ensure they don't design a system in which there is a limited number and circle of people who can win, because such a design would simply repeat the mistake of Eastman's old appraisal system. In rewarding and recognizing success, Eastman complements monetary with intrinsic rewards. Letting people know they make a difference to the company pays dividends.

Eastman has attempted to reinforce positive behaviours by taking care not to be manipulative. This it has achieved by nurturing a spirit of respect, openness, teamwork and trust. These are the fundamentals laid down in The Eastman Way, which has helped to drive the company from one success to another.

Source: Milliken, W. F. (1996). The Eastman Way. *Quality Progress*, October, 57–62.

Case Study 8

First Union: designing and using employee segmentation

Astute marketing executives have been quick to see the opportunity in using the techniques of internal marketing to institutionalize an outward looking sales culture, build strong internal support for marketing programmes and campaigns, as well as add that little bit extra to their total marketing efforts. For many, the practice is a new one, but they are fast learning that it is an important one. Traditionally, the emphasis was solely directed toward capturing customers. Now marketing executives are seeing that there is another half to the programme of capturing and retaining customers, and that this missing half is inside the organization, namely internal marketing. The missing half is derived from the recognition that employees, more than anything else, affect the external customer maintenance process. With this new realization, smart marketers have begun to search for ways to involve employees to execute the marketing plan. This focus includes employees who do not perceive themselves as being part of the marketing process, such as non-customer-contact employees, who in the course of a week's work may never see a single customer. Consequently, marketing budgets and energies have started to be redirected to these so-called internal customers.

First Union bank, of the USA, has learnt that the concepts and techniques of external marketing are usefully transposed to the internal context. Goals of planning, segmentation, differentiation and promotional strategies can all be accomplished effectively with a well-conceived internal marketing mix.

First Union has found that the techniques of market research are very helpful in the task of getting to understand and know employees. Traditional external skills and techniques can be easily deployed internally to increase internal understanding and knowledge. Particularly useful are employee opinion research, attitude surveys, leadership and communications studies (of internal publications), focus groups, and feedback systems. Newer methods that have been used by First Union that add to the traditional ones are such techniques as climate studies and 'deep sensing' sessions, where executives use small groups and dialogue sessions to discover feelings that employees have about their organization.

First Union is also involved in identifying executives with strong intuitive skills, who are particularly perceptive about employees' concerns, and encourages them to share their feelings about employee attitudes and wants with bank management. For example, First Union management identified several employees who were employee sensitive to provide a first indication of how employees will react to change of policy and procedures. First Union has found them to be an invaluable source of initial insight, and uses them on a regular basis.

Once First Union managed to get over the traditional assumption that all employees are the same and therefore communicated and treated them in only the broadest terms, they started to find many differences. The way to surface these differences was to consider that the employee base is composed of groups or segments with many different interests. Once First Union began to think in terms of differentiating their employee base, they began to see how they could tailor internal marketing programmes to segments to achieve the outcomes they wanted.

First Union has utilized both demographic and psychographic analysis to segment the employee base, and discovered much useful information. The range of criteria to segment the internal market is dependent on the questions being asked, but most useful amongst these are criteria such as age, sex, education, family status, race, income and job function. Psychographic segmentation criteria have included elements such as perceptions, attitudes, beliefs and values about work, relationships, and approach to life. Internal segmentation has helped the internal marketing team not just appreciate the differences, but also to use these to design more effective communication programmes and think up specific ways of motivating targeted segments toward customer consciousness. One of the insights emerging from the internal probing was that age is a major differentiator. Employees under 30 are different from those over 30. Typically, those over 30 tend to be more loyal and more conservative, while those under 30 have far less conservative views, are more willing to experiment and cope better with change (structural, technological, as well as environmental). Through this appreciation, it was possible to design a different communication approach for these two employee segments and utilize a different means of reaching out to them.

First Union found a highly credible means of communication: employee television. First Union found that the under-30 group, which makes up about two-thirds of its employee base, believes that television has a high level of credibility as opposed to print media. Additionally, they place high value on the convenience of communicating via television as opposed to daily travelling long distances to attend meetings.

First Union also discovered that simplistic segmentation of the employee base is not sufficient. They need to track and understand what is going on with employees. An important factor to track is to ask what workplace and career issues are important to employees. The changes that have occurred in this respect within the financial sector are fairly dramatic. For instance, a large proportion of employees now enter the profession as graduates, they are younger and with the intensely competitive environment they are also very fickle in their loyalty to the firm. All this information is important in trying to design 'job product' packages for employee motivation and customer consciousness. Knowing where employees are coming from makes this task that much easier.

By arming itself with deeper insights about its employees, First Union found that it could create better communications and motivational programmes to create customer-led quality products and service. By gathering factual information, employees' jobs did not become easier, but they became better and more fulfilling.

Source: Sullivan, M. P. (1985). Exploring the untapped resource of internal marketing. *American Banker*, **150** (30 October), 4–6.

GTE Supply: developing and running an internal survey instrument

GTE Supply negotiates contracts and purchases a wide range of goods needed for telephone operations. The goods range from office supplies to telecommunications fibre optics. The majority of the company's customers are part of the parent company's internal network of GTE local telephone companies (telcos). GTE Supply manages around 200 warehouses nationwide and is primarily responsible in the installation, support and maintenance of telcos.

Until the mid 1970s, GTE had managed its GTE telcos in a decentralized and, it may be said, in a somewhat disorganized manner. In an attempt to standardize and track installation and maintenance materials, the company decided centralized controls would improve consistency and also at the same time reduce costs. This led to the formation of GTE Supply, which is headquartered in Dallas, Fort Worth, Texas. Nevertheless, GTE also appreciated that centralization does not necessarily guarantee improvement, and it could easily amplify existing problems.

Soon after its creation, GTE Supply customer-contact employees began to report complaints from customers about price, delivery and employee attitudes. This led GTE Supply to systematically survey internal customers. This was done not simply as an exercise to fulfil requirements of some formal programme, such as quality, but because it was believed that there would be two benefits: firstly, improve the visibility of the group within the company and, secondly, the actions would counteract the depersonalizing aspects of the supply process automation, which had been undertaken to improve accuracy and reduce costs.

The development of the internal surveys became an instrumental part of GTE Supply's Quality Improvement (QI) process. By using the surveys to identify internal customer needs, and by publicizing the results and by keeping track of the trends over time, GTE found that it could see how well it was progressing in achieving critical aims set by leadership. The so-called critical items included such things as:

- implementing customer advocacy, education and feedback pro-grammes;
- stocking the correct items;
- improving communications;
- improving quality;
- encouraging teamwork and involvement;
- recognizing employees;
- striving for a single efficient system;
- instituting an integrated distribution network;
- implementing a supplier management process;
- benchmarking operations.

By paying careful attention, GTE Supply was able to develop a systematic and highly effective process of obtaining and using its information from internal customers. This is very important in large organizations, where it is easy to fall into the trap of focusing on narrow physical and financial objectives that are far removed from the needs of the employees they serve. The dialogue created by the process helped GTE Supply make partners of hitherto adversarial groups, and increase customer satisfaction as well as reduce costs.

GTE Supply's internal survey instrument came to be seen as an important method for listening to the voice of internal customers in the dispersed GTE Supply network. It became a central part of the QI effort, in its ability to act as a diagnostic and motivational tool to improve the company's performance.

Internal survey instrument

The survey was constructed with care, to ensure that it was not open to internal criticism and cynicism that often goes hand in hand with such initiatives. The strongest safeguard against cynicism was the vice president's promise that actions would be taken on the results of the survey. There was a strong call to action from the top leading people to perceive it as a serious tool for driving improvement.

In designing the instrument, GTE Supply set up internal focus groups as well as conducting general internal market research to define key concepts relevant to their service environment. These concepts were then used to create a list of performance criteria against which GTE Supply's performance could be assessed. The rating uses a five-point Likert scale, with the anchors: excellent, good, average, below average, poor. The respondents rate the following parameters:

- provides complete information;
- understands customers' needs;
- does the job right first time;
- provides timely responses to questions and requests;
- anticipates customers' needs;
- keeps customers informed or updated about problems or solutions;
- avails itself to contact with customers;
- has subject matter expertise;
- makes it easier to do business with;
- meets due dates;
- has a spirit of co-operation;
- follows up on service;
- provides clear written communication;
- provides clear verbal communication;
- gives customers an opportunity to provide feedback;
- tells customers whom to call with questions;
- is courteous;
- initiates and approves changes.

Additionally, three questions attempt to probe a more global perspective of the company's performance. These are:

1 How do you rate the overall quality of service provided by GTE Supply over the last 12 months: excellent, good, average, below average or poor?

2 Would you say the overall quality of GTE Supply is 'much worse', 'worse', 'about the same', 'better' or 'much better' than 1 year ago?

3 Comparing its overall quality to the price of its products and services, how would you rate the value GTE Supply offers: excellent, good, average, below average or poor?

To get individuals to elaborate on these questions, each is followed by 'Why did you say that?'

Finally, individuals are asked: 'What improvements, if any, could be made by GTE Supply?'

The survey is administered by an outside company, which is experienced in conducting internal customer surveys by phone. At the beginning, the survey was run annually, but it then moved to a quarterly run. This enabled GTE Supply to be more responsive and serve the needs of those responding. Since the survey is internal, the response rate was high. Over time, the survey has become part of the job responsibilities of managers, indicating the level of support for the survey process.

Data into actions

The collected data are presented and examined under two formats:

- Quantitative data, which are used to compile longitudinal trends, and compare performance differences across telcos and different subgroups.
- Qualitative data, which are used to provide more detail and substance. All managers are required to read the qualitative responses.

The quantitative data help define priorities, while the qualitative data help to identify motivations and highlight any unusual or unanticipated issues.

At year-end, detailed reports are given to senior management, who use the information to define future objectives. Regional managers then use these to develop action plans. Once all action plans have been prepared, these are checked to see that they align with strategic objectives. Next, employees are then made responsible to implement the plans, and the outcomes of the implementation effort are tracked and evaluated. Plans are adjusted if they do not deliver to expectation.

GTE Supply has managed to get a great many benefits from the internal survey. It has improved communication between management and staff, which has consequently led to increases in efficiency and effectiveness. The enhanced flow of information has helped to decrease costs by:

- improving forecasts of customers' supply needs – allowing GTE to plan ahead;
- decreasing inventories – telco managers seeing higher responsiveness from GTE Supply no longer need to stockpile;
- eliminates unnecessary or inappropriate supplies;
- improves economies of scale.

Additionally, the improved communication and sense of higher empowerment leads to higher levels of customer satisfaction because:

- telco employees have a channel to express their dissatisfaction, highlight their needs, etc.;
- new products are developed and introduced in a timelier manner;

■ contact is established between GTE Supply staff and telco staff, such that if problems do arise they are rapidly communicated and addressed.

Lessons learned

GTE Supply's internal survey and associated QI actions transformed it from one of the worst performing to one of the best regarded companies within GTE's portfolio. On the way, a number of valuable lessons were learnt.

On management of quality, GTE Supply learnt:

■ The QI process does not have to be driven by a formal quality programme.
■ Commitment and involvement of leadership is critical.
■ Centralized HQ does not necessarily interfere with employee empowerment. Quite the opposite, it may enhance it, by providing aggregating and standardizing information, and then encouraging local units to create their own action plans for improvement.
■ The depersonalization part of automation can be countered via a good communication process.

On the improvement side, the company found out that:

■ Effective communication can lead to outstanding performance outcomes.
■ Combination of formal communication processes in which the internal survey is a focal point helps the assimilation of new organizational units into the company's quality improvement culture.
■ Shared aims are facilitated between suppliers and internal customers, so benefiting strategic alignment.

On the mechanics of the process, GTE learnt that:

■ Satisfaction surveys should be geared toward the respondents rather than the sponsors.
■ Quantitative information must be supplemented by qualitative information to draw more rounded conclusions and assessments.
■ A survey is effective only if actions are taken. Just collating data is never sufficient. Action must be preceded by objective setting and clear communications.

GTE Supply also learnt that there are differences between external customers and internal customers, and these differences must be taken advantage of:

- Partnership with internal customers is greatly facilitated by closeness, frequent meetings and common organizational aims.
- The ease of identifying and the long-term availability of internal customers should be used to build a stakeholder constituency to improve performance.
- External customers are concerned with matters other than those of the company, so the data collected need to be translated inwardly via processes such as Quality Function Deployment (QFD). For internal customers, on the other hand, the survey is just the beginning of a dialogue.

The biggest and most important lesson that GTE Supply learnt from their effort was that listening to internal customers is very important if real improvements are to be realized in external customer satisfaction. Internal listening is complementary to external focus.

Source: Drew, J. H. and Fussell, T. R. (1996). Becoming partners with internal customers. *Quality Progress*, October, 51–4.

Lutheran Brotherhood: building skills and competencies through internal marketing

Lutheran Brotherhood is an $8 billion financial services business head-quartered in Minneapolis. It has 1500 employees located in its home office and 1700 out in the field.

When word around the office surfaced that the sales force at Lutheran Brotherhood were using their laptop computers as deadweight in their car trunks during the winter, it was clear it was time to update what once were cutting-edge computers and software (purchased three and a half years ago).

In their search, development and implementation of a new easy-to-use laptop computer system that would help increase the productivity of its sales force, the company adopted a company-wide focus based on team-work among departments. This approach eventually led to peers teaching each other the new technology. The outcome? In just 5 weeks, almost all 1500 members of Lutheran Brotherhood's sales force learned how to use the new laptop technology. All signs indicate the training programme was a huge success: not only was there positive feedback from the sales representatives, but the company's sales have also began to rise since the new laptops were introduced. Although it would be unwise to attribute the sales rise solely to the implementation of new technology, it clearly seems to have made a significant contribution in one way or another. Within a period of 6 months, sales figures rose an average of 25 per cent compared to the same period in the previous year.

In developing the peer training programme, Lutheran Brotherhood initially were aware that two elements were going to be key in the successful introduction of the new systems:

- direct sales force participation in developing the programme to ensure they would have a sense of ownership in the new technology;
- interdepartmental involvement from employees throughout Lutheran Brotherhood.

In recognition of this, the company formed a 21-member task force, consisting of MIS and marketing professionals. The task force spent 6 months researching laptop computers before selecting the Toshiba 3100SX. To accompany the hardware, the members developed customized software to help representatives undertake client needs analyses as well as show how various combinations of the company's products can help meet those needs. Client management software to help sales representatives organize and store information on contracts, names and addresses of clients, and personal information was also integrated into the package by the task force team.

To support the training effort, an internal marketing plan was developed to generate some excitement and anticipation for the new technology, while minimizing any employee anxiety. The internal marketing campaign included:

- frequent correspondence to district representatives about their upcoming training, at what came to be called LBU (Lutheran Brotherhood University);
- news articles in company publications to help the sales force visualize themselves successfully using their new laptops;
- positive word-of-mouth generated by the deployment team and the field test group.

The internal marketing effort was sustained at a high level throughout the training sessions. For example, a music video would be shown at the beginning of every LBU session. It featured Lutheran Brotherhood executives in ponytails and spiked hair, jamming and lip-synching to original music written for LBU. The video also showed a district representative (from the district undergoing training) using the laptop successfully and easily.

Ruth Bash, the company's assistant vice president of field technology, noted that 'The video used the MTV treatment and it was definitely well-received. At a couple of LBU sites, it received standing ovations.'

The task force set the training initiative rolling by first training a 110-member deployment team, which consisted of individuals from every major functional area of Lutheran Brotherhood. To get direct feedback from experienced users, the deployment team then selected a pilot group of eight sales representatives from throughout the country. The pilot group used the new laptop daily, suggested ways to simplify and improve the software programme, and provided ideas on structure for the mass training.

When it was time for the mass training to begin, members of the pilot group helped launch the training sessions. They even assisted in the classroom. Craig Darrington, manager of field force training and development, responsible for the co-ordination of the LBU training agenda stated: 'The credibility of what we were doing was enhanced by the support and input from the pilot group.'

The training sessions took place at eight LBU locations set up at college campuses throughout the country. The choice of college campus was made to foster a relaxed and focused learning environment. Approximately 1900 people (1500 district representatives and their assistants) attended the 3-day sessions. A student–teacher ratio of 10:1 was maintained to ensure that all trainees received the help they needed. Three people served as trainers in each classroom. One person demonstrated on a laptop computer the steps being discussed, while the other two trainers served as roving experts walking around the classroom to answer individual questions. In addition, at each LBU site, there were also at least two technical experts who walked from room to room to answer technical questions and solve hardware problems.

The training sessions were designed to combine intensive hands-on training. The sessions were designed to include fun and build camaraderie. The company wanted trainees to become not only knowledgeable about the new systems and technology, but also eager to use them. To ensure this, the company:

- Developed a video to be used during the training that featured a brief walk-through of each major capability of the new software and showed applications in a business setting. Additionally, the video was filmed on location at sales offices throughout the country, so that it featured recognizable members of the sales force at work on the new laptops in their offices.

- Showed testimonials from sales representatives from the pilot programme to demonstrate peer support for the new technology. This also helped the sales staff visualize themselves using the new technology successfully.

- Developed an ongoing support to users of the new technology. The company maintains a toll-free hot line for agents to call when they have questions, features follow-up material in a monthly newsletter and plans to do a second generation of training.

At the time, the new technology introduction was the largest training project ever undertaken by Lutheran Brotherhood. Its success highlighted to the company that, by careful internal marketing, employees can do just about anything in just about any length of time.

Source: Obenshain, V. (1992). Peer training yields speedy results. *Personnel Journal*, **71** (4), April, 107–10.

Midland Bank: improving customer service through internal marketing

The banking sector has been pushing to improve customer service in its attempt to overcome negative consumer perceptions. The desire by high street banks to position themselves as providers of high quality service providers came after many years of criticism that they were failing to care for their customers.

Many banks attempted to improve their image. One of the actions by Midland, now part of the HSBC group, was to revive its 'Listening Bank' slogan and launch a campaign highlighting its customer service to change perceptions. In the mid 1990s, the bank released TV commercials featuring an employee in the role of a superhero solving customers' problems. This theme was quickly mimicked by competitors.

In their attempts to shake off their poor public image of the late 1980s and early 1990s, many banks initiated programmes of internal marketing, training and customer service. The success of these programmes led the banks to claim improvements in customer service. Despite the claims, however, the evidence is not entirely clear-cut, since there are some studies that suggest the persistence of high levels of consumer discontent. For example, in a 1997 survey conducted by NOP, it was revealed that 31 per cent believed their banking service had improved, compared with 54 per cent who felt it had stayed largely the same, while 14 per cent felt it was worse than ever. According to senior researcher for the Consumers' Association Neil Walkling, there seems to have been little change in the situation. 'The service you get is still a bit of a lottery. It is very difficult for banks to maintain uniform service when they have so many branches, but an increased use of telephone banking should improve the situation.'

Despite this, Midland believes that as a result of its initiatives its customer service has evolved and improved over the years. Andy Stephens, head of customer service at Midland, highlighted that customer care has become a strategic imperative for the company. 'Banks have never been the most popular beasts, but 3 or 4 years ago we were getting some very bad press so we decided to become more customer focused. We said if we are going to compete in this market with all these new competitors coming in, like Virgin, then we are going to have to get better.'

In response to the competitive challenges from new operators like Virgin, Tesco and Sainsbury's, and the growing expectations of customers, Midland introduced numerous new services and made improvements to existing ones, examples of which are:

- rapid expansion of cash points, placing them at third party sites such as stations and supermarkets;
- introduction of telephone and PC banking;
- reducing queues in branches by updating the bank's computer systems;
- cutting back on the number of charges customers are liable for.

The backcloth to these changes has been the heavy emphasis on employee development. Midland's 40 000 members of staff all underwent a 1-day customer service training course, which each individual had to pass. Midland also began to use mystery shoppers to check and improve employee skills in dealing with customers. Following this, Midland claimed that the number of complaints it received fell 36 per cent year-on-year in 1996, while customer satisfaction rose from 82 per cent in 1995 to 90 per cent in 1996. Other high street banks such as Barclays, NatWest and Lloyds TSB followed suit and introduced similar changes, and all claimed improvements in performance.

One driving force for internal change has been First Direct, which Midland launched in 1989. In many ways, First Direct revolutionized the financial sector and its innovative approach rightly received high praise for service quality.

First Direct

Midland's offshoot First Direct adopted an approach of natural communications in its internal marketing programme. Sue Pollitt, internal marketing manager at First Direct, believes the key to successful internal marketing is to ensure that it doesn't become too stage-managed: 'What we do is make sure people feel they can speak out and have a dialogue with anyone in the business. We have done focus groups with our staff about how packaged we want our internal marketing to be and they don't want it. They prefer the rawness of the communications we have at the moment.' The closest First Direct gets to a 'pre-packed' programme is ensuring everyone has an informed understanding of the company's plans and priorities, and they have a chance to question senior management on a face-to-face basis in an entirely open way. According to Pollitt, 'It's also about hiring the right people: we do believe that if we actually see our people as representing the brand and influencing our customers' regard of First Direct we are naturally going to make sure we recruit the right people, who might not have the skills and knowledge required, but have a natural empathy.'

First Direct is as imaginative with its own staff as it tries to be in reaching and building relationships with its external customers. When creating its external customer programmes, the company always tries to look for what Pollitt calls the 'icing on the cake' for staff. First Direct attempts to be creative in trying to fulfil the needs of employees. For instance, it took advantage of the fact that its meeting rooms are empty in the evenings to hold classes in all sorts of subjects (for example, Spanish and guitar lessons were the most popular) and it was not that costly to set up because the company was easily able to use its purchasing power to negotiate good rates. First Direct knows that these innovations are not enough to keep people continually on board, because just like external markets the needs of the staff keep evolving. Employee needs change as they get used to what is on offer. Politt makes the point simply: 'We are trying to achieve a bit of a wow factor with our internal audience, just as we would like our people to achieve this with our external audience.'

Sources: Barrett, P. (1997). Banks lend an ear to service. *Marketing*, 16 January, p. 16. Mazur, L. (1999). Unleashing employees' true value: employees can be your company's most valuable marketing asset. *Marketing*, April, pp. 22–4.

Nations Bank: using external marketing as part of the internal marketing programme

In 1992, a merger between NCNB Corp. with C&S/Sovran led to the birth of Nations Bank, USA, as a $119 billion institution. The newly formed bank decided to use internal marketing to send a message to its employees.

Nations Bank chose an advertising campaign to communicate its message to its employees. The cost for a 90-second advertising slot was close to $600 000. The advert went out during this year's Orange Bowl football game, broadcast nationally by NBC on New Year's Day. While this is a large sum of money for any advert, it was a particularly large sum when the target audience was only 58 000 people. For Nations Bank it was worth the expense to send a message to employees that the bank was committed to lending to the local community. Before the game's airing, all Nations Bank employees were urged to 'invite [Chairman] Hugh McColl into your living rooms'.

The advert was only a small part of Nations Bank's effort to help employees understand their new company, where it is going and how they fit into its future. Internal marketing has proved to be a vital component in mega-bank mergers. The reason is simple: before two companies officially combine and launch a marketing campaign aimed at the general public, their employees must have a unified vision of why the merger is good. Rusty Rainey, the NationsBank executive vice president, who came from NCNB and is handling the merger transition, explained: 'You market to your customers through your employees, so your employees come first.'

Another internal marketing action, one that Rainey considers the most important element in managing the transition successfully, was when NCNB arranged for its senior officers to visit C&S/Sovran employees at all levels. NCNB first used this tactic in 1988, when its bid for First Republic Bank Corp. was accepted by the Federal Deposit Insurance Corp.; NCNB dispatched 200 top-level employees to every First

Republic Bank office in Texas and sent yellow roses to its 15 000 new employees.

Personal appearances by senior executives were an essential part of the internal marketing of the merger. During the 2 months following its August merger announcement, NCNB's chairman High McColl travelled across the South to visit with C&S/Sovran and NCNB bankers, and returned with pockets full of business cards on which employees had scrawled questions regarding the merger; the questions were later answered in employee publications. With these visits, Rainey notes, McColl was saying: 'I care enough to come to your place and meet you.'

Source: Faber, D. (1992). A pitch for togetherness. *Institutional Investor*, **26** (3), March, 22.

Norwich Union: improving efficiency through internal customer management

Often, when companies have attempted to introduce a competitive element in the supply and purchase of services available internally, they have found it has surfaced inter-personnel frictions, which heralded serious repercussions throughout the business. Norwich Union's attempt at introducing such change within its legal division is an example of how internal marketing can help the transition.

Traditional practice at Norwich Union mandated use of the company's 40-strong legal section, except in certain special circumstances. No charge was made for services provided. All this changed when John Flynn, then head of department, made a policy decision to make the department more acceptable to its users, since perceptions across the company were that the legal section was poor at customer relations. The decision was made to try to get a measurable improvement in the legal section's operation and in its user satisfaction.

The first step of this undertaking involved conducting an image study, among the department's clients, to establish a flag-post of current status. The study segmented users of the department's services as light, medium and heavy across a variety of service categories, such as commercial conveyancing to litigation. The study highlighted the areas in which the department was considered deficient, especially in terms of skills, responsiveness and efficiency. The study also revealed a number of misconceptions which clients held about the department, and highlighted that there was less than clear knowledge of the full range of services that the legal section was currently providing and could be providing.

The findings led to immediate actions to rectify areas where criticism was justified. In conjunction with the remedial actions, an image campaign was launched to change perceptions where they were ill founded. A marketing plan was developed, which included 'getting to know you' (two-way presentations), in which the legal department set out its services and answered questions on facilities, skills and plans. Following this, internal clients were asked to summarize their own activities and problems. This then began joint discussions to see how relationships and interactions could be improved to the benefit of both sides. From issues raised and suggestions, the legal department, just as with many private legal practices, began production and circulation of a brochure and newsletters on a regular basis. A customer care programme was also introduced, which included a regular analysis of complaints. To deal with any points arising from these surveys, a rectification and zero-defect system was set up. Twelve months after the campaign, a check for overall progress was conducted. The results of this revealed a vast improvement in both the image of the department and the quality of client relations. As for the internal clients, they signalled improvements in efficiency as a consequence of the new approach.

From its internal marketing efforts, which began in the legal section, Norwich Union learnt that just because the customers are internal it does not mean (though it was often unwisely assumed) that all the information required about them is known or is obtainable. Indeed, neither proposition is wholly true.

From their experience, it was seen that one basic technique for successful internal marketing in this context was that of networking. Networking involved using contacts and the contacts' contacts to offer the service and to encourage referrals. Norwich Union found that to effectively engage in this requires two things:

- First, *know yourself*. One basic question that has to be answered is whether every potential and actual internal client knows every aspect of every service that is and can be provided. The problem is that often even the departments themselves do not know or appreciate their own range or the quality of their offerings, so it is not surprising that clients do not know it either. The point is simple: if potential clients do not know what you are offering and can offer they cannot buy it.
- Second, *know your client*. The internal marketing department has to take steps to ensure that they understand their current and potential client in depth. They must appreciate their problems, policies, aspirations and activities. Only after such understanding has been compiled and assimilated is it possible to start active internal marketing actions such as internal promotion, etc.

In tackling the network challenge, the company had to address a number of barriers:

- *Territorialism*. Many managers were brought up with silo mentalities, and tended to be very protective of clients. They did not wish to expose their own business to the risk that another department or operating company would fail to satisfy the client and thereby jeopardize their relationship.

■ *The 'what's in it for me?' syndrome.* It was crucial to be able to highlight benefits to the referral agency; otherwise, they saw no reason to expose themselves to risk. One way was to highlight long-term reciprocity. If this could be demonstrated then the battle for co-operation was largely won.

■ *Personality clashes and internal competition.* The company had to address not just turf mentality, but also battles of promotion and career progression implication as a consequence of moving from individual competition to get up the corporate ladder to team-based collaborative success.

Whilst none of these barriers was insuperable, they needed direct consideration and sustained action to ameliorate and remove their negative effects.

Source: Wilson, A. (1995). The internal marketing of services: the new age surge. *Logistics Information Management*, **8** (4), 357–63.

Provena: improving service quality in the healthcare environment

Provena Covenant Medical Centre is a 280-bed healthcare facility in Urbana, Illinois. Provena has come to appreciate that quality customer service in hospitals includes more than just patients. Every employee – including physicians, executives, nurses and maintenance workers – plays a vital role in improving customer satisfaction.

Provena has taken a number of steps to ensure that all their employees know how they contribute to Provena's goal of superior customer service. These are outlined below.

Communicating customer service standards

Provena communicates to all its employees the importance of customer satisfaction and that each person plays a role in providing the highest service possible. Provena has established hospital-wide customer service standards to help employees see how they can contribute to customer satisfaction. Provena has centrally set overall customer service goals to improve satisfaction ratings, but lets each individual department establish its own goals. For example, employees in the laboratory have set their own standards for filling various requests for tests within a specified period of time to a specified level of accuracy.

Another method Provena uses to get employees to understand how they contribute to customer satisfaction is to embody a strong customer service mentality within its mission statement. A well-defined vision and mission and a strong set of corporate values help to drive behaviour. Provena devotes considerable time in its mission to highlight Provena's aim to treat everyone that comes to them (patient as well non-patient) with respect and dignity. Provena strongly believes that if all their employees are treated with respect, they will respond in kind to those they care for, particularly patients and their families.

Training for customer service is continuous and is used to reiterate the tenets of Provena's customer-driven mission. Provena stresses that every employee, executive, volunteer and physician is expected to make quality customer service a central part of his or her work. This emphasis begins on the very first day of employees joining the institute in new employee orientation sessions. Additionally, Provena makes adherence to customer service standards a significant part of an employee's performance evaluation. These standards and goals are regularly reiterated. For instance, Provena has an annual Re-certification Day, at which employees review and are tested on all of the relevant competencies for their job, including customer service goals and expectations.

Addressing the needs of internal customers

Employees who do not come into direct contact with patients often find it difficult to see how their work plays a part in customer satisfaction. Provena's primary focus is on the service it provides directly to its patients, yet it does not lose sight of the fact that its 'customers' include not only patients and their families, but also hospital employees (clinical and non-clinical) and volunteers. For example, one of the satisfaction goals of the maintenance staff is to respond to all repair requests within a specific time period. In this case, the customer is defined as other departments within the hospital.

Another example is in the setting up of a physician hotline, so physicians can contact administration with concerns they have about the quality of patient care. In this case, physicians are the customers. These initiatives are driven by the clear belief that providing quality service to internal customers ultimately results in higher service quality to patients.

Recognizing superior customer service at all levels

Provena knows that by recognizing superior customer service it helps employees see the results of their efforts. Recognition reinforces customer service standards and the mission of the organization. For example, every meeting at Provena typically starts with a brief period to discuss 'Mission Moments'. Provena's 'Mission Moments' let employees, committee members, executives, physicians, volunteers and others share an example of how people in the organization fulfil the mission of Provena. A typical 'Mission Moment' might be sharing a note or a letter from a patient or family member reporting on the extraordinary care they received from a staff member.

Measuring results

At Provena, everyone is seen as an active agent in service quality delivery. The results of this orientation are extremely transparent in the organization's success.

Since 1994, Provena has been part of a regional patient satisfaction benchmarking group. Every year, Provena sets a specific satisfaction improvement goal. This is monitored by the benchmarking agency by collecting information through an ongoing series of telephone interviews with recent users of Provena's in-patient and out-patient services. Provena's efforts have been so successful that, in 1999, they won the benchmarking agency award for the highest level of patient satisfaction among all hospitals in the region.

With healthcare becoming so competitive, it has become increasingly important for hospitals to provide high quality service care. Provena attributes its success to helping employees at all levels to recognize their contributions to quality customer service. This it has achieved by looking to and managing its internal customers.

Source: Friedman, D. H. (2000). Quality customer service: it's everyone's job. *Healthcare Executive*, May/June, 4–9.

St Luke's Hospital: the role of internal marketing in implementing a knowledge-based system

St Luke's Hospital in Chesterfield, Missouri, USA, is a 493-bed opera-tion, which handles an average of 170 000 out-patient visits and 20 000 in-patient visits annually. St Luke's also operates a 120-bed skilled nursing and residential care facility, three urgent care centres, as well as offering home health services and an affiliated hospitals' dialysis centre.

Sensing changes in its environment, St Luke's set up a task force, which included physicians, administrators and key users, to evaluate existing systems and define a future direction. The task force came out with a strategy emphasizing empowering caregivers (one of its most valuable resources) to provide the high level service required for success in this sector. St Luke's strategy to deliver this was one that required it to be at the leading edge of available technologies. This led the hospital to imple-ment information systems that empowered caregivers with the patient data they need. In January 1993, St Luke's went live with a self-developed Patient Information Network System (PINS) to provide caregivers infor-mation in a graphical format using client/server computing. St Luke's then began to look toward the next step, not only putting data in front of caregivers, but also transforming the data into information they can use. This led to its decision to develop and implement a computer-based patient record (CPR) system.

The role of IT in patient care service quality

Comments by George Tucker, chief of the Department of Surgery and chairman of the hospital's Medical Executive Committee, highlight the logic behind the decision to implement a CPR system:

'I see the hospital functioning as an information exchange – we gather, compile and interpret data. Paper-oriented information-exchange processes are antiquated. Physicians spend most of their time gathering information [by] reviewing voluminous paper charts and tracking down patient information on the phone or in various parts of the hospital.

The computer-based patient record provides instant access to patient information. Patient information is presented in perspectives not available in a paper environment. I can sit at a terminal and look at a broad perspective of a patient's medical condition or I can look at detailed information including lab or pathology results. Looking at the patient's history this way, I can pull in histories and physicals, discharge summaries or operative notes for a specific patient.

The computer-based patient record helps us formulate long-term care plans and objectives, and then lets us evaluate outcomes and our treatment of the patient. We can compare outcomes for a single patient or group of patients.'

St Luke's has followed a six-step methodology (called CREATE) to implement its CPR system.

Step 1. Create an internal marketing and education strategy

Involving stakeholders (physicians like Tucker) was the first step in planning CPR implementation. It was important to remember that toolsets must be designed with user involvement, in this case caregivers who understood the benefits of this new technology.

After enlisting involvement from key stakeholders, an internal marketing and education strategy was developed to convey what the future delivery system was, what it could do, how it could be used and what were its benefits across the hospital departments. The internal marketing efforts were strengthened by continuous communication and education throughout the organization. The internal communications were used to present the benefits of the CPR system to administrators, caregivers and support personnel.

Step 2. Research, plan and build the communications infrastructure

Once there is initial support for the new system, the next step is to build an enterprise-wide network to support the CPR.

Step 3. Evaluate the data you now have available electronically, as well as the data you want to make available electronically

With the infrastructure in place, it was necessary to consider which data were relevant and important to provide over the network. Without a complete understanding of the data, data will remain data – not information. This process was helped by creating a life cycle for the data, and considering the following aspects:

- source of the data;
- quality of the data; and
- purpose(s) of the data.

The next step was to define the improvement paths available for the data. For example, to make it possible to electronically extract quantifiable results from dictated reports.

Step 4. Assemble a battle plan for your institution

Next, it was necessary to form integration teams and formulate departmental strategic plans based on compiled administrative and informed caregiver objectives. When assembling teams, it was important to ensure that there was informed involvement, because what is at stake is the basis of the organization's long-term future. The future must fulfil all stakeholder requirements – from the clinical to the financial end of the continuum.

Step 5. Team with your vendor

It is usual, unless one has an unlimited budget, to team up and create a partnership with a vendor. There are many systems out in the marketplace, so the decision requires careful scrutiny and selection. St Luke's decided on First Data's First Empower solution because the system most closely matched the hospital's needs.

Step 6. Expand upon the model

The task then was to integrate existing data into the hospital's new information model. Following this there was a move to enhance the model contents with newly computerized information from best-of-class departmental or institutional systems.

With its successful internal marketing and education strategy, it was possible to unleash the true power of CPR in the hospital. This sharing of knowledge raised the quality of service and also helped the hospital to become more learning orientated.

Technology enables but internal marketing makes customer focus happen

Healthcare providers like St Luke's are faced with tremendous challenges for delivering excellence in patient care. The use of information technologies such as the computer-based patient record is increasingly playing a role in setting higher standards of service delivery. The success of new technologies is, however, based on effectively embedding them into the organization. This means getting employees to overcome their fear of new technology, getting them to understand how they could benefit from it and showing them how to use it efficiently.

Source: Steiniger, V. (1994). Checklist helps C-R-E-A-T-E a successful CPR. *Health Management Technology*, **15** (11), 37–41.

Terminix International: using internal marketing to energize the company

Terminix International is a division of Service Master Co., USA. The company is in the business of pest control.

The challenge facing Terminix offices around the country was to improve customer retention by reducing the number of cancellations and 'allowances' for business. Allowances largely account for times that Terminix does not service an account, such as when a family is out of town and does not have the house sprayed one month. Improved customer retention means increased business, which Terminix believes is achieved by delivering strong customer service.

Terminix vice president of marketing, Clayton Spitz, says the company has had a strong commitment to customer service for a long time. However, Terminix started a programme in 1994, called Customers for Life, focusing on customer retention. Terminix decided to take its efforts to a higher level by developing an internal marketing programme for employees. The programme was designed to help employees become more customer oriented. It was developed and launched with the aid of the consultants, GS America.

According to Scott Vogel, director of promotional marketing for GS America, giving advice to Terminix: 'What's key in this programme is trying to motivate technicians. Technicians are your best sales people.'

The promotion got under way on 18 January in 370 Terminix branches around the country. 'Kick-off kits' with streamers and balloons were sent to each branch, along with collateral pieces. In-house and collateral pieces included humour and primary designs to communicate ideas for the promotion.

Vogel said: 'We want to keep it simple, so you can walk by it and get a message.'

As part of the internal marketing programme, branches were divided into categories by their percentages of cancellation. Posters were designed to display cancellation and allowance percentages, and highlight the targeted improvements that were set by managers at each Terminix branch.

At the end of each quarter year, amounts were to be tallied and winning branches named.

The promotion was prize-driven, with each employee at a winning branch receiving such items as gym bags, coolers and pocket knives. Employees at the winning branches were then to be entered in sweepstakes at the end of the year for larger prizes like vehicles and cruises. Even though service technicians and managers were the primary targets for the promotion, all employees at branches were included in the competition for prizes. Spitz pointed out that the reason for this was simple:

> *'All of this is a team effort...It's all pulling together, and it's everybody's responsibility to save a customer. Customer retention is a team concept'.*

Terminix executives wanted to sponsor a promotion that would involve all employees. They wanted to put together something where everybody in the operation is rewarded when a branch is successful. This meant designing a promotion where literally everybody in the company could win.

Additionally, since the promotion was to run over such a long period, it was necessary to make sure that the campaign did not lose momentum. Therefore, it was decided that GS America should conduct telemarketing surveys throughout the year. As Vogel said:

> *'A year is a long time, and I think keeping in touch each quarter...will give us the pulse of what's happening. All this pomp and circumstance is nice, but it's not effective if it doesn't sell results.'*

Terminix will evaluate GS America at the end of each quarter to be sure the promotion remains effective.

Source: Hollis, K. (1995). Terminix uses internal marketing to better business. *Memphis Business Journal*, **16** (40), 6 February, 13.

Thomas Cook: developing internal customer orientation in the purchasing function

The 1991 Gulf War sparked safety concerns, which hit the travel business hard. For the first time in its 150-year history, travel company Thomas Cook recorded a major slump in its profits, resulting in all round redundancies. The signal was clear for action. The consultancy arm of Coopers & Lybrand was contracted to assess the predicament. After examining the cost structure of the company, it became evident that the purchasing function was poorly organized and not taking advantage of the strength associated with the company's overall spend. Buying took place in an uncoordinated manner and there was an absence of policy to drive decision making. An internal study arrived at similar conclusions.

Following the investigation, Thomas Cook appointed Alan Fenwick as head of purchasing. Fenwick inherited a small central department that was handling only a fraction of the total corporate purchasing spend, and even this was dissipated on low strategic value items. His task was to create a new team and to organize the different purchasing activities into a coherent whole and thereby improve the cost structure.

Turnaround actions

The first step that Fenwick took was to improve external supplier quality by closely monitoring the standard of supplier relationships and service. Current relationships and performance were so poor that users often ignored preferred contracts. Fenwick took action to rationalize this in a process that he called 'hacking through the jungle'. This emphasis on external quality improvement yielded dramatic improvements in the first few years. Suppliers were reduced to 2500 by 1996, from a base of 7000 in 1992 (at a time when the company only had 7000 UK employees). By 1996, the top 10 per cent slice of suppliers accounted for 90 per cent of orders, which was far removed from the earlier position. These simple changes in the purchasing process led to savings of £3.5 million in the first year and £2.75 million in the next.

Internal marketing initiative

By 1995, however, Fenwick realized that for further improvements the company would have to switch to more sophisticated goals. The initial cost savings had been important to stop immediate declines, but long-term success could only be achieved by better 'internal marketing'. Internal marketing was seen as a way of selling the purchasing function's added-value potential to the rest of the organization. This approach would get purchasing to become more involved and do so in a more flexible and holistic manner. As chance would have it, this recognition, fortunately, coincided with a change in the organizational reporting structure: moving from the financial director to the strategic marketing director instead.

Knowing and managing around attitudes and culture

Thomas Cook's culture of local empowerment meant that purchasing had to win the confidence of internal customers (those employees who may wish to use purchasing) rather than grabbing their current domain through the exercise of power. In one sense, as Fenwick noted: 'My competitors are the customers; they can use me or do it themselves and if I give them a hard time – through bureaucracy or poor information – they disappear very quickly.' Given that these internal customers could easily revert back to doing it themselves, as of old, meant that the central purchasing would have to prove itself on results rather than the aggressive self-publicity, which was not likely to go down well in the Thomas Cook culture.

Fenwick quickly became aware that one of the biggest barriers to effective internal marketing was the traditional attitude that purchasing professionals held of themselves. Purchasing agents were pretty brilliant at being customers, but seemed to be almost useless as suppliers and being customer focused themselves. Fenwick attended to this by getting the purchasing team to produce its own mission statement on customer relationships. The team also underwent customer care training to reorient their attitudes to be service-led. The attitude shift also meant moving away from simply recognizing paper-based qualifications, such as CIPS diplomas, to customer-focused attitudes. The comments below highlight the change in sentiment that was slowly coming through as a result of the new initiative.

'In the old days when I was recruiting, the first on the list of "must haves" was a CIPS diploma. Now the real "must have" is a customer-focused attitude.

The last two people I've recruited hadn't worked in purchasing before and didn't know what the department does. They came from the customer call centre and are red hot on customer service. They have made a major difference to the way the department performs. The best feature they provide is that they really take ownership of the problem – it might be a simple request but they make sure it's done. Those of us from a purchasing background may not be so good at that. They have reoriented our attitude to one of customer focus.

The perfect person is someone with a CIPS diploma and the customer focus, but by God are they rare. We interviewed purchasing managers with 20 years' experience who were terrible – nothing wrong with their purchasing skills but their attitude to customers was terrible. It's easier to recruit a non-buyer and teach them buying than the other way round. I have six people with CIPS diplomas... not short of people who can teach. What I've not got enough of is this customer-focused attitude.

One woman has no experience of purchasing but has a no-nonsense approach and a superb customer-focused attitude. She has asked about going on the CIPS course but I would rather she did more service training – to go on "train the trainer" courses and be the facilitator in this department.'

Developing internal customer consciousness

Internal market research showed the internal customers of purchasing were being let down in some very basic ways. According to Fenwick: 'People found it hard to do business with us. You ask a buyer what he or she should be providing and they'll say negotiation, sourcing – all the fancy stuff. Ask any customer and they say delivery, troubleshooting, expediting, being informative, having a help desk – all the basic stuff.' This led to the development of service-level agreement for customers – answering the phone quickly, being available, etc. All very simplistic, yet it was the beginning of the customer focus revolution. Soon thereafter, a tracking system for internal customer satisfaction was introduced and it threw up many insights about the varied and contradictory needs of customers.

This experience brought out that customer care is about the simple things – knowing what they want and providing it – rather than putting all your energy into investing in expensive purchasing systems. In addition, the purchasing department began to learn about customer consciousness by examining others for best practices. One of the best sources for learning was the purchasing department's suppliers and their salespeople. Fenwick noted: 'They are trooping through the office every day and using the same techniques we need to use. Every buyer can tell you who a good salesperson is – I have encouraged my people to learn from the good ones.'

Internal customer segmentation

As had taken place with supplier relationships, it was just as vital to identify key customers – in terms of spend, decision-making power and current relationship with purchasing. This was addressed by a number of approaches.

One initial exercise was to segment the internal customer base into prospects, crawlers, joggers and racers: prospects being those who avoided the purchasing function and racers being the closest of partners. The task was to focus on the areas where purchasing was getting least work, whilst ensuring they kept the racers fully satisfied.

This segmentation was enhanced by the use of a matrix framework examining value against risk, as used commonly for evaluating products or suppliers. The framework allowed the identification of, for example, customers who were critical for reasons of credibility. 'A high profile manager, who may not be spending a huge amount of money, but who has purposely avoided us, would be a high level target. We have a few customers like that and they are high on our list.' At the same time, the framework allows the identification of some customers who are too inefficient to target. 'You might have a prospect who is so unique that they won't want us and we won't want them either. If the first model was the only analysis they would go high on the list, get a lot of attention and waste everyone's time. My aspiration is not to control every penny of our spend. I tell all our customers I only want to be involved where we both feel I can add value. If the customer is doing a superb job, wherever they are on the matrix, all I will offer is advice and training.'

Internal product development

To be successful, purchasing needed to continuously offer value to their customer. This meant developing internal products and services to fit closely to the changing needs of the internal customers. Customer needs analysis was made an ongoing process to keep track of changes as they occurred in the company and the external marketplace.

Part of increasing the value-adding potential was in identifying the key services that customers want. By considering the issues the team began to offer a tailored solution, with users cherry-picking the areas of purchasing and supply with which they needed most help. It became possible for their customers to either buy a cradle-to-grave product or pick and mix. One of the most popular 'products' was checking terms and conditions of contracts. This appealed to many customers who had not considered using purchasing before. 'The market research manager would spend a lot of money but never dreamt we had anything to add. One of the first things in our selling campaign was health-checking the small print.'

Another popular 'product' that was developed was expediting. In this 'product/service', the customer chooses the supplier, and sources and organizes it all. However, if they encounter problems then purchasing has the expertise to sort it out. For instance, sometimes internal customers would want purchasing to get tough with a supplier while they remained at arm's length to come in and dress the wounds.

A big advantage of the 'Expediter product' approach is that it allows the team to demonstrate its value and win user confidence. This allowed the relatively new purchasing team to increase their own confidence and move up the learning curve. For the new team one big fear was of over-promising and under-delivering. For this reason, one team manager was assigned a specific 'delivery not promise' project to ensure contracts perform. Purchasing did not want to get internal customers excited and then fail to live up to their expectations. This would close the door and no amount of internal marketing would reopen it. Fenwick relates an experience of one supplier failing to give a customer the information they needed. 'In the customer's mind the supplier is useless and it will take years to change that. One bad response can destroy a great supplier. The risks are enormous, so we are going slowly.'

End outcomes

Over the longer horizon, the purchasing team aims to develop close relationships between internal customers and their external suppliers. This is a strategy many traditional purchasing departments are reluctant to follow because they fear that they will do themselves out of a job. Fenwick doesn't subscribe to this belief: 'I think that's unfounded – we've got better things to do with our time than merely get between customer and supplier.'

Fenwick is intensely proud of the record of the purchasing team at Thomas Cook and firmly believes that internal marketing has been fundamental in creating customer consciousness and ultimately its overall success.

Fenwick believes that the Thomas Cook team's progress presents a challenge to the rest of the profession. As he notes: 'I haven't found a real customer-focused purchaser, apart from the team working for me.

That is the real issue for the profession. Even in manufacturing, more buyers will not have the divine right to purchase, they will have to prove they can add value. Managers who refuse to see that will be at risk. . . People are waking up to the fact that internal marketing of purchasing is becoming the issue today. And there is more rubbish spoken about it than anything else. There are high profile people in the profession who profess it but don't do it – you just have to speak to the customers!'

Source: Edwards, N. (1997). Selling me softly. *Supply Management*, **2** (4), 13 February, 30–2.

TMC: structuring the internal marketing process

In marketing the Thomas & Mack Centre (TMC), located at the University of Nevada – Las Vegas, almost as much effort has gone into marketing the building to the employees as has gone into marketing the building to the public. TMC's General Manager Pat Christenson drove the initiative on the belief that internal marketing is as important as external marketing.

Pat Christenson discerned that: 'At TMC, service is really our only goal.' To achieve this aim, Christenson set about developing an extensive internal marketing to motivate employees and raise service results. Christenson named the initiative as *'We Can Make a Difference'*. Christenson's internal marketing plan began with the development of a mission statement, which set the goal for the centre and its workers.

Mission Statement:

> *'To the Las Vegas community and its guests we provide*
> *diverse, distinct events with quality professional services while*
> *progressively managing a clean, safe, well maintained and self-*
> *supporting facility.'*

The mission statement embodied what Christenson strongly believes in, but he appreciates that for it to mean anything it is his responsibility to ensure that his employees believe in it too. 'If your people aren't in tune with what you expect, then it's all for naught' he said. 'We decided that we were going to turn the marketing plan inward; we're going to focus on the employees.'

To help with the initiative, Christenson found an ally in M. L. Smith, a professor at the University's School of Hotel Administration. Smith helped with the design of the programme, and acted as motivator and facilitator of training. The goal of internal marketing was simply to exceed customer expectations.

TMC's internal marketing initiative is captured in the activities and steps described below.

Start at the top

Christenson emphasizes that internal marketing programmes have to start at the top of the management ladder. 'It starts at you and above you. You need to make the commitment and get a commitment from your boss – a commitment to time and resources. If you have that commitment and you start, no matter what your resources are it will pay off.'

Involve everyone

Christenson suggests involving everyone is very important: 'Don't you write the plan, get the people who do the jobs involved. They probably have a better understanding of what needs to be done.'

By getting employees to input into the plan, it is more than likely that they become committed to it by their own accord. Full-time employees are not the only ones who need to be involved. Guests, clients, part-time workers and contracted workers can all contribute. They are all very useful in helping to identify which areas need attention and what are the best motivating tools.

Know yourself (understand your strengths and weaknesses)

A key stage in TMC's internal marketing plan was to take a close look at itself. This allowed TMC to find out who they really were; what was the building's history, its legacy, its competition and the perception of its service, its potential?

By looking at the history of the building, its perception and its performance record, it became possible for managers to have a better idea of what the goals should be and how to achieve them. In this way, problems are identified and opportunities fleshed out. Only after this appreciation can mission statements or objectives be developed.

Strategic objectives and actions

After determining the mission, a strategy needs to be designed and a clear action programme defined. The action programme can include schedules, budgets, assignments and other details. Once a plan is in place, it needs to be monitored, feedback needs to be obtained and it needs to be reviewed regularly.

Christenson identified a number of organizational objectives for TMC employees. He wanted to motivate them by providing them with a positive work environment, establish corporate commitment, incorporate ongoing training and develop a strong reward programme. His insight was based on the realization that how he treats his employees determines how they treat their customers.

To achieve this, a number of internal marketing actions were developed, as outlined below.

Communicating

Christenson started to hold a monthly staff breakfast, where key issues and objectives are addressed. The breakfasts were attended by an average of 125 employees. 'We give information. We update what's going on. They like to know, and that way we don't have to deal with rumours' said Christenson.

The breakfasts also motivate employees by including recognition and rewards. The breakfasts are made into fun events. 'We encourage creative presentations' stated Christenson. 'We really do have a lot of fun. We try to keep this business as fun as possible.'

Additionally, a quarterly newsletter is used to spread praise and information. It is a high quality colour brochure, which is sent to every employee. It was used to convey the message that they are important.

Training and competence building

The internal marketing programme stresses competence enhancement. TMC runs training sessions on such topics as guest services, leadership and communication. Learning modules were also developed for more specific topics such as alcohol training, disability awareness training and working during the Grand National Rodeo.

Being part of the 'family'

In order to foster understanding, senior staff takes time to work alongside juniors. For example, they have worked as ushers, and even do shifts in the parking lot.

Recognizing and rewarding

Employees are recognized for their outstanding work, with nominations for the Spirit of Service award. Five nominations lead to a pin, which many employees wear proudly. 'If there is something that they do that is phenomenal, they'll get the pin right away' says Christenson. Along with the pin comes another reward, dinner for two.

Rewards are customized to employees. For example, when the clean-up crew did a spectacular job, as a reward, they and their families were the invited guests in a VIP suite for a circus show. The ticketing office was once treated to dinner at the Hard Rock Cafe, and each got a cafe T-shirt.

Employees are also rewarded for the hard work by being paid well. 'One thing that I think is important is to be fair in payment' says Christenson. 'When we have been successful, we need to pass it on. We also don't extend people over their bounds. We hire the right amount of people and pay them well and give them a positive work environment.'

Active listening

Employee suggestions are highly encouraged, and for every suggestion that is implemented, an employee gets two free tickets to the TMC event of his or her choice. The suggestion of the month gets dinner for two at a local restaurant.

Measuring and acting

Feedback is crucial for improvement. Managers need to conduct internal market research to complement external market research. They need to talk to their guests as well as treat their employees like guests. They need to listen to the needs of both. It is important to get multiple angles of feedback because even if it appears that employees are doing excellent work, guest perceptions, employee self-perceptions and management perception of the job that employees can and often do vary significantly. Using multiple feedback makes for a more complete understanding, and thereby leads to better improvement actions.

Outcomes

The goal of an internal marketing programme was not just to make employees happy, but also to make the employees happy about their jobs so that they will do them well.

The sector is highly competitive and consumers are not just sophisticated but have a lot of choice. This makes them highly demanding. As Smith highlighted: 'Everything in our business is tied to service. Service is king. The focus has changed from the product to how you make me feel when I come for the product.'

And Smith goes on to note: 'Quality service deals with the quality guest experience. Providing service is an art. Providing service profitably is a science. Cutting costs is not going to help you create excellence.'

Source: Ray, S. (1993). Creative internal marketing pays off. *Amusement Business*, **105** (8), 22 February, 11–12.

Case Study References

Atlantic Richfield Company
Svenning, Lynne and Ruchinskas, John (1986), 'Internal "Market Research" Program is yielding successful vidoeconferencing for ARCOvision', *Communications News*, Feb. 1986, 23/2 pp. 48–52.

Aydlotte and Cartwright Inc
Schonbak, Judith, (1991), 'Internal marketing worth every cent', *Business Atlanta*, Oct 1991, 20/10 pp. 16–17.

Barclay Card Services (BCS)
Mazur, Laura (1999), 'Unleashing employees' true value: employees can be your company's most valuable marketing asset', *Marketing*, April 1999, pp. 22–24.

Barnado's
Welch, Jilly (1988), 'Barnardo's points way to HR and marketing link-up', *People Management*, 4/1, pp. 13–14.

Boatmen Trust Company
Ottinger, William F. (1991), 'Making the case for Trust', *Bank Management*, Nov 1991, 67/11 pp 37–40. Anon (1992), 'Internal incentives boost trust referrals'. *Bank Marketing*, April 1992, 24/4, pp. 42–44.

CSX
Blanchard, Roy H. (1993), 'Change – or die', *Railway Age*, March, 194/3, pp. 64–5.

Eastman Chemical Company
Milliken, Weston F. (1996), 'The Eastman Way', *Quality Progress*, Oct 1996, pp. 57–62.

First Union
Sullivan, Michael P. (1985), 'Exploring the untapped resource of internal marketing', *American Banker*, Oct 30, 1985 v150 pp. 4–6.

GTE Supply
Drew, James H. and Fussell, T. R. (1996), 'Becoming Partners with Internal Customers', *Quality Progress*, Oct 1996, pp. 51–54.

Lutheran Brotherhood
Obenshain, Victoria (1992), 'Peer Training Yields Speedy Results', *Personnel Journal*, Apr, 71/4, pp. 107–110.

Midland Bank

Barrett, Patrick (1997), 'Banks lend an ear to service', *Marketing*, Jan 16, 1997 p. 16.

Nations Bank

Faber, David (1992), 'A pitch for togetherness', *Institutional Investor*, March, 26/3, p. 22.

Norwich Union

Wilson, Aubrey (1995), 'The internal marketing of services: the new age surge', *Logistics Information Management*, 8/4, pp. 357–63.

Provena

Friedman, Diane H. (2000), 'Quality customer service: It's everyone's job', *Healthcare Executive*, May/Jun, pp. 4–9.

St Luke's Hospital

Steiniger, Vince (1994), 'Checklist helps C-R-E-A-T-E a successful CPR', *Health Management Technology*, 15/11, pp. 37–41.

Terminix International

Hollis, Kerissa (1995), 'Terminix uses internal marketing to better business', *Memphis Business Journal*, Feb 6, 16/40, p. 13.

Thomas Cook

Edwards, Nick (1997), 'Selling me softly', *Supply Management*, Feb 13, 2/4, pp. 30–32.

TMC

Ray, Susan (1993), 'Creative Internal Marketing Plans Pay Off', *Amusement Business*, Feb 22, 105/8, pp. 11–12.

Index